Train Your CEO Brain

For my mother

How to shape your
brain, shape your life
and shape the world

Train Your CEO BRAIN and Become Your Best Self

Margriet Sitskoorn

Translated by Mischa Hoyinck and Robert Chesal

Vakmedianet

Photography: Irene Sitskoorn Fotografie
Graphic design and illustrations: AnneMarie Adriaans
Layout: Justus Bottenheft
Translation: Mischa Hoyinck and Robert Chesal, Word's Worth
Editor: Nienke van Oeveren, Boekredactie
Printed in the Netherlands

ISBN 978 94 6276 218 3

www.vakmedianet.nl

Table of Contents

Preface

This book is intended to help you achieve your personal goals. Your goals may have to do with yourself, your job, your company, your family or the world around you. Perhaps you set these goals a long time ago, but they never came within reach. Maybe they slipped through your fingers because you allowed yourself to be sidetracked by everyday concerns, temptations in your immediate environment or fossilized behavioral and emotional patterns. This may have led you to think that you don't have control over your own life, or that something or someone else is in the driver's seat.

This book is useful regardless of the specific goals you have in mind. It doesn't matter whether you want to start a new business, enroll in a degree program, do a better job raising your children or stop smoking. What does matter is that your own effort can make a difference.

There are goals I can't help you with. If you want to win the lottery or turn back the clock, you're reading the wrong book. However, if you want the awareness and practical training you need to stop feeling like a puppet on a string, this book could be the game-changer you've been waiting for. It can help you develop into a puppet master so you'll no longer feel like a marionette. You could say this book is about leadership. You will learn to captain your own ship, steer your own behavior, and even guide others who you are responsible for.

I decided to write this book based on the personal problems and questions raised by people who attended my lectures and workshops. Another motive was my observations of the world around me; I see things happening both locally and globally that give cause for concern. Although we hear a lot about healthy living, wealth and care for others, it seems that people are experiencing greater levels of stress, sinking deeper into debt and leading unhealthier lifestyles than ever before. We read about mass unemployment and poverty, businesses going bankrupt, systemic problems in the banking and insurance sector, longer and longer waiting lists in healthcare, declining education standards and the list goes on. It seems we often make the wrong choices, both in our individual lives and as leaders, managers and parents: choices that prevent us from securing a successful and sound future for all of us.

This sobering summary is not all, because the suffering on a global scale demands our attention too. Around the world, people are being killed, maimed and displaced in unprecedented numbers by armed conflict. We see human trafficking, child prostitution, terrorist attacks, drug wars, environmental destruction and epidemics. It seems like an unstoppable path of self-destruction. What's more, most of us have seen video images of these horrible events: images we can no longer unsee.

The internet may well have created a global village where time zones and borders no longer matter, where everyone can be in touch with one another. And yet, growing numbers of people are feeling the opposite: a gap between themselves and others that is becoming harder to bridge. Widening divisions are causing many to retreat into a defensive stance, in which they can only see things from their own perspective. Some are prepared to give their lives and take others with them, just to maintain their worldview. This is the paradox; although we have achieved great technological progress, our emotional and social development seems to lag behind.

Gamemaster

Many of us feel life in today's world has become far too fast, too unpredictable, and too demanding. We wonder how to cope. How do I avoid going crazy from all the information I am bombarded with every day? How do I deal with the changes continually happening all around me? How do I stay healthy, grow, achieve more at work, make my business a success and do a good job of raising my children in this world? Despite all these daunting challenges, we see people around us who flourish amid this constant change, who despite all its problems seem to be more successful and happier than ever.

The common denominator is that many people feel tossed about by forces beyond their control. We all want to reclaim our position as master of the game. To put it as a question: How do I develop the right skills to be successful in this new world? I use the word 'success' in its broadest sense: in terms of private life, business, the physical self, thoughts, feelings and actions. Success on my own terms, in other words: having something to offer to my immediate surroundings or even the wider world. How can I teach myself and others to make the right choices more often so we can rid this planet of stupidity, step by step, and together create a more successful world? In a nutshell: How do I make the most of my potential and achieve my goals? That is the question I explored. In this book, and in the EFFECT program, I present the answers I found.

How to use this book

Train Your CEO Brain consists of three sections: (self-)knowledge, growth and impact assessment. These sections are subdivided into chapters. Each chapter begins with a quotation that captures the chapter's essence and a paragraph summarizing what you will learn. Next, I let you experience the feeling of being a puppet on a string, manipulated by all kinds of internal and external forces. The goal is for you to feel the main thrust of the chapter so you will retain its content long-term. Then I explain, step by step, how to develop the key areas of your brain and how to enhance the skills you need to take control of your life.

In the first chapter, 'A Goal to Set Your Sights On', you will lay the foundations for the work to be done in the rest of the book. This is where you set your own goal. This chapter is all about acquiring the basic knowledge you will need from

This book is about leadership; about steering your own behavior and guiding others you are responsible for.

now on. You will learn how to set a goal that increases your chances of success, but also that setting a goal is not enough. You'll see that it is just as important to have the motivation and the right skills to achieve your goal. If you don't want to do this preliminary work yet, but would rather read on first, that's fine. Come back to Chapter 1 when you are ready and skip ahead to Chapter 2, which focuses on the VUCA World.

Chapter 2, 'The VUCA World', explains the important changes that are shaping today's world. Many of us have not adjusted our skills or assumed the right mindset to deal with this new world. This accounts for much of the disquiet, chaos and helplessness we often feel and the choices that undermine our own efforts to achieve personal goals.

In Chapter 3, 'The CEO Brain', I explain why you need to develop a specific part of your brain, the prefrontal cortex, if you are to survive in our new world. In evolutionary terms, this is the most recently developed part of our brain. The general area and the networks it is connected to are associated with such capabilities as adaptation to change, planning, learning from feedback, out-of-the-box thinking, forming an opinion or vision, making complex decisions, prosocial behavior, feeling motivated and regulating emotions. Another name for this part of the brain is the executive or CEO brain. Many studies have shown that when the networks of the prefrontal cortex and the skills related to these networks are well developed, success in life is more likely. And that means any kind of success, whether it has to do with your job, health, education, relationship, or just plain happiness.

Chapter 4, 'A Recipe for Success', reveals that you are actually suffering from a mild prefrontal cortex dysfunction and that you frequently fail to steer your own course in the midst of outside forces. In this chapter, you will learn which character traits and skills are known to foster success and wisdom and you will rate yourself for each of these. You will also learn how brain plasticity and exposure to new experiences, information and training help us to grow in the desired way and to adapt to a changing environment. You'll discover that you can literally change the brain's structure and performance, not just for yourself, but also for others. This creates not only big opportunities, but also big responsibilities. As you shape your brain, you also shape your life and the wider world.

In Chapter 5, 'Pitfalls', you will see why many of us fail to change, even when it is clear that we should do so because our current behavior gets us into trouble and does not produce the results we envision for ourselves or others. In this chapter, you will experience firsthand the mechanisms that keep you from attaining your goals. This will help you understand and overcome the forces that lead you to make unwise decisions. The insights and exercises in this chapter will prepare you for the journey toward your goals. You will learn to recognize the pitfalls, avoid them, and hopefully even pre-empt them.

These first five chapters focus on (self-)knowledge, both theoretical and self-reported. The next six chapters will explore growth.

Each of the growth chapters will deal with a scientifically proven method of stimulating the prefrontal cortex. You will learn why each method is so important and how you can master it. I will discuss the benefits of an enriched environment, and how you can optimize your ability to focus your attention. Other methods include the secret of a good night's sleep, and why physical exercise shapes not only your body and muscles, but your brain too. You will discover how the future and the present are connected and how integrating this knowledge into your behavior can help you achieve your goals. You'll also learn what the key factors are in the development of children's frontal lobes. And I will discuss the importance of allowing yourself time to change.

EFFECT Program

Because this book is meant to be of immediate use to its readers, Part II will focus on the conditions you can create yourself:

Environmental Enrichment
Flow Focus
Fixed Sleeping Pattern
Exercise
Connecting Today with Tomorrow
Time

Taken as a whole, the methods to create these conditions comprise a coherent program known by its acronym, EFFECT. In each chapter, you will find exercises that I call PFC Exercises (PFC = Prefrontal Cortex). These will have a positive influence on the development of your prefrontal cortex and the executive tasks it facilitates.

The final section of this book, focusing on impact assessment, consists of a single chapter: 'The Effect'. This is where everything you will have learned comes together: your goal, path, motivation, pitfalls and skills. You will see that you have gained a lot of knowledge about the human brain, about the achievement of goals and the difficulties you will face along the way, and ultimately about yourself. By the time you reach this chapter, you will probably have devoted time to the EFFECT program and to developing your CEO brain. Therefore you will be a lot closer to reaching your goals. This final chapter will reveal that you have not only been working toward your current goal, but also toward a whole range of other objectives you may have.

Personal commitment

This book can help you achieve your goals by offering you theoretical knowledge that raises your awareness, and exercises for self-development. You will also be asked to complete tests and watch videos. I chose to structure the book this way because research has revealed the importance of personally committing to the information you learn. This makes the entire process more pleasant and helps you grasp and retain the information better. Furthermore, personal commitment helps integrate what you have learned into your thinking, emotions and behavior. This optimizes personal growth and maximizes the odds of attaining your goals.

Most of the questionnaires in this book are not clinical psychological tests. They are intended to get you thinking and to lend you some perspective on your own feelings, thoughts and actions. Should you be interested in exploring these issues in more depth, I would suggest that you look for psychological tests that are used for clinical assessment or contact a psychologist who can assess you.

I wrote this book in an easy-to-digest style to increase the likelihood that you will actually use it and get real results. The knowledge and the accompanying exercises will enable you to develop your CEO brain and achieve your goals. Not everyone will progress at the same pace. But everyone will benefit from devoting time to enhancing their executive skills. This book is for leaders, managers, teachers, lecturers, parents and other child caretakers, administrators and all others who wish to take responsibility for their own lives and for a part of the world around them. It's about self-knowledge, self-reflection, and personal growth. By reading this book, you are taking a step toward shaping your own brain to make the most of your potential. You are putting yourself in a position to become successful in various ways: in your private life, in your professional career, and socially, with an eye to the interests of others.

This book is meant to help you train your CEO brain and grow toward your best self.

MARGRIET SITSKOORN
November 2015

‘It’s hard to remember that this day will never come again. That the time is now and the place is here and that there are no second chances at a single moment.’

Jeanette Winterson

goodreads.com

PART I **Introduction**

This section of the book will give you insight into your own goals and the reasons why it is often so difficult to achieve them. You will learn about the many forces in the outside world that act upon you and often determine your thoughts, feelings and deeds without you even realizing it. This section will also discuss the skills and traits that increase your chances of success in life, and describe the parts of the brain that regulate them. As you read, you will begin to realize that if you want to stop being a puppet on a string, you will have to develop these areas of your brain and consciously learn the skills they govern. Part I is the foundation supporting Part II of the book, which will show you how to develop your brain and the skills related to success.

PART I
GAINING SELF-KNOWLEDGE

What do I want to accomplish in life?
Why is it so hard to achieve my goals?
What skills do I have to work on
to be successful?
What internal and external forces
do I need to be aware of?

‘If you want to live a happy life, tie it to a goal, not to people or things.’

Albert Einstein

goodreads.com

Chapter 1 **A Goal to Set Your Sights on**

In this chapter, you will set and clarify your goals. You will learn how to articulate your goals in a way that enhances your chances of success. This chapter will show you that the journey can in fact be broken up into stages, and you will get an idea of the obstacles you can expect along the way. Next, you will commit to your goal or choose a different one.

SELF-KNOWLEDGE

How do you get there?

Look at the image and try to find the way using only your eyes, so don't use your finger to trace the lines as you make your way through the maze toward the center.

This maze is based on the figures designed by Artificial Intelligence pioneers Marvin Minsky and Seymour Papert. Most people are unable to see which path actually leads to the center. Illustrations like these show us the limitations of our observational skills. We are often incapable of getting an accurate first impression. Sometimes, all we need is more time to gather more information. The maze is a metaphor: we don't always know how to attain our goal beforehand because we simply can't see and know everything. We need to spend time gathering information and developing skills.

Gathering information

Usually, when you've set yourself a goal, you assume you can achieve it. But you don't always know how to get there or whether you have the skills to complete the journey. This could lead you to choose the wrong path, because you might not see the big picture, base your decisions on the wrong information, or get distracted by whatever you encounter along the way. If this happens, you will invest a lot of energy, but your efforts will fail. All your work will likely lead to more of the same; you'll wind up on dead end streets, frustrated and disappointed, and sometimes even worse off in terms of health, wealth and well-being. Achieving a goal is like a well-planned vacation. It pays to do more than just get in the car and start driving; you're better off also putting energy into gathering information and preparing for possible problems before charting your route. This chapter will help you do so when setting your goals.

SELF-KNOWLEDGE

Setting your goals

Take a moment to think about the following questions. They are about your life's goals and dreams, and they are the guiding principle that will help you apply this book to your own life. Pick out the questions that matter to you, answer them as fully and honestly as possible, and add some questions of your own if you like. By doing this, you will learn something about your goals in life and why they are not immediately within reach. Think hard about what really matters to you. Don't let yourself be guided by what you ought to say, or ought to want. If you feel yourself resisting this idea, ask yourself where this resistance is coming from or skip ahead to Chapter 2.

1 How do you define personal success? ....

Why do you find the things you've named important? ....

2 How do you define personal happiness? ....

What can help you achieve such happiness? ....

3 What do you want to achieve in life?

Is something holding you back? If so, what?

4 What do you want to achieve career-wise?

Is something holding you back? If so, what?

5 What do you want to achieve in terms of your friends / family?

Is something holding you back? If so, what?

6 What do you want to achieve for the greater good?

Is something holding you back? If so, what?

7 What do you want to achieve in terms of your personality (traits)?

Is something holding you back? If so, what?

8 What do you want to achieve in terms of your physical health?

Is something holding you back? If so, what?

9 What do you want to achieve in terms of your hobbies / leisure time?

Is something holding you back? If so, what?

10 What do you want to achieve in terms of education or personal growth?

Is something holding you back? If so, what?

11 What do you want to achieve in terms of wealth?

Is something holding you back? If so, what?

12 What do you want to achieve in the short run?

Is something holding you back? If so, what?

13 What do you want to achieve in terms of ______ (fill in the blank)?

14 What do you want to achieve in terms of ______ (fill in the blank)?

Is something holding you back? If so, what?

Some of the things holding you back could be rephrased as goals. Suppose you'd like to exercise more often, but you usually skip it because you're tired or would rather have some family time. You could then rephrase your goal as 'to have more energy'. Go down the list you've just filled out and check for these 'hidden' goals. You might be able to find several obstacles that could be turned into goals. Later, we'll discuss how you can prioritize your goals.

SELF-KNOWLEDGE

Your main goal

Now it's time to rate how successful you've been at reaching these goals so far. If you added extra questions in the previous step, add the appropriate variables to the list below. You can rate the variables using a scale ranging from 'None' (meaning not at all successful) to 'Somewhat successful' to 'Quite successful' to 'Very successful'.

Then rank the variables in order of importance. In other words, give the variable you value most a 1 (e.g. your work), and the one you value most after that a 2 (e.g. your family), and so on. This will show you in which areas you are doing well by your own standards, and which areas need more attention and effort.

Successfulness	None	Somewhat	Quite	Very	Ranking
Work	☐	☐	☐	☐	______
Family	☐	☐	☐	☐	______
Friends	☐	☐	☐	☐	______
Education	☐	☐	☐	☐	______
Leisure	☐	☐	☐	☐	______
Physical health	☐	☐	☐	☐	______
Wealth	☐	☐	☐	☐	______
Happiness	☐	☐	☐	☐	______
Personality traits	☐	☐	☐	☐	______
For the greater good	☐	☐	☐	☐	______
______	☐	☐	☐	☐	______
______	☐	☐	☐	☐	______
______	☐	☐	☐	☐	______
______	☐	☐	☐	☐	______

Now that you have some background information about yourself, it is time to answer the million-dollar question: What is your main goal in life? What do you want to work on right now?

My main goal is ______________________________

____

____

____

____

____

____

Three components

Achieving your goals depends on three crucial aspects, according to Wilhelm Hofmann at the University of Chicago's Booth School of Business.

1 Articulate and monitor

First and foremost, you need to know what thoughts, feelings, behavior or external results you want to achieve, in other words exactly what goal you are trying to attain. You have to visualize this goal and keep it in mind, and continually monitor whether you are getting any closer to attaining it. Let's suppose your goal is to continue to speak in a normal tone of voice when someone does not immediately do what you want them to do. You must take notice when such an event occurs, visualize yourself continuing to speak in a normal tone of voice and monitor whether you are actually getting better at this.

2 Motivation

Secondly, it is crucial that you are sufficiently motivated to put energy into achieving your goal. In other words, it takes more than wanting to keep your temper; you must also be willing to work on it.

3 Skills

Thirdly and lastly, you need the skills to map out and stick to the path toward your goal and to overcome the obstacles and temptations you come across along the way. For example, you need to realize that you tend to lose your temper when you are tired and things don't go your way. This realization might lead you to conclude that you need to restructure your life so that you are better rested and better able to maintain a normal tone of voice when frustrated.

To achieve your goals you need to meet all three preconditions: being able to put your goals into words, being motivated, and having the right skills. If you know what you want, but lack the motivation and the competency to monitor your progress, you won't get very far. On the other hand, if you are highly motivated and have certain skills, but you don't know exactly what you want, you won't achieve much either. Likewise, if you know what you want, but you are not able to motivate yourself, you won't reach your goal.

How to articulate your goal

It turns out that the way you articulate your goals increases the odds of actually achieving them. So let's rephrase your goals and optimize their wording. Some of the best methods for doing this can be found in the work of Gabriele Oettingen and Traci Mann. Oettingen and Mann discovered that people tend to use one of three ways to set goals:

You can achieve your goals only if:

- you are able to articulate the goal you want to attain;
- you have the right motivation;
- you have developed the appropriate skills.

1 They visualize the future they want to achieve and all the nice things that go with it. For example, after I get that promotion, I will drive an Audi R8, get lots of attention and travel the world.
2 They focus on all the pitfalls along the way. For example, I'll never be able to afford that car, because my co-worker is going for the same promotion and my boss likes her more.
3 They use a combination of the previous two visualizations. They concentrate on the goal without forgetting about the stumbling blocks along the way.

You could call the first group of people *optimists*, the second *pessimists* and the third *realists*. Research has shown that the first two approaches – optimism and pessimism – do not correlate very strongly with achieving goals, while the third one does. The third approach is especially effective when you define the obstacles very clearly and design a roadmap for overcoming them, Oettingen writes. For example, you could reason as follows: in my current workplace, I will never get the chance to earn enough to be able to afford an Audi R8, so I will go back to school and find another job. That's quite a radical roadmap, of course, but you get the idea and it also applies to less radical steps. For example, if my goal is to lose 6 pounds and I know that once I open a bag of chips I won't stop eating, I should simply not open that bag, or better yet, only go shopping on a full stomach and stop buying chips altogether.

By setting rules, you're more likely to nip certain temptations and problems in the bud. I will come back to this in greater detail in Chapter 5, 'Pitfalls'.

As Oettingen and Mann write, it's best to formulate your goals in positive terms, that is, in terms of what you do want instead of what you don't want. This will enable you to keep your eye on your goal and your roadmap, and monitor your progress. When you describe your goal as something you want to achieve, you can determine exactly when you have achieved it. Having a clear endpoint makes it easier to draw up a clear roadmap to help you achieve that goal. In other words, 'I want to go to the gym three times a week' is a better goal to set than 'I don't want to lie on the couch watching TV with a bag of potato chips every night'.

Oettingen and Mann also describe how to phrase your goals in terms of hitting a certain target – 'I want to raise $10,000 for that charity' – or in terms of developing a skill – 'I want to improve my fundraising skills'. The former is a performance goal, while the latter is a mastery goal. Evidence suggests that mastery goals motivate you more, and in the long run help you achieve greater success, than performance goals. Learning a skill (a mastery goal) will stand you in good stead for the rest of your life, of course, but defining an endpoint is harder in this type of goal-setting. Now let's rephrase your goal and come up with a roadmap.

Rephrasing your goal and drawing up a roadmap

SELF-KNOWLEDGE

Phrase your goal in a realistic manner, using the 'I want to...' structure. Be as concrete as possible about what you want to achieve, so you will know when you have achieved it. Also write down what benefits you expect to reap, what you need to do to achieve it (roadmap), and what pitfalls (obstacles/temptations) you expect to encounter.

Goal: I want to ______________________________

I will have achieved my goal when ______________________________

How do I benefit from this goal? (What is the reason I am setting it?) ______________________________

What do I need to do to achieve my goal? ______________________________

What obstacles and temptations can I expect to meet along the way? ______________________________

Once you have articulated your goal, you need to estimate how motivated you are, so you can assess your commitment. If you fail to do so, there will be a gaping hole between setting your goal and achieving it: you're saying you want to achieve something, but not doing what's necessary to actually achieve it.

Motivation

Take another look at how you described your goal, your roadmap and the obstacles and temptations you expect to encounter. Then read the five statements below and check the one that best reflects how motivated you are to reach your goal.
Try not to fool yourself. If you are not terribly motivated, be honest and admit it to yourself, because it is simply not very realistic to set a goal if you're not prepared to do what's necessary to achieve it. You can spare yourself a lot of the frustration resulting from wanting something that is not going to happen.

1 I always drag my feet when there is something I have to do to reach my goal. ____ ☐
2 If I feel like it, I do what's necessary to achieve my goal, but I know I often won't feel like it. ____ ☐
3 I'll try to do what's necessary to reach my goal about half the time, but I'm not going to upset my life for it. ____ ☐
4 I resolve to do everything I need to do to achieve my goal, but I expect to have some problems some of the time. Some of the time equals ... times.[1] ____ ☐
5 I'm unstoppable and will do whatever it takes to attain my goal. ____ ☐

If you've checked statement 1, 2 or 3, you should seriously ask yourself whether it is realistic to think you will attain your goal. As Wilhelm Hofmann writes, motivation is one of the three factors that are indispensable to reaching your goals. Statements 1, 2 and 3 all reflect a lack of motivation. So you can either set another goal, for which you are motivated, or you can try to increase your motivation.

Statements 4 and 5 reflect sufficient motivation. If you run into an obstacle or temptation, think of what you need to do to attain your goal and reread what you filled in above. This will shore up your determination.

If you have checked statement 4 or 5, write it on a flashcard and carry this with you, so you can take it out at moments of weakness to reread the statement and renew your commitment to your goal. If you checked statement 4, keep track of the number of times you've felt tempted and monitor whether you've reached the number you filled in above.

---

1 Decide beforehand how many times 'some of the time' is. If it is close to half the time, check statement 3 instead. This number does not represent the number of times you may succumb to your weaknesses, but how many times you foresee having to face a temptation or obstacle and overcome it.

Objective assessment of your motivation

So far, you have given a subjective assessment of your motivation. A more objective way of assessing it is by keeping track of how much time per day you actually spend on attaining your goal. Saying you are highly motivated to achieve a goal needs to go hand in hand with spending a substantial amount of time working toward it.

Keep track of the number of hours you spend every day working toward your goal.

Goal: ....

....

....

....

....

....

Number of hours spent on goal in week 1
Monday ....
Tuesday ....
Wednesday ....
Thursday ....
Friday ....
Saturday ....
Sunday ....

Number of hours spent on goal in week 2
Monday ....
Tuesday ....
Wednesday ....
Thursday ....
Friday ....
Saturday ....
Sunday ....

Number of hours spent on goal in week 3
Monday ....
Tuesday ....
Wednesday ....
Thursday ....
Friday ....
Saturday ....
Sunday ....

For any additional weeks, you can keep track of the hours in your (electronic) calendar.

Before I delve into the VUCA world in the next chapter, I want to impart another interesting bit of knowledge about motivation. Motivation can be intrinsic or extrinsic. If it is you who wants to change or achieve something, you are intrinsically motivated. If, however, you think others expect you to change or achieve something, for which you will receive some external reward, you are extrinsically motivated.

SELF-KNOWLEDGE

Type of motivation

Ask yourself whether you are intrinsically or extrinsically motivated to attain your goal, or whether both types of motivation are at play. It is not always easy to distinguish between the two. Check the box that best fits your motivation. If necessary, refer back to the answers you wrote down when defining the benefits you expect to gain from achieving this goal.

I am:

- ☐ Intrinsically
- ☐ Extrinsically
- ☐ Both intrinsically and extrinsically

motivated to achieve my goal.

A large-scale study by Koestner and co-authors shows that people who are intrinsically motivated to achieve a goal are more likely to display the behavior needed to achieve it. So if you are intrinsically motivated to reach the goal you have set, you have made things much easier for yourself.

Clarifying your goals and ensuring you are motivated to work on them are two of the three variables Hofmann considers indispensable to reaching goals. Hofmann's third variable pertains to the skills you need to successfully bring your plans to fruition. Those skills and the extent to which you already possess them are the topic of the next two chapters.

The Red Queen's Race

'Well, in our country', said Alice still panting a little, 'you'd generally get to somewhere else if you run very fast for a long time, as we've been doing.' 'A slow sort of country!' said the queen. 'Now here, you see, it takes all the running you can do, to keep in the same place. If you want to get somewhere else, you must run at least twice as fast as that.'

Lewis Carroll

Through the Looking Glass

Chapter 2 **The VUCA World**

This chapter illustrates the many important changes taking place in our society. These changes make big demands on us, and therefore on our brains. They sometimes demand too much of us, more than we can handle. As a result, we end up sick or falling badly behind. In this chapter, you will discover that we need to develop particular skills to prevent changes from taking over our lives.

Overtaxing the brain

Find a chair, take a seat and put both your feet on the ground. If you are left-handed, write the number 9 in the air with your left hand; if you are right-handed, do the same with your right hand. Now put your hands on your lap. If you are left-handed, lift your left foot up and turn your ankle, moving clockwise. Do this with your right foot if you are right-handed. Easy, right?

Now do both at the same time. So remain seated, and if you are left-handed write a 9 in the air with your left hand while turning your left ankle clockwise. Do this with your right hand and foot if you are right-handed.

How did that go? I bet something went wrong somewhere. Either your ankle did not make a neat circular motion but did something haphazard, or the 9 in the air was distorted. You may even have drawn it backwards. The reason these two easy tasks are no longer so easy, is that you are overtaxing a certain part of your brain. I deliberately asked you to combine these particular tasks because they both require the use of your premotor and motor cortices.

Unless you've had extensive practice carrying out two independent tasks, like a musician has, you'll find that you are requiring more than these parts of the brain can handle. When you ask too much of the brain, it can no longer fulfill its tasks properly, and this causes inefficiency and mistakes. This exercise is a metaphor for the price we pay when multitasking, a demand imposed on us by the complex world we live in.

The Red Queen hypothesis

I chose to open this chapter with the Red Queen's quote from *Through the Looking Glass*, because it contains two important insights that form the basis for successfully achieving the goals you have set. Firstly, the quote makes clear that both humans and their environment are continually changing. That has always been the case; change, paradoxically enough, is a constant. Change is the foundation of development and as such indispensable for progress (even if change, in and of itself, does not always have a direction or a goal). Secondly, the quote shows that if you fail to adapt to your environment or the Zeitgeist, you may suffer as a result. Carroll's Red Queen's race has even inspired an evolutionary hypothesis known as the Red Queen hypothesis: in order for an organism to survive and reproduce in an ever-changing environment where competing organisms keep adapting to these changes, this organism will also have to adapt and develop.

Chances are, this idea will not strike you as new. The principle of the survival of those who are best at adapting to their (changing) environment is often encapsulated in Herbert Spencer's phrase "survival of the fittest" – even though this originally referred to natural selection. You might be tempted to dismiss all this as common sense, but I think it is important to give it due emphasis, because experience has shown that we tend to ignore these insights. Be it consciously or unconsciously, we tend to think that we adjust effortlessly and seamlessly to the changing times. This conscious or unconscious conviction leads us to believe we don't need to work on those crucial changes. As a consequence, we end up feeling either tossed about by forces we have no control over, or, worse, like we're doomed and will never get anywhere – as the Red Queen quote indicates.

Unfortunately, failing to adjust is a very real problem. Businesses go belly up because they wait too long to adopt new technology (remember Kodak, Nokia and BlackBerry?). People experience personal failures because they are unable to handle an overload of information, temptation and choices (think of burn-outs, heart disease and addictions). Groups fall out of step with the times by clinging to traditions and values that once determined their identity, but are now obsolete and untenable (recall, for instance, how the leaders of the Communist Bloc didn't notice that their empire was crumbling until it was too late, or that the American auto industry was eclipsed by Japanese carmakers when it failed to embrace more efficient technology, or how some people in the southern US still protest the removal of the Confederate flag and other symbols associated with slavery – over 150 years after slavery was abolished).

Rapid change

This immediately provokes questions. For instance, if change is so important and has always been a constant, then how is today different from before? Are today's changes fundamentally different from those in the past? If so, how? And how do we need to adapt in order to ensure our survival and continued development?

In response to the first question, we can conclude that our time distinguishes itself from earlier eras in history by the information overload we are exposed to every day, whether we like it or not. This information overload has been made possible by the technological progress that allows us to store, share and access information on an unprecedented scale. We can now access new information anywhere anytime, but there is far more information available than we can remember or respond to. In some people, this causes stress, fatigue, attention deficit and anxiety. Daniel Levitin has discussed this phenomenon – its causes, consequences and possible solutions – in his book *The Organized Mind: Thinking Straight in the Age of Information Overload.*

All the new information we have also enables us to make changes rapidly and frequently, sometimes even before previous changes have had time to prove their usefulness. So, while this information has increased the turnover rate of everything in life, it has not necessarily added more value. Instead, it can leave us feeling like we are living in a permanent state of instability. New products, technologies, theories, regulations, opportunities and constraints are replacing each other at breakneck speed. What's new today is old school in a week. What's true today is outdated tomorrow. What's possible today is overdue in a month.

Let me give you some examples of developments that have influenced our thoughts, emotions and actions. This list is not exhaustive, of course, because there are simply too many new developments. But let me start with Industry 4.0.

Industry 4.0 refers to an industry focused on flexibility and speed in the development of new products and manufacturing technologies. We are witnessing a revolution in design, manufacturing and distribution. Far-reaching digitization of information on products and processes makes it possible to collect and collate large amounts of data. 3D printing now enables us to 'print' practically anything: from clothing to weapons, from artificial limbs to entire homes! In the field of industrial robotics, robots are outperforming people in both speed and precision. Network-centric production systems are connecting people and equipment in new ways. This fourth industrial revolution is giving rise to the Internet of Things.

The Internet of Things denotes all sorts of new opportunities for entrepreneurs and consumers across all industries, because the number of smart products (thinking tools) keeps growing and so does the number of smart devices connected to the internet. These days, far more apparatuses than people are communicating with each other and their environment. All these machines (computers, cars, toys, refrigerators, etc.) are collecting data (through digitization) and can keep us informed of past and present statuses and possible future scenarios. This enables us to control activities and processes using the most accurate information available online. For example, if your refrigerator is running low on particular foods, the fridge can generate a shopping list and order those products delivered to your door. Likewise, continuous monitoring will show when certain parts of a machine need replacing before they break down and cause downtime on the whole production line. Similarly, if your health is at risk, continuous monitoring of your blood and urine levels will reveal possible critical levels and alert your doctor or pharmacy so treatment can start immediately.

This fourth industrial revolution is giving birth to new product functions, services and business models, such as drones that deliver packages, usage-based insurance such as pay-as-you-drive and pay-how-you-drive, and, of course, the sale of 3D models for 3D printers. All these new developments are sometimes subsumed under the heading of 'disruptive technologies'. In the best-case scenario, such technologies give rise to disruptive innovation: innovations that open up new markets and new opportunities. However, these technologies have also created great problems, because certain companies, ideas or manufacturing methods are suddenly rendered obsolete unless they adopt the new technology. Therefore, this new era is also referred to as the Age of Innovation: an era not shaped by power and knowledge, but by those who continually innovate.

In addition to disruptive technological innovation, there is also social innovation. Organizations and individuals are interacting in changing ways. Of course, we as individuals always were our own most valuable resource (at least, ideally speaking), but these days employees have become the most important capital that organizations have at their disposal: human capital. And like all other capital, they require investment. Static knowledge is obsolete. Employees need to develop dynamic knowledge, because we live in a world where conflicts are generally settled by brainpower rather than physical force. This is true of political struggles, business competition and conflicts between military powers, but it even comes into play when applying for a building permit in a nature reserve.

Although I usually find truth in proverbs and sayings, the expression 'What is learned in the cradle is carried to the grave' is a bit outdated, at least as far as static knowledge goes. Obviously, the expression still applies to learning how to adapt to change. In the past, the trades that people learned during their schooling and internship lasted them a lifetime. But today, there are so many changes afoot and the pace of change is so rapid that working and learning are now intertwined, or at least they ought to be. This development (combined with other social changes) is causing businesses to evolve into people-centric systems. The result is that four activities – working, learning, innovating and doing business – are inextricably linked.

This interlocking set of four activities applies not only to the business community, but also to your personal life. In order to lead a good life in this day and age, you need to stay abreast of new information and learn new skills. You need to continue to develop yourself, which will enable you to think of and initiate new things that contribute to your life and to society. Therefore, we as a society must invest even more in the development of human capital. We must more actively pursue education, knowledge transfer and data exchange. This is not always easy, as trust and breaches of trust have become a big issue in our big data society, where every scrap of information about us is apparently stored in huge databases that can easily be linked for further investigation.

Resisting all this 24/7 availability, opportunity and intrusion is far from easy.

Job quality and full utilization of talent have become deciding factors, but so has quality of life. We are concerned with our work-life balance; we deal with flextime, continuous education, parental leave and drastic career changes. Many businesses have introduced Results Only Work Environments, where employees are free to decide when and where they work and are responsible for their results rather than the hours they work. People are being given different responsibilities, both at work and beyond. Not only are they responsible for managing their own time, but their work environment is also changing with shifting notions of hierarchy and leadership on the work floor. In their private lives, they also have more autonomy and responsibility than ever before, as they are expected to select their utilities, health insurance and internet providers, and to decide when and where they wish to work remotely.

And that is not all. Continuing globalization and the emerging sharing economy, which is gaining a foothold through the many online sharing portals, are upsetting the apple cart even more. A recent report from the Dutch Marketing Innovation Platform PIM, entitled *Welcome to the age of homo socius*, refers to a new reality, where sharing – of experiences, opinions, knowledge and assets – is becoming more important than owning. We can benefit enormously from other people's efforts and let others benefit from our knowledge and hard work. Wikipedia, Twitter, open source software, various communities and Facebook give us access to an endless flow of expertise (as well as nonsense!) generated by others.

Social enterprise has found new avenues, such as crowdfunding and co-creation. From a neurological point of view, sharing is a very rewarding primary need that deeply affects our economy and society. It is the antidote to greed, waste and us-them thinking, which are nonetheless still big, destructive forces. I am not entirely sure whether the sharing economy is based on the need to share or on the desire to get something on the cheap and to commercialize everything you own. It could be greed, in other words, or a combination of these two contradictory impulses.

In a related development, knowledge is becoming ever more specialized and the complexity of things necessitates ever more collaboration and coordination, whether this concerns heart transplants, dealing with terrorism, or the development of a vaccine or drug against infectious diseases. Furthermore, we seem to be living in a world where the sky is the limit and choice overload has become a problem, as Alvin Toffler first argued in his 1970 book *Future Shock* and Dutch journalist Maarten van den Heuvel showed in his recent documentary and book *Vrijheid, gelijkheid, broederschap.* [*Liberty, Equality, Fraternity*]. Actor-centered learning – tackling difficult, ambiguous questions that involve self-interest (e.g. what do I consider the best balance between caring for the environment and securing a good income) – has gained in importance, while we see a decline in veridical decision making – involving questions that can be answered in a clear-cut, non-ambiguous manner that does not involve self-interest (e.g. what types of garbage go into the paper waste bin).

It seems as we can have and be anything we want, as long as we work hard enough or give good fortune a helping hand (although I am still struggling to understand how the latter is supposed to work). We no longer even have to settle for the looks Mother Nature gave us. We can change and tweak almost anything we don't like: our faces, boobs, buns and bellies. We live in a young, tight, fast society and that requires time and money. We need pills and surgery and injections and personal trainers to keep up. And that takes time and money, which we often don't have because of all the other requirements, obligations and temptations we face.

Addictions are lurking everywhere: behind the game console, in the supermarket, in webshops and in our never-ending work. Resisting all this 24/7 availability, opportunity and intrusion is far from easy. That requires an antidote in the shape of skills like the ability to suppress undesirable responses, adaptability, long-term rather than short-term thinking, social skills and self-reflection, to name but a few. Our brain has the capacity to learn these skills, but tends to be underdeveloped, and that makes resisting all these temptations so hard.[2]

Not only has everything apparently become faster and more complex, our communication has also fundamentally changed. In the digital age, we do not, as Daniel Levitin describes, need to sit down to carefully formulate our thoughts on paper, then walk to the mailbox and mail a letter that will be opened and read two days later. Instead, we put pretty much anything we're thinking, however impulsive, in an email, text message, tweet or Facebook post because these channels present so few obstacles.

Things that cost barely any time or effort intrude upon our lives every second of every day, whether we have the energy to deal with them or not. Pertinent and irrelevant information alternate in rapid succession and are hard to tell apart at first, or at all. Somehow, we need to make sense of it all. Being in constant touch with everyone all over the planet changes our idea of time and space. We can attend a meeting in our hometown while talking on screen to people on the other side of the Earth, where it is nighttime, and at the same time chat to a third person who is somewhere else entirely. In that sense, we live in a timeless, placeless world, as described in Thomas Friedman's bestseller *The World is Flat*. The youngest generations tend to see the world on screen rather than seeing the world directly, as the older generations are still used to doing. This must result in differences between people and how their brains function, and how they think, feel and act. Interesting books on this topic are Richard Restak's *The New Brain* and Nicholas Carr's *The Shallows*.

2 For a more detailed explanation, see Sitskoorn, *Passies van het brein*,2010, [Passions of the Brain].

Our core identity
All these changes and more have caused notions like privacy, sexuality, location, time, social group, information, knowledge and facts to evolve (or should I say devolve) into new definitions and experiences. I just summed those up in one sentence, but if you think about it for a minute, that's quite a radical change. These notions make up our core identity. Questions that come up in the context of these shifting notions include:

- Who am I?
- Where do I belong?
- What is and isn't mine?
- What is real and what is fiction?
- What defines me?

We tend not to think too hard about these questions, and usually we come up with only partial answers. Yet we feel these are fundamental questions. The questions are substantive, but the answers ambiguous or absent, leading to insecurity, helplessness, lethargy, aggression and procrastination. Such feelings only increase the pressure you experience, and that pressure affects your ability to think logically. This is the start of a vicious cycle of unproductive behavior and negative consequences.

The VUCA World

In the USA, this rapidly changing, stressful world is referred to as VUCA World, a blanket term using an acronym that stands for Volatile, Uncertain, Complex, Ambiguous. The term originated in the US Army in the 1990s. Each of the words in VUCA has its own meaning, but there are some overlaps too. Let me run down the list.

Those who can cope with the VUCA World can explain new situations and show others the way through vision and innovation.

Volatility stands for the nature, dynamics and rapidity of change (see, for example Charles and Jayne May in *Are you VUCA ready?*). A great example of this was the sudden bankruptcy of Lehman Brothers. On September 10, 2008, Lehman Brothers posted a $3.93 billion quarterly loss because of faulty mortgages. The CEO put the bank up for sale, and shares plummeted. Four days later, the US government refused to bail out Lehman Bros. On September 15, the bank filed for bankruptcy, triggering a world stock market crisis. Within days, AIG, the world's biggest insurer, and industrial giants like General Motors teetered on the brink of bankruptcy.

Uncertainty stands for the unpredictability of events now and in the future, and the extent to which we are aware of what is going on in the world. Today, many questions we ask ourselves reflect that uncertainty: What impact will terrorism and the refugee crisis have on my personal life? Will I keep my job in the current economic climate?

Complexity stands for the number of variables that can play a role in an event at any given moment, and the confusion caused by this. We are capable of gathering more information than ever before, at great speed. But at the same time, we still have to assess the value of this information and put it in its proper perspective. This only increases the complexity and makes things even harder to understand.

And last but not least, *Ambiguity* stands for the lack of clarity in the state of affairs, the confusion of cause and effect, and the vagueness that can result from this.

The VUCA world has caused the demise of many products and companies. Kodak lost a lot of market share when photography went digital. Traditional telecom providers lost out to WhatsApp and Skype, which, like Facebook and Instagram, drastically changed the way we communicate. Newspapers have been struggling to adapt to the digital age and many retailers are having trouble competing with webshops, to name just a few examples. And the impact of VUCA is not limited to the world of business. It is also evident in healthcare, education and other areas of society.

Those of us who are good at dealing with VUCA characteristics are better at dealing with today's world. They are ready for what is about to come. They are better equipped to use the opportunities offered by the VUCA world and to chart their own course. These are the people who know how to interpret the new situation and who can guide others through vision and innovation. They can make us feel comfortable in a changing world.

New skills

All these changes demand a lot of our brains. Old skills, like concentrating and shifting our attention from one matter to another, need improving. But we also need to develop new skills, like effectively selecting and critically evaluating information from the incredible abundance of available data, and applying it in an organizational context or in our personal lives. This requires flexibility, creativity and innovative power, but also skills like knowing when to relax and shield yourself from outside stimuli.

These are also known as '21st century skills'.[3]

In *21st Century Skills: Learning for Life in our Times*, Bernie Trilling and Charles Fadel describe the skills we need in today's world. They distinguish three types of 21st century skills that all children should be taught in school: 1) learning and innovation skills, 2) digital literacy skills, and 3) life and career skills.

Learning and innovation skills comprise:
- Critical thinking and problem solving;
- Communication and collaboration;
- Creativity and innovation.

Digital literacy skills comprise:
- Information literacy: knowing how to effectively and efficiently access information; how to critically and competently evaluate information; and how to accurately and creatively use it.
- Media literacy: understanding how to use the most appropriate media tools and sources available for learning; and how to use various media to create effective and persuasive products to convey your message. This means understanding how and why information is disseminated by various media and being able to utilize the most appropriate media to spread your own message and achieve your own goals.
- Information and communication technology (ICT): knowing how to effectively apply the latest technology.

Last but not least, *life and career skills* comprise:
- Flexibility and adaptability
- Initiative and self-direction
- Social and cross-cultural skills
- Productivity
- Accountability
- Leadership
- Responsibility

Trilling and Fadel's book clearly explains which skills students need to develop in order to work and live in this century. Obviously, those skills are not only beneficial for the next generation, but for all of us!

---

3 http://www.p21.org/our-work/p21-framework

The CEO brain

The previous section made the point that we are indeed dealing with wholesale changes that deeply affect our lives, health and happiness. Clearly, we will somehow need to adapt to keep up or achieve anything. But the question is: How? Can we even adapt? Or are we doomed to succumb to stress, despair and a downward spiral? Fortunately not. We can adapt, of course. But we do need to take action to adapt more effectively. What action? In a nutshell: we need to develop our prefrontal cortex.

Evolutionarily speaking, the prefrontal cortex is a relatively young area of the brain with connections to the entire brain. The region is associated with skills like flexibility, planning, learning from feedback, creativity, logic, complex decision-making, self-reflection, prosocial behavior and emotion regulation, to name just a few. This part of our brain is also known as the executive brain, or CEO brain. This is because the degree to which this area and its attendant skills are developed is a strong predictor of personal and business success. Those who develop their CEO brain and skills are very successful at adapting to the demands of life today. Those are the people who excel. To them, the new world is not confusing, fatiguing or destructive, but brimming with opportunities for development.

From puppet to puppet master

Scientists all over the world are devising methods that develop the executive brain and the executive skills. This book summarizes part of the knowledge gathered so far and makes it accessible, so you can use it to your own advantage. By doing so, you can start feeling like a puppet master rather than a puppet on a string. You can learn to be a leader, capable of guiding not just yourself but others too. If necessary, you'll be able to point others in the right direction and chart a course toward development and better business organization, or even better prepare your own children for their life and self-actualization. It is time for us – in this smart world, with all its smart tools – to develop smart brains, so we can develop smart thinking, smart feeling and smart acting. This will give us smart organizations, smart kids and smart lives. In short, it is time to develop our CEO brain.

The next chapter will deal in more detail with the CEO brain, its attendant skills, and the characteristics that have been linked to success. But before we get to that, I am going to ask you to do an exercise that will increase your self-knowledge and help pave the way. It should be clear by now that the many changes in our environment are pushing people out of their comfort zone. This triggers all sorts of emotions and behaviors that can hamper or even block us from adapting to the new reality. This book too will regularly push you out of your comfort zone. Even Chapter 1 may have had that effect on you. To help you deal with this, I would like you to fill out the following questionnaire, even though your first reaction will probably be to resist. But let me assure you: ultimately, you will benefit from it almost every day.

We will need to learn some new skills and unlearn others. Break old patterns.

Out of your comfort zone

SELF-KNOWLEDGE

When was the last time you were pushed out of your comfort zone? Think what your response is like when you feel uncomfortable. Do you start making lame jokes? Do you refuse to do certain things? Do you get loud, or do you go very quiet?

To get you started, I have listed a few options below. Check the box if you think a statement applies to you. I have also left room for you to supplement the statements with your own specific responses. If you find it hard to characterize your reactions, ask someone who knows you to characterize your behavior when you have to do things you're not familiar with or are uncomfortable doing.

When I get pushed out of my comfort zone:

- ☐ I start shooting holes in whatever is suggested
- ☐ I start joking around
- ☐ I withdraw from the situation
- ☐ I think: I can just wait this one out
- ☐ I refuse to do certain things
- ☐ I get loud
- ☐ I go very quiet
- ☐ I act like I know better and start looking for arguments that can block the proposal or idea
- ☐ I stop listening
- ☐ I try to obstruct things through intimidation
- ☐ I ridicule the other
- ☐ I look for allies to justify myself
- ☐ ______
- ☐ ______
- ☐ ______
- ☐ ______
- ☐ ______

This exercise is intended to teach you how to stay one step ahead of yourself. Development and change by definition require leaving your comfort zone. It does not matter whether you are dealing with a natural development (going from crawling to walking upright) or with an externally induced development, like when technological changes force the company you work for to overhaul its information process, or when a reorganization leads to changes in your job description. The point is you need to adapt.

Once you know how you tend to react when you have to leave your comfort zone, you can use that knowledge to overcome the fear or helplessness that have stopped you in the past and move forward.

‘It is change, continuing change, inevitable change that is the dominant factor in society today. No sensible decision can be made any longer without taking into account not only the world as it is, but the world as it will be. This, in turn, means that our statesmen, our businessmen, our everyman must take on a science fictional way of thinking.’

Isaac Asimov

‘My Own View’ (essay)

Chapter 3 **The CEO Brain**

This chapter deals with what are known as cold and hot executive skills, why they are so important and what the CEO brain is. In the pages ahead, you will estimate the strength of your own executive skills, which will give you more insight into your own performance.

SELF-KNOWLEDGE

The Riddle of the Gnomes

Look at the illustration above. You see four gnomes on a staircase. Each of them is wearing a hat. Two of them are wearing a solid grey hat, and two are wearing a striped hat. The gnomes can only see straight ahead. They are not allowed to communicate with each other in any way. The gnome at the top of the stairs is standing behind a closed door that no one can see through. No one can see that gnome, and that gnome can see no one else.

The gnomes know that two of them are wearing grey hats and two are wearing striped hats. None of them knows which hat they themselves are wearing, but they can each see the hats worn by those standing in front of them. The first gnome who figures out which color hat he is wearing will win € 10,000. Which gnome can be the first to know with the greatest degree of certainty which type of hat is on his head: Gnome 1, 2, 3 or 4 and why?

You can find the answer at the end of this chapter (see page 75).

The riddle above is a difficult logical puzzle that makes you think. However, it is not a riddle that has anything to do with your personal ambitions or desires, so in a sense this task is not connected to your feelings. We call the capacities required to complete this type of task cold CEO skills or cold executive skills. When a task requires you to call upon your cognitive abilities and is also directly connected to your emotions because it is linked to something you would love to achieve or have, or that you are afraid of, we call the capabilities you need hot CEO skills or hot executive skills (see page 65).

Marshmallow Experiment

Imagine you are a child and you have been put in a room where you are about to be subjected to a psychological test. A researcher comes in and places a marshmallow on the table. 'This marshmallow is for you,' the researcher tells you. 'You may eat it, but if you wait until I get back – I need to leave but I will be back soon – then you will get two marshmallows instead of just one.' What would you do?

This was a real experiment, and the children who were given this test showed a wide range of reactions. Some popped the marshmallow into their mouths before the researcher even finished speaking. Some waited briefly, but ate the marshmallow the moment the researcher left. Others sniffed it, or nibbled it, doubtlessly betting that this would not be noticed. Those who did manage to wait used different strategies. Some kept looking away from the marshmallow or used their fingers to count, while others became physically very active or froze in their seats and stared straight ahead.

The marshmallow question seems arbitrary, but isn't. The ability to leave the marshmallow alone indicates something profoundly important: the capacity to withstand the desire for instant gratification and the willpower to hold out for maximum returns. We know this thanks to Walter Mischel, who in the 1960s conducted this experiment, and to the follow-up studies on the same children, which revealed incredible results. Mischel originally carried out the marshmallow experiment to see which techniques children use to resist temptation. As expected, some children ate the marshmallow right away, while others managed to hold out until the researcher returned.

Researchers tracked the progress of some of these children, and years later, when they were in secondary school, made a fascinating discovery. The children who had shown willpower in the experiment were now more successful students. Compared to the children who gave in to temptation within 30 seconds, those who were able to wait 15 minutes before eating the marshmallow got much higher scores on their SATs, the standardized test used by US universities to assess student applicants.

Other researchers, such as Angela Duckworth, showed that willpower is a better predictor of educational success than IQ and test scores. Particularly the combination of willpower and a clearly articulated goal – if I wait, I will get two marshmallows – tends to increase the chances of achieving the stated goal. Just like we saw in the previous chapter.

Clearly, marshmallows are not the point. The experiment is merely a metaphor for the temptations you are not able to withstand, the ones that prevent you from achieving your goals. Perhaps the marshmallow symbolizes your unstoppable urge to drink, or the demands of your job that you never say no to, or the excuses you make so you don't have to treat the other fairly, or the colleague you fantasize about but who will end up giving you more trouble than happiness if you succumb to that scenario. The marshmallow stands for the surrender to a temptation for short-term satisfaction, while it would be better to resist because changing your behavior will benefit you far more in the long run.

Your marshmallow

SELF-KNOWLEDGE

Recall the goal that you are trying to achieve. Describe the marshmallows that stand in your way: the sources of instant gratification that you tend to give in to and which prevent you from succeeding.

My marshmallows are ______________________________

On YouTube you can find all kinds of interesting videos about the marshmallow experiment[4] that clearly show how waiting for something better, bigger or nicer is

4 For example, www.youtube.com/watch?v=QX_oy9614HQ.

very difficult when you have a source of instant gratification right in front of you. In Chapter 5, 'Pitfalls', I will show you what you can do to lessen the temptation. I will first explain what executive skills are and why they are crucial to achieving your goal. I will also show you what gnomes and marshmallows have to do with your CEO brain.

Executive skills

In the previous chapter, I showed how the VUCA world makes heavy demands on us. Perhaps I didn't even need to make this clear, as you live every day of your life in the VUCA world. You have almost certainly felt its force acting upon you in your own experience. If we are to be successful in this rapidly changing world with its information overload, we'll have to learn to enjoy a new kind of game: the challenge of change. We will have to look further outside ourselves than we are accustomed to, and reflect more on our own behavior. We will also have to dare to let go of our thought patterns, like: 'It is what it is', or 'You can't teach an old dog new tricks'. We will have to develop skills like planning, flexibility, selecting the right information, learning from feedback, suppressing all kinds of impulses, self-regulation, relaxation and out-of-our-box thinking. In neuropsychology, such capacities are collectively referred to as executive skills.

Executive or CEO skills is an umbrella term for a whole range of capabilities. Roughly speaking, we can say they enable us to monitor and regulate our emotions, thoughts and behavior in such a way that we can successfully adapt to a changing environment and achieve our goals while feeling healthy and happy. Executive skills ensure that we make the right decisions and persevere when things get tough or tedious. They enable us to suppress our impulses, to keep our primary emotions in check, and to learn from feedback, to name but a few examples.

Three core executive skills

The executive skills are defined and categorized in many ways. An article by Akira Miyake and co-authors presents three basic elements that can be found in nearly all descriptions of executive skills. The same conclusions can be found in a report from the National Scientific Council on the Developing Child and the National Forum on Early Childhood Policy and Programs. This report is available from the website of Harvard University Center on the Developing Child.[5]

The three core executive skills are: working memory, self-control, and cognitive and mental flexibility. For each of these elements, I will provide the Council's definition[6] and an explanation with examples.

5 http://developingchild.harvard.edu/resources/reports_and_working_papers/working_papers/wp11/

6 Building the brain's 'Air Traffic Control' system: How early experiences shape the development of executive function, p. 2.

Executive skills help us to make the right decisions, persevere when things get tough or tedious, suppress our impulses, keep our primary emotions in check, and learn from feedback.

1 Working memory

"The capacity to hold and manipulate information in our heads over short periods of time. It provides a mental surface on which we can place important information so that it is ready to use in the course of our everyday lives."

Your working memory enables you to access information and use it to achieve a certain goal. It enables you to rely on more than just direct observation – what you see, feel or hear at a given moment – and to use everything you know and have learned to achieve some future goal. For example, you need your working memory to mentally calculate a sum, to return to a topic of conversation if you've been interrupted, to remember what you've already done when you stop writing an article or cooking a meal to look something up online, or to run down the list of things you need to do when opening a new webshop.

Your working memory ensures that your life makes sense, because it keeps track of what has gone before and can bring that to bear on what is happening now or what is going to happen in the future. In other words, your working memory links your past to your present and future, keeps your sights set on your goals and adjusts your course. It can rearrange things so you understand them better, and it can integrate new information with existing information, enabling you to execute tasks ever better. Furthermore, your working memory enables you to come up with totally new ideas, because it allows you to draw a connection between concepts that initially seemed unrelated. Without your working memory, you would not understand a thing and would not be able to create anything at all. It is a skill we tend to ignore, but it should be at the top of our development goals list.

Based on the work of Latvian-born cognitive neuroscientist Elkhonon Goldberg, we now also regard our ability to select the right information from the abundance we are faced with as an important aspect of working memory. The ability to select is an indispensable skill in the VUCA world, as is the ability to update this information when there is a shift in our ideas or environment and new requirements become operative. Think of the countless times a day you rely on your working memory. Everything you want to do, whether you're preparing for a meeting, finishing a workout, or ferrying kids from school to extracurricular activities, involves your working memory to some extent. People with a good working memory are better able to adapt to the demands they face and juggle tasks (which requires switching between tasks and information) without feeling overtaxed.

2 Self-control

"The skill we use to master and filter our thoughts and impulses so we can resist temptations, distractions and habits, and to pause and think before we act."

Temptations and impulses keep you from attaining your long-term goals

The importance of this skill is clear right away. This is the skill that enables us to transcend our wish for instant gratification, to ignore and withstand the strongest stimulus in our environment or in ourselves, and to aim for the long term. Our ability to control our impulses ensures we don't always say the first thing that comes to mind, that we don't hit a person who insults us, and that we don't jump into bed with the man or woman next door just because we feel like it.

3 Cognitive or mental flexibility
"The capacity to nimbly switch gears and adjust to changed demands, priorities, or perspectives. It is what enables us to apply different rules in different settings."

Those who have these executive skills are better able to adapt to a changing environment, are more prone to see new opportunities, and are also better equipped to anticipate danger. Clearly, these people are more likely to be successful than those who are stuck in a rut and unaware of important things in their environment. Think of this skill as the ability to change your tone depending on whether you are talking to your children or your peers. Or suppose a friend calls to say he's just been fired; cognitive or mental flexibility enables you to be comforting and supportive instead of boasting about your latest success. This skill also includes being able to see and admit that you were wrong about something and not blaming the outside world or someone else for adversity in your life.

These executive skills are often complementary. Together, they can help you achieve your goals.

Very Active Psychology

SELF-KNOWLEDGE

In 2002, University of Twente and Erasmus University Rotterdam started a project intended to teach students about all sorts of psychological phenomena through direct exposure. This project was very successful, in my opinion. It offered various programs that allowed students to take online tests that gave them firsthand experience of psychological phenomena and taught them about the underlying concepts. The programs developed for this goal were named ZAPs. ZAP is an acronym for *Zeer Actieve Psychologie* (Very Active Psychology). Some of these ZAPs called on students' executive skills. And although the project ended in 2004, the ZAP website is still accessible for general use. So go to zap.psy.utwente.nl[7] and try the various ZAPs to get some direct experience with the three core executive values. To test your self-control, you could try the Stroop color test or the Simon effect. To test your working memory, you might want to do the Brown-Peterson task. Another useful website is www.mathisfun.com, where you can

7 http://zap.psy.utwente.nl/

test your cognitive flexibility by trying the Tower of Hanoi.[8] For more fun executive skills tests, visit www.cognitivefun.net.[9] There you can find go/no-go-tasks (self-control), the Corsi-block test, the Backward Digit Span-task and N-Back-tasks (working memory).

Don't forget to write down your scores when you do these tests, because I will refer to them in the last chapter of this book.

Task	Score

Once your working memory, self-control and cognitive flexibility are well developed, you will be better able to achieve your goals. Imagine your goal is to exercise more. Your working memory enables you to keep your sights on this goal, even when you get distracted by other things. Your ability to control your impulses ensures you don't sit down on the couch with a chunk of Brie and a glass of wine, but makes you feel strong enough to actually go to the gym. And if you don't have enough time to go to the gym, your mental flexibility helps you think of an alternative, like going for a 30-minute jog instead.

Consciously goal-oriented behavior

Executive skills are also associated with consciously goal-oriented behavior as opposed to automatic behavior. Your executive skills are what enable you to respond intentionally to the situation (it is raining) in combination with your own plans and motivation (I've always wanted to dance in the rain) by doing what

8 www.mathsisfun.com/games/towerofhanoi.html

9 www.cognitivefun.net/

it takes (going out in the rain) rather than responding on automatic pilot (take cover or stay inside). Obviously, the tasks you carry out purely on automatic pilot or solely based on your executive skills are few and far between. Most tasks are a mix of both. So, you rely on different networks in your brain. If you had to do everything intentionally, that would take an enormous amount of energy and time. If you did everything on automatic pilot, however, your behavior would be completely predictable and rigid, and you would be unable to adapt to new situations.

It is not hard to see how important executive skills are, not just for you personally, but for people in all walks of life and for our society as a whole. It is important for the national government and the healthcare sector, for charities and for the business community.

Goldstein and Naglieri's classification

Returning to the goals you set in Chapter 1, you are probably wondering which executive skills you need to achieve those. This is where Sam Goldstein and Jack Naglieri's classification comes in handy. They have defined executive skills as the degree of efficiency with which someone gathers knowledge and solves problems in various areas. In their *Handbook of Executive Functioning*, they subdivide executive skills into more components than the three I described earlier. They define nine important elements of executive functioning, namely:

1 Focusing, retaining, releasing and dividing attention
2 Regulating emotions
3 Flexibility (ability to deal with change)
4 Inhibitory control
5 Task initiation
6 Organization
7 Planning
8 Self-monitoring
9 Using your working memory

These skills are pretty self-evident. If you go back and reread this list, I bet you will be able to identify right away why they are so crucial for attaining your goals. Let me say explicitly that regulating emotions also includes the ability to cope with stress. As you probably know, you will face setbacks and encounter unhelpful people in almost any endeavor in life, which can make your short or long-term ambitions harder, or in some cases even nearly impossible, to achieve. This will no doubt trigger negative emotions. But your brain (and in particular the networks involving your prefrontal cortex, including your anterior cingulate cortex) can regulate these emotions and decrease stress. This skill greatly influences how happy you are with your life and also helps people to coexist peacefully.

Three additional skills

I would like to add a few extra executive skills that I consider indispensable, because Goldstein and Naglieri's list disregards how other people can affect you and vice versa. After all, we usually execute our plans in a social environment rather than in isolation. We might want to move up the corporate ladder, say, or to effect social change in our community. Perhaps we want to start a business in a foreign country. Achieving any of these goals requires cooperation, competition, leadership and communication. In any social environment, executing your plans or achieving your goals depends on more than just your own actions and pursuits; it also depends on what others do and aspire to. To assess this social interplay, you need a realistic image of yourself, but also of others.

1 Forming a realistic self-image

The first skill I am adding is the ability to form a realistic self-image. You need that to make realistic plans, to chart, and to stay the course so those plans become reality. Here is a true story that illustrates this point. You might have read about Sujit Kumar, the chicken boy from Fiji, in my earlier book *Het maakbare brein* [The Mutable Brain], or heard about him in the media.

The Chicken Boy

After his mother's death and his father's murder, Sujit's grandfather locked him up for years in a chicken pen, where he had little or no human contact. Eventually, a social worker found and liberated him, but for lack of suitable alternatives, brought him to an old people's home. There, Sujit was tied to a bed, neglected and abused for 20 years. This is where Elizabeth Clayton found him in 2002. She took him in and surrounded him with incredible amounts of love and care.

Although Sujit has since, with the help of all his caretakers, made great progress in terms of motor skills, social skills and emotions, it remains unclear whether he has developed a sense of self. Because he is unable to talk or clearly sign and has no other way of answering questions, it seems impossible to find out whether he is self-aware. In animal behavioral studies, researchers use the mirror test developed by psychologist Roger Gallup in 1970 to assess whether animals recognize themselves. In the mirror test, animals are put in front of a mirror, sometimes after they have been surreptitiously marked on their forehead. If an animal connects its own movements with what it sees in the mirror, as evidenced by touching the mark on its forehead, this indicates that it probably understands that the mirror shows its reflection and not another animal. Some primates, and probably some elephants, dolphins and even one bird species – the Eurasian magpie – show some degree of self-recognition.

Based on Sujit's response to his reflection, we don't think he is self-aware. He is fascinated by the mirror, but does not react to his reflection in a way that suggests he recognizes himself. He will caress and kiss his reflection, for instance, but if you put a mark on his forehead without him noticing, he neither tries to touch that mark, nor does he show surprise at its presence. Other behaviors do not indicate that Sujit has a sense of self either. This lack of self-image is one of the reasons for the absence of certain developments in Sujit, such as problem solving, planning or deferring gratification. Sujit seems to continually live in the moment, controlled by the need for instant gratification, which amounts to the need to experience pleasure and avoid pain. Based on these needs, Sujit wants to satisfy the urge that arises in the moment, like eating when he feels hungry or sees someone else eat, or the urge to avoid something, like someone who is angry or a burning fire. His lack of self-awareness is one of the reasons he will always remain dependent on others.

2 Capacity for theory of mind

We know that having a self-image, and preferably a realistic one, is important for our ability to develop. But just knowing what makes you tick and what abilities you have, is not enough. You also need to have some idea of what makes others tick. This is the second additional skill I am adding to the list. What do other people want? What are their intentions? What are they going to do and how will they react to what you are doing or to other stimuli from their environment? What consequences will this have for them and for you?

You need to be able to look into someone else's mind, as it were, and read the emotions, intentions and thoughts in there in order to incorporate them in your own plans and actions. What does she think when I say I love her? What is that company or nation going to do now that they know I've run out of money, or now that I'm rallying my troops? What will her move be if I move my rook to this square on the chessboard and how will this influence the game? These are all important questions that have an impact on the failure or success of your plans. The ability to assess other people is a skill that makes a successful mother, CEO, general or politician and ensures good social interaction between people in general. This ability to assess other people's thoughts, feelings, actions and expectations is known as theory of mind. (Some researchers subsume theory of mind under cognitive flexibility, but because I want to give it due emphasis, I treat it as a separate category).

Other people will come up with a theory on your thoughts, actions and feelings and take those into account in their actions. So, you will also have to form a theory of mind about other people's theories of mind about you! Some people are exceptionally good at this. There is a great anecdote about Winston Churchill that illustrates the importance of theory of mind.

Winston Churchill

One night, at a dinner for foreign dignitaries from the British Commonwealth, Churchill was approached by one of the waiters, who told him that one of the honorable guests had pocketed an antique, silver saltshaker. What was Churchill to do? If he confronted the guest directly, he would cause him public embarrassment and possibly trigger a diplomatic incident. If he waited until after dinner, the guest would likely deny the theft and the saltshaker would be gone.

Churchill took action in a way that required quite a bit of theory of mind. He quickly pocketed the matching silver pepper pot and as the dinner drew to a close, sidled up to the dignitary in question and surreptitiously pulled out the pepper pot, saying: "Unfortunately, I think they've spotted us. I guess we'd better put them back." He put the pepper pot on the table, prompting his guest to do the same, and in so doing avoided political scandal while also ensuring the return of the stolen object.

The thief probably knew full well that Churchill had seen right through him, but also understood that Churchill's action offered him an opportunity to extricate himself from the situation without losing face. All in all, a lot of theory of mind going on there.

The executive skills you need to deal with complex events are different from those you need to deal with isolated actions like solving Rubik's cube or building a toolshed. For the type of plans that involve trying to get other people to do something, theory of mind is an indispensable executive skill.

3 Prosocial behavior

With theory of mind comes another important skill: prosocial behavior. Prosocial behavior means taking not only your own interests into account, but also those of others. As a result of this behavior, you show respect for other people, you are able to help them without expecting anything in return, and you do not harm them, even if you stand to gain large amounts of money, honor or possessions by doing so. Prosocial behavior means understanding that a healthy society requires everyone to see beyond personal gain. It means you don't just come up with excuses to do whatever you want, while you know you are exploiting, harming or denigrating others. Many people find it hard to show prosocial behavior (even though most people are convinced they are good at it, proving that a significant number of us have an unrealistic self-image). A lack of prosocial behavior is at the root of human trafficking, discrimination, economic crises, environmental pollution, quarrels between neighbors and bullying, to name but a few widespread social ills. That is why I have added this skill to Goldstein and Naglieri's nine executive skills.

Now that you have a clear theoretical overview of the main executive skills required to perform well, it is time to turn to your own executive skills, to see which ones you have and which you need to work on. I will now ask you to fill out several questionnaires. Obviously, this requires some self-knowledge and above all, a willingness to answer truthfully.

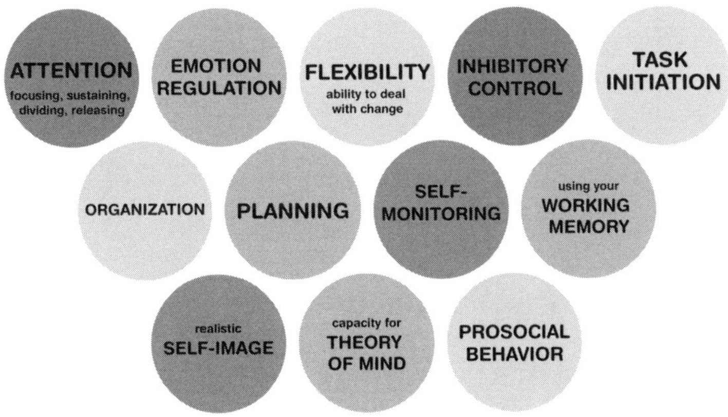

Twelve executive skills

Assessing your executive skills

To help you thoroughly assess your own abilities, I've included a table listing executive skills and several problems you might encounter if you haven't mastered each particular skill. This is based on a table designed by Dawson and Guare that appears in Goldstein and Naglieri's *Handbook of Executive Functioning*. Feel free to expand this table if you think of other problems caused by incomplete mastery of a skill.

	Skill	Problems caused by incomplete mastery
1	*Attention: focusing, sustaining, dividing, releasing*	Being easily distracted. Not deciding what to focus your attention on, but letting internal or external stimuli determine this. Finding it hard to finish a task. Getting stuck in activities that no longer serve a purpose and just generate negativity (thoughts, feelings). Problems with focusing, sustaining and releasing attention can lead to addiction, because you are incapable of directing your attention away from temptations.
2	*Emotion regulation (includes coping with stress)*	Getting upset easily. Having a short fuse. Getting anxious because of small incidents. Getting stuck in negative emotions. Having temper tantrums or rages. Being unable to put something behind you. Being unpredictable, volatile.
3	*Flexibility (ability to deal with change)*	Perceiving change as an affront. Feeling a lot of resistance when required to make changes. Continuing to do something, even if it has (partly) ceased to be productive. Being rigid. Finding it difficult to deal with open-ended tasks. Being able to think of only one solution to a problem.
4	*Inhibitory control*	Acting on impulse. Making inappropriate remarks. Responding immediately to all external stimuli. Getting into trouble with the law, in social situations and/or financially. Not thinking about the consequences of your actions.
5	*Task initiation*	Not meeting deadlines. Procrastinating. Endlessly postponing tasks. Doing everything at the last minute. Giving priority to short-term pleasure over things that have to be done.
6	*Organization*	Lacking structure. Having a messy desk/house. Regularly being unable to find things. Not having a fixed place for things. Jumping into tasks without proper preparation.
7	*Planning*	Being unable to subdivide a large goal into smaller milestones. Not knowing what to prioritize. Not achieving goals. Appearing chaotic. Feeling chaotic. Having trouble establishing a daily routine.
8	*Self-monitoring*	Not achieving goals. Not knowing what you have left to do. Not asking yourself or not honestly answering the question 'How am I doing?' Making careless mistakes. Being tired all the time. Rushing and skimping.

Skill	Problems caused by incomplete mastery
9 *Working memory*	Often forgetting things you need. Forgetting deadlines. Having trouble applying things you've learned. Forgetting what you have to do. Having trouble selecting relevant information. Forgetting instructions. Having trouble multitasking.
10 *Realistic self-image*	Overestimating yourself. Underestimating yourself. Bragging. Getting into trouble because you are unable to deliver on your promises. Being disappointed a lot. Blaming others for things that go wrong, coming up with a lot of 'yes, buts...' . Underestimating tasks. Finding it hard to set realistic goals. Not starting anything because you think you're not good at anything.
11 *Capacity for theory of mind*	Being unable to put yourself in someone else's shoes. Steamrolling other people's feelings. Seeing things only from your own perspective. Not understanding why people get upset.
12 *Prosocial behavior (keeping others' interests in mind)*	Always securing the best or the most for yourself. Making decisions that benefit you, but harm others. Letting your own short-term gain prevail over long-term gain for others.

Score your own ability for all twelve executive skills on a scale ranging from 'Incapable' to 'Bad' to 'Pretty good' to 'Good'.

Self-assessment	Incapable	Bad	Pretty good	Good
1 Attention: focusing, sustaining, dividing, releasing	☐	☐	☐	☐
2 Emotion regulation (includes coping with stress)	☐	☐	☐	☐
3 Flexibility (ability to deal with change)	☐	☐	☐	☐
4 Inhibitory control	☐	☐	☐	☐
5 Task initiation	☐	☐	☐	☐
6 Organization	☐	☐	☐	☐
7 Planning	☐	☐	☐	☐
8 Self-monitoring	☐	☐	☐	☐
9 Working memory	☐	☐	☐	☐
10 Realistic self-image	☐	☐	☐	☐
11 Capacity for theory of mind	☐	☐	☐	☐
12 Prosocial behavior (keeping others' interests in mind)	☐	☐	☐	☐

In order to test your self-knowledge (because opinions tend to differ), ask someone you trust and who knows you well to score you on these 12 executive skills. This person should let themselves be guided by how well they think you've generally mastered these skills.

Assessment by someone else	Incapable	Bad	Pretty good	Good
1 Attention: focusing, sustaining, dividing, releasing	☐	☐	☐	☐
2 Emotion regulation (includes coping with stress)	☐	☐	☐	☐
3 Flexibility (ability to deal with change)	☐	☐	☐	☐
4 Inhibitory control	☐	☐	☐	☐
5 Task initiation	☐	☐	☐	☐
6 Organization	☐	☐	☐	☐
7 Planning	☐	☐	☐	☐
8 Self-monitoring	☐	☐	☐	☐
9 Working memory	☐	☐	☐	☐
10 Realistic self-image	☐	☐	☐	☐
11 Capacity for theory of mind	☐	☐	☐	☐
12 Prosocial behavior (keeping others' interests in mind)	☐	☐	☐	☐

Check whether these scores match your own, and whether you agree with the other person's assessment of you. Adjust your own scores if you find the other person's assessment more accurate. Then write down your goal and use the information you've gathered through this step as feedback for your goal.

- Determine which executive skills you will need in order to achieve your goal by checking the appropriate box ('not at all', 'a little' or 'absolutely necessary') in the 'Skills needed to achieve goal' list on the next page.
- Next, look at each skill and assess whether you have it (taking the other person's assessment of your skills into account). If you possess this skill, check the 'Able' box.
- Check whether you can expect difficulty on the path toward your goal. Do you possess all the skills you need? If you come across a skill you need (either 'a little', or 'absolutely'), check the 'Problem' box.
- Look at the 'problem' boxes you've checked and see which unmastered executive skills are likely to cause problems on the path toward your goal. This description might seem a bit complicated, but if you take a look at the list, you will immediately see what you're supposed to do.

Goal: ....

Skills needed for goal	Not at all	A little	Indispensable	Able	Problem
1 Attention: focusing, sustaining, dividing, releasing	☐	☐	☐	☐	☐
2 Emotion regulation (includes coping with stress)	☐	☐	☐	☐	☐
3 Flexibility (ability to deal with change)	☐	☐	☐	☐	☐
4 Inhibitory control	☐	☐	☐	☐	☐
5 Task initiation	☐	☐	☐	☐	☐
6 Organization	☐	☐	☐	☐	☐
7 Planning	☐	☐	☐	☐	☐
8 Self-monitoring	☐	☐	☐	☐	☐
9 Working memory	☐	☐	☐	☐	☐
10 Realistic self-image	☐	☐	☐	☐	☐
11 Capacity for theory of mind	☐	☐	☐	☐	☐
12 Prosocial behavior (keeping others' interests in mind)	☐	☐	☐	☐	☐

These questionnaires can help you assess how well you have mastered the various skills. This is known as self-assessment. These are not official psychological tests. They are simply intended to make you think about your executive functioning and anticipate where you can expect to run into problems. To obtain an objective assessment of how good you are at the various executive skills you would need to undergo a full neuropsychological evaluation. I will discuss ways to improve your executive skills in Part II of this book.

Hot and cold executive skills

The riddle of the gnomes and the marshmallow experiment at the beginning of this chapter both call on your executive skills. However, there is a crucial difference between the two tasks and this difference is the guiding principle for dividing executive skills into two categories. The riddle of the gnomes calls on your cold executive skills. Cold executive skills are the skills you use to achieve a goal in a relatively context-free, non-emotional environment where analytical abilities count. These are also the skills you need to solve a puzzle, or to remember the numbers for your calculations.

The marshmallow experiment calls on your hot executive skills. Hot executive skills evaluate, steer and control stimuli and tasks that are personally, emotionally charged. As a child, you are sorely tempted to eat your marshmallow, but you know you will get two if you can wait a little while. Your brain seems to tell you to wait. But at the same time it tells you to eat, and everything in your body and your emotions seem to be geared toward eating that marshmallow. Emotion, motivation, instant gratification, inhibition and long-term rewards are the main ingredients in this dilemma. This mixture creates the circumstances where we need our hot executive skills to withstand temptation.

So, you use hot executive skills to achieve your goals while emotion, motivation and short-term rewards (such as money, sex, food, attention or status) are at play. Sometimes, achieving your goal requires you to ignore short-term pleasures (such as eating that marshmallow this instant). For example, you want to lose weight, but in order to achieve that goal you have to resist numerous temptations every day. Or you are saving up for something expensive, so you need to stop impulse buying for a while.

Adults, too, are faced with tasks that put their hot executive skills to the test. One of these is called the Iowa Gambling Task, originally developed by Antoine Bechara and Antonio Damasio, but now available in countless variations. In the original task, you are given $2,000 in fake money and then asked to take a card from one of four stacks in front of you. Every card you draw tells you whether you are winning or losing money. Two of the stacks let you win large amounts right away, but later annihilate your winnings by dealing you even larger losses. In other words, as the game progresses, you start losing money. The other two stacks of cards initially reward you with smaller winnings, and also contain losing amounts that are smaller than your winnings. If you draw cards from these two stacks, you eventually win money.

Healthy adults discover how the game is set up and start drawing mainly from the stacks that provide the smaller winnings, but even smaller losses. Patients with damage to the ventromedial prefrontal cortex – the innermost, lowest part of your prefrontal cortex – continue to draw cards from the high stakes stacks. They appear not to be able to change their behavior, even after suffering large losses following their large winnings. In other words, these patients have trouble integrating later results into their behavior, making their behavior less adaptive.

Adaptive behavior

Antoine Bechara also demonstrated that we can predict beforehand whether or not patients will show adaptive behavior. Patients whose ventromedial prefrontal cortex is damaged as well as healthy subjects show the same perspiration reaction when drawing a winning or losing card. However, healthy subjects also start perspiring more before drawing a card from the losing stacks. You could see this as an anticipatory response, a sort of gut feeling that guides your behavior (actually, a ventromedial prefrontal cortex feeling, but that doesn't exactly roll off the tongue). Patients whose ventromedial prefrontal cortex is damaged do not show this anticipatory response. They seem not to get this cautionary negative feeling when they draw a card from the wrong stack, which might explain why they continue to display their high-risk behavior after their initial wins.

We can transfer this knowledge to our own less pathological, but still ailing prefrontal behavior. We can take the patients' non-adaptive behavior in the Iowa Gambling Task as a metaphor for our own failure to learn from past mistakes in our everyday lives. For example, we have repeatedly experienced that if we let ourselves be guided by our emotions and the need to prove ourselves right in a discussion, either at home or at work, we will end up in a fight instead of displaying problem-solving behavior. Yet we continue to do the same. Or, we know that if we continue to eat junk food, we will ingest too much salt and sugar instead of healthy nutrients. Still, we do not change our behavior, because we get pleasure from the convenience of junk food and from the salt and sugar in the food itself. Just like patients whose ventromedial prefrontal cortex is damaged, we continue to show behavior for which we will eventually have to pay the price.

Antonio Damasio and co-authors showed that patients whose ventromedial prefrontal cortex was damaged often displayed behavior that can be classified as (acquired) sociopathy or anti-social personality disorder. People with this disorder show irritable and aggressive behavior, have trouble adapting to the usual norms, are often impulsive and insensitive and have trouble planning, making them prone to get into trouble. In other words, these patients have problems with many of the executive skills.

Executive skills and your goal

Some studies have shown that hot executive skills – responsible for assessing, processing and regulating emotionally loaded stimuli – are important for being socially successfully, while cold executive skills – responsible for assessing, processing and regulating non-emotionally loaded stimuli – are related to intelligence. However, other studies have shown that these conclusions might be too simple. There is also evidence that there is a correlation between lower intelligence and a lesser ability to ignore a small instant reward in favor of a larger deferred reward. This is corroborated by the SAT scores in the marshmallow experiment. In daily life, hot and cold executive tasks are usually not strictly divided, so you will often need both types of skills to succeed at a given task.

In order to achieve almost any goal, you need to take the following sequence of steps:

1 Defining and setting your goal
2 Charting a course toward your goal, including *a*) the steps you need to take and *b*) the problems you expect to encounter
3 Executing this plan, step by step
4 In case of unexpected events, adjusting your plan (or goal)
5 Determining when you have attained your goal.

You can only take all of these steps if you are proficient in both hot and cold executive skills.

Executive skills don't suck the joy out of your life. They remove the drama, the conflicts with yourself and others, the failures and the sick-making habits from your life.

Executive skills ensure that we can keep our sights on the horizon and will not fall for our short-term needs and temptations. I will discuss this in more detail in Chapter 5, 'Pitfalls'. These skills help us escape the constraints of the present, the past and even the future. They enable you to take control and to feel less like a puppet on a string that can only respond to its environment in set ways. Executive skills allow us to create things and make things happen, and to reach our goals, even against all odds. Of course, this in turn creates future pressure. Suppose, for example, that you want to graduate (at some point in the future). That means you will now have to start studying for your exams, which is likely to cause you some stress in the present. Yet, your executive skills will enable you to cope with this feeling and avoid chronic stress, burnout or worse.

The prefrontal cortex

Memory of the Future

Some 30 years ago, Swedish neuroscientist David Henschen Ingvar coined the term 'memory of the future'. This might sound like a contradiction in terms, because in order for you to remember something it must have happened first. Yet this is the perfect term for what I want to explain here. Ingvar's phrase refers to our ability to remember our plans for the future and the behaviors we will need to show in order to carry these out (a type of working memory). Ultimately, this term refers to the ability to actually imagine, anticipate and create a future. This notion is close to what Isaac Asimov, in the statement I quoted at the beginning of this chapter, called 'a science-fictional way of thinking.' In the paper introducing the notion of the memory of the future, Ingvar also wrote that these skills have to do with the (pre)frontal cortex. People who have sustained brain damage in this area actually lose their future, he argued, because they become indifferent and inactive. They can no longer foresee a future and act upon this vision, which in a sense makes them just like Sujit Kumar, the chicken boy.

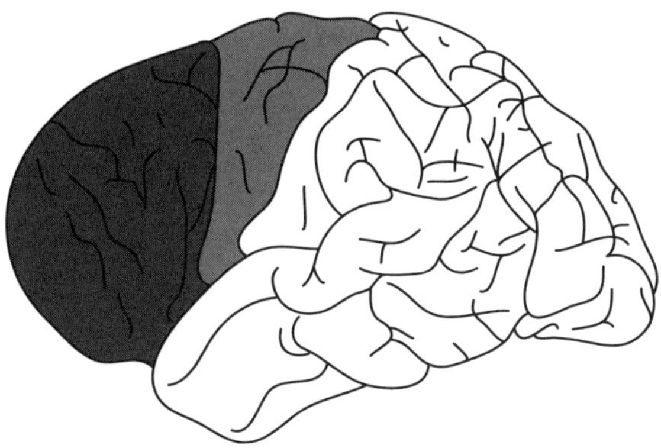

The prefrontal cortex (dark grey): an area you can develop

At this point, I will propose the rather blunt thesis that I first put forward in my earlier book *Passies van het brein*: that all of us are to some extent suffering from a dysfunctional prefrontal cortex. After all, as individuals we all find it difficult at times (and the number of times differs from one person to the next obviously) not to give in to short-term temptation, regardless of whether the specific temptation is to eat junk food, buy the latest gadget, or go to bed with the ski instructor. And so we all in some way undermine our long-term goals (of losing weight, saving money or not hurting our life partner). At a societal scale, the same prefrontal dysfunction manifests itself in the sale of bad mortgages, human trafficking and child prostitution, and directly or indirectly profiting – through investments – from arms sales and environmental pollution.

The anatomy of the prefrontal cortex

Executive skills appear to be related to the most complex characteristics of human behavior and are mainly, but not exclusively, linked to the frontal lobe, the prefrontal cortex and the neural pathways from this area to the posterior and medial/subcortical areas of the brain, as I explained in Chapter 2, 'The VUCA World'. The prefrontal cortex is the anterior part of the frontal cortex and is located in front of the (pre)motor cortex. The frontal cortex comprises about one third of the total cerebral cortex, making it the largest area of the brain.

There are various ways to parse the prefrontal cortex. One frequently used division is according to histological (cellular composition), or cytoarchitectonic mapping. In this system, the cerebral cortex is divided into morphologically distinct areas that are numbered. The most popular categorization is Korbinian Brodmann's map, which is why the 52 areas this German neurologist identified are also known as Brodmann areas.[10] Scientists disagree about exactly which Brodmann areas are part of the prefrontal cortex. Studies have shown that brains vary greatly in terms of the morphology of their prefrontal cortex. In other words: no two brains are the same, even though we behavioral scientists and therapists sometimes act as if they are.

You could also categorize the prefrontal cortex based on the other areas of the brain that it projects to, or based on the biochemicals involved in this process. For the purposes of this book, it is sufficient and most expedient to simply divide the prefrontal cortex into an upper (or dorsal) part, a lower (or ventral) part and an orbitofrontal part (the part that is above and behind your eye sockets, the orbitae). The lateral area mainly receives a lot of information from your senses. The dorsolateral prefrontal cortex seems to be associated with cold executive skills in particular, while the ventromedial and orbitofrontal parts of the prefrontal cortex primarily appear to play a role in hot executive skills. The foremost part of the

10 https://en.wikipedia.org/wiki/Brodmann_area

prefrontal cortex, called the rostral prefrontal cortex, appears to be especially important for coordinating different tasks, i.e. for multitasking.

In order to clarify the names of the various areas a little, I am including a short glossary of terms:

> Dorsal = upper, top (the back side on a quadruped).
> Ventral = lower, bottom (the belly on a quadruped).
> Rostral = in het direction of the nose.
> Lateral = side, outer.
> Medial = middle, inner.

The anterior cingulate cortex is often mentioned in the same breath with the prefrontal cortex because this part of the brain also facilitates executive skills (even though, strictly speaking, it is not part of the (pre)frontal cortex). This area seems to function as a connection between the frontal lobe and the limbic system (which is important for emotion and pleasure); it plays an important part in identifying errors and conflicts in a reaction.

Medial and lateral areas

The dorsal and ventral parts of the prefrontal cortex can be divided into the medial parts (those on the inside) and the lateral ones (those on the outside of the cortex). The orbitofrontal areas overlap with the medial areas of the prefrontal cortex and have many connections to the system in your brain related to perceiving and regulating emotions and areas associated with long-term memory. The terms orbital prefrontal cortex and ventromedial prefrontal cortex are sometimes used to refer to the same area of the brain.

Obviously, the distinct parts of the prefrontal cortex do not work in isolation but rather as part of a variety of networks, which also involve the posterior and medial parts of the brain. The prefrontal cortex is extremely well connected to areas associated with emotion, punishment and reward, motor skills, sensory information and the integration thereof, but also with areas that regulate our most basic functions, such as breathing and our heartbeat. This is precisely why this area is so well equipped to regulate our emotions, thoughts and actions, to give us new ideas, to make us focus on the future, to make us aware of our own impulses and to compel us to introduce necessary changes.

Development

Evolutionarily speaking, the prefrontal cortex is the most recently developed area of the brain. It developed on top of the areas of our brain that developed earlier, which are all also still active and influencing our emotions, thoughts and actions. These influences can be contradictory. You experience that on a daily basis, for example, when you say you want to do one thing (be patient), but actually do another (lose your temper). Those evolutionarily older areas, such as the thalamus, the amygdala and the nucleus accumbens, are more geared toward the rigid, rapid and standard processing of information and toward directing standard reactions to stimuli, like fight, flight, avoid or approach. They accomplish this by making us feel strong emotions and desires that often prompt stereotypical, automatic actions and reactions. The evolutionarily older brain areas are also geared toward the short term instead of the long term.

The development of the cortex, and the prefrontal cortex in particular, has enabled the brain to become more flexible, adaptive, social and long-term oriented. This area of the brain enables us to do something other than what our older brain areas prompt us to do. It even allows us to regulate how these older areas function. This knowledge makes it possible to refute the common dogmas that crime, abuse and stupidity are innate and can never be changed. The first part of this sentence is true. Yes, those things are innate. But the second half of the sentence is nonsense because the opposite – the good, the wise and the ability to outsmart those destructive urges – are also innate. And even more importantly, we can change our feelings and behaviors. My earlier publications *Het maakbare brein* and *Passies van het brein* explain this in greater depth.

The structure of the brain may well explain why we can feel so stuck in dilemmas like 'I want to enjoy this (alcohol, money, sex, etc.) this instant' or 'I am feeling so fill-in-the-blank (angry, hurt, stressed out, excited)' even though I know it is bad for me in the long run and I shouldn't let this sense of urgency dictate my actions, feelings and thoughts. After all, the brain is not a brand new model, but has developed gradually and still contains legacy systems. The short-term urges and responses of the older parts and the long-term considerations of the newer parts are exerting their influence simultaneously. This might explain why your thoughts, feelings and actions sometimes feel so contradictory, and why it can be so hard to achieve the goals you have set.

Michelangelo

According to an intriguing hypothesis, Michelangelo was way ahead of his time and in the early 1600s already aware of the importance to humanity of the prefrontal cortex and its attendant skills. He is thought to have hidden this knowledge as a secret code in 'The Creation of Adam', his famous fresco on the Sistine Chapel's vaults. The fresco depicts the biblical story of creation from the book of Genesis and shows God giving life to Adam, the first man. In 1990, physician Frank Lynn Meshberger published a paper in *The Journal of the American Medical Association* deciphering Michelangelo's imagery and arguing that the fresco depicted not only Adam and God, but also a third 'character' that we had overlooked for centuries. Meshberger convincingly shows how God, the angels and God's gown form an accurate anatomical illustration of the human brain, including several sulci (the grooves on the brain's surface), the brainstem, the vertebral artery, the pituitary gland, the optic chiasm, the pons, the spinal cord and the cerebellum (see the image on the next page).

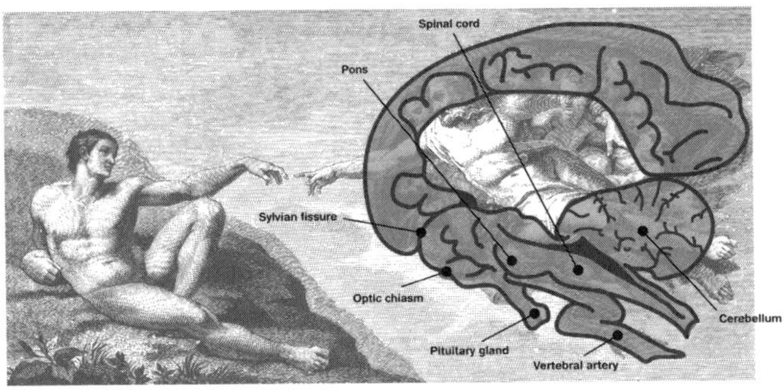

Michelangelo's secret code in The Creation of Adam.[11]

Meshberger disputed the common interpretation of the fresco, writing that it did not depict God bringing Adam to life because Adam's eyes are already open and he looks very much alive. Instead, he argued, God is passing the gift of *intellect* to Adam through that outstretched finger and arm protruding from his gown (an image that represents the frontal lobe). Intellect: that which makes us wise, allows us to transcend the present, to be creative and proactive. So in Meshberger's view, God turns Adam into *homo sapiens*, a wise human being. I endorse this interpretation, but replace the word 'intellect' with 'executive functioning' that would have made Adam the Homo Sapiens Verus, the truly wise human, or the human being that posesses all the qualities that make us human.

Meshberger bases his conclusion in part on a sonnet in which Michelangelo describes the intellect as the divine gift from God. God passes this gift through his fingertip, which almost, but not quite, touches Adam's fingertip. Receiving this intellect is what enables humans to 'plan the best and highest' and to 'try all things received', as Michelangelo writes in his sonnet:[12]

---

11 Sources: www.psychologytoday.com/blog/hide-and-seek/201207/the-creation-god www.nslc.wustl.edu/courses/bio3411/woolsey/2011/JAMA-1990-Meshberger-1837-41.pdf

12 Tusianai J., (1960). *The Complete Poems of Michelangelo*. New York, NY: Noonday Press; pp. 146-147.

After the divine part has well conceived

Man's face and gesture, soon both mind and hand,

With a cheap model, first, at their command,

Give life to stone, but this is not achieved

By skill. In painting, too, this is perceived:

Only after the intellect has planned

The best and highest, can the ready hand

Take up the brush and try all things received.

You could see the space between God and Adam's fingertips as a synaptic cleft. Nerve cell protrusions called axons conduct electrical impulses from one cell to the next to transfer information between cells. In the process, the cell protrusions do not actually touch each other. There is a gap in between that is known as a synaptic cleft. Meshberger argues that the gap between God and Adam's fingers in Michelangelo's painting alludes to this cleft. But how would the artist have known about this? According to lore, Michelangelo dissected and studied corpses, learning a great deal about the human anatomy, including that of the brain. This might explain the accuracy of the secret code in his fresco.

We could expand on Meshberger's analysis. By passing the new, the extraordinary, the intellectual to Adam's left hand, God is stimulating his right hemisphere in particular. This is how a lot of signals are transmitted: from the left side of the body to the right hemisphere and vice versa. Control of the human body works the same way: from the right brain hemisphere to the left side of the body and vice versa. There is growing evidence that exposure to new information and the acquisition of new knowledge mainly involves our right hemisphere. The left hemisphere comes into play once skills and responses have become ingrained. The fresco, therefore, may in fact depict the transfer of knowledge from God's right hand (using his left hemisphere, a metaphor for God's omniscience) to Adam's left hand (sending signals to his right hemisphere, a metaphor for the reception of new information he must still learn to use).

Obviously, we can't know whether this hypothesis about The Creation of Adam is right. What we do know is that in the centuries since the painting of the fresco, many studies have shown how important the prefrontal cortex is and how key this area is to learning the skills that make us truly human and ensure that our societies can become social, viable and inclusive communities. The next chapter will focus on the skills you need to become successful and wise.

SELF-KNOWLEDGE

Solution to the Riddle of the Gnomes

The right answer is Gnome #2. Neither gnome #3 nor gnome #4 can see any of the other gnomes and consequently cannot know which hat any of them is wearing.

Gnome #1, however, sees two gnomes ahead and knows that #2 is wearing a grey hat while #3 is wearing a striped hat. However, this information is of no use; he knows there are two grey hats and two striped hats, so he still doesn't know whether he is wearing a grey or a striped one. Therefore, Gnome #1 stays put.

Gnome #2 sees that the gnome ahead of him (gnome #3) is wearing a striped hat. Based on this information alone, he cannot deduce what color his own hat is. So he waits and waits, until he notices that none of the other gnomes is moving. Not even the gnome directly behind him. This provides him with a key piece of information. Because the gnome behind him (#1) is not jumping down to collect his prize, this must mean that #1 doesn't know what color hat he's wearing. Therefore, he must be seeing two different hats in front of him (if he saw two of the same color, he would immediately know what color hat he had on). And because gnome #2 can see that gnome #3 is wearing a striped hat, he can conclude that his own hat is grey. He jumps down from the stairs and wins the € 10,000 prize.

‘Between stimulus and response there is a space. In that space is our power to choose our response. In our response lies our growth and our freedom.’

Source unknown

Chapter 4 **A Recipe for Success**

This chapter teaches you something about your prefrontal cortex. You will learn that your behavior is highly predictable. You will discover which skills you need to be successful and steer your own course.

One-minute marionette

SELF-KNOWLEDGE

Stand in a doorway and lift your arms sideways until the backs of your hands reach the doorposts. Flex your muscles and push as hard as you can with the backs of both hands against the doorposts. Pretend you want to push the doorposts out. Now slowly count to 30. Then relax your muscles and immediately take a step forward to see what happens. You'll be amazed.

If there is no convenient doorway to use, you can also do this by pushing the back of one hand against a wall.

If you did this exercise right, you will feel your arms effortlessly raising themselves as if you were a puppet on a string. The reason for this is simple. When you were in the doorway and pushed your hands against the doorposts, you used your muscles just as you would have if you had lifted your arms. The doorposts prevented you from lifting them any higher, despite all your effort. When you stepped forward, your muscles were still flexed, even though you tried to relax them, so without the restraint from the doorpost, they rose on their own.

Obviously, this exercise, which I first read about in Vicki Cobb's *How to Really Fool Yourself*, is a metaphor for the fact that you are not always in charge of your own actions, and that many of the forces steering your life are beyond your understanding or control.

Mechanisms

Frontal lobe patients

We don't know all there is to know about executive skills and the prefrontal cortex, but science has discovered a great deal so far. Initially, our knowledge came from studying patients with a frontal lobe injury.

Countless studies have shown that people with such injuries have trouble suppressing urges and show concomitant, socially undesirable behavior. In such 'frontal lobe' patients, behavior and emotions are steered by immediate internal and external stimuli, leading to behavior aimed at instantly gratifying short-term urges, but harmful to the patient's long-term or even short-term interests. Such patients have trouble focusing and sustaining their attention for the time it takes to complete a task. Some show great rigidity and are unable to release their attention once focused on something. As Elkhonon Goldberg describes in *The New Executive Brain*, the disorders that result from an injury to the (pre)frontal lobe can be divided roughly into two categories: perseverative behavior and field-dependent behavior.

1 Perseverative behavior

A person with perseveration has an inability or a decreased ability to switch from one activity to another, even in a situation that clearly requires this. People with this disorder continue a behavior that was appropriate for a particular situation well after the situation has ceased to exist. For example, when asked to cross out the Ps on a sheet covered in lowercase letters P, B and Q (pbqpppqqbqp-bqqpbbpq and so on), they might continue to do so even after the experimenter has asked them to switch to crossing out the b's. Or when asked to complete the pattern below, they only draw triangles, because that is the first thing they drew and they are unable to change or alternate the patterns.

Try to copy the pattern below without lifting your pen from the paper.

Perseveration seems to occur primarily after damage to a patient's left frontal lobe, but in fact we all suffer from some degree of perseveration. An example is when you keep yelling at a loved one (perseverative behavior) or won't let go of your anger (perseveration of emotion), even after they have sincerely apologized for some minor misstep. We also perseverate when we continue to judge someone for the way they used to be, even though he or she has truly changed over the years.

2 Field-dependent behavior

We speak of field-dependent behavior when someone cannot complete a task or achieve a goal because they keep getting distracted by what is happening around them. Field-dependent behavior seems to occur mainly in patients whose right frontal lobe has been damaged. Field-dependent behavior is not internally motivated but rather steered by external stimuli, which prevent the patient from achieving goals. Some of my patients with this disorder would drink from my teacup or start reading a book on my desk, simply because their eye fell on it and they associated it with the act of drinking or reading.

The opportunity prompted by the relationship between an object (teacup) and a subject (arm and mouth) is called affordance (drinking), a term coined by James Gibson in the 1970s. The behavior an affordance evokes in these patients was termed utilization behavior by French neurologist François Lhermitte. Utilization behavior is also common in people without a frontal lobe injury, but is not recognized as such and therefore also not considered pathological. Examples of such behavior in normal life include impulse buying or letting your day be filled by the laundry, the dishes and the plants rather than what you need to do, like the taxes. Obviously, I'm speaking from personal experience here. You do these things simply because they present themselves to you, because in sight is in mind, as it were, and not because you planned it that way.

Some field-dependent patients imitate the behavior of people around them. If they see someone scratching their cheek, they also start scratching their cheek. If they hear someone laugh, they do the same. This type of copycat behavior is known as echopraxia. This too is something we all suffer from, to some extent. When I address an audience, I sometimes deliberately scratch my cheek and see many people copying my gesture. It is easy to come up with countless run-of-the-mill, harmless examples of echopraxia, like growing a beard because it's the current fashion, botoxing your face because the rich and famous do it, or speeding, drinking Nespresso, wearing a particular brand.... and the list goes on. Some examples are more harmful, however, such as joining others in bullying someone at school, or supporting a hate-mongering politician just because he seems to be gaining popularity.

Some field-dependent frontal lobe patients repeat verbatim what they hear other people say. If you ask them 'What's your name?', they'll consistently repeat your question instead of answering it. This parroting behavior is known as echolalia. Repeating one-liners you've read on the internet or in the paper, or repeating and forwarding gossip you haven't bothered to check, are everyday examples of this.

Although such everyday examples of perseveration, echopraxia, echolalia and utilization behavior are clearly not pathological, they can partly explain why you fail to do what is necessary to achieve your goals. Sometimes, an ability to respond quickly to external stimuli comes in handy, of course. If your roof is leaking, it makes sense to immediately take action. Similarly, you may need to instantly adjust to changing circumstances when crossing a busy road. However, in a world of temptation and information overload, you would soon lose your mind (and your life) if you responded to every external stimulus. Disregarding distraction and following an internal plan, responding only to pertinent information, are important survival skills.

It's easy to tell successful people and unsuccessful people apart; the former can choose whether or not to react to certain stimuli, while the latter seem to have no choice but to react to external stimuli. Even though they might still perceive their actions as the result of free will, we can all agree that these patterns limit their range of possible behaviors and hence the ability to shape their own, and others', present and future.

Flexible and wise response

It is useful to realize that our behavior is often informed by perseverative and field-dependent behavior. We're wired that way; the evolutionarily older parts of the brain are primarily guided by direct internal and external stimuli. The pre-frontal cortex developed later in the process of human evolution. In conjunction with several other parts of the brain, it enabled us to transcend field-dependence and perseveration. Yet those old forces still tug on us, especially if we do not learn to focus on the long term. Elkhonon Goldberg summarizes the evolution of the brain as a behavioral repertoire ranging from involuntarily responding to past or present stimuli (field-dependence) with certain behaviors, thoughts and emotions (perseveration), to having the ability to follow an internal, long-term plan while ignoring distractions. In order to do the latter, you need to be able to deduce what is the most important stimulus at any given time, so you can adjust your plans and their execution if need be. If you can do this, you will gain an increasing ability to learn proactive behavior.

Stereotypical response

If you have well-developed executive skills, you can proactively rather than reactively take part in your own life, the world, the present and the future. I realize it must sound strange to read the phrase 'to proactively take part in your own life', but this is something I am sure you don't often do, even if you are convinced otherwise. All too often, we respond reactively or reflexively to stimuli, making us a puppet rather than a puppeteer. At a basic level, you could say these responses work like this: I'm hungry so I eat something; he says something nasty so I feel insulted; she turns me on so I make a pass at her. You often do this without really considering the possible long-term consequences of this behavior for yourself or others.

Although it is easy to see how this *stimulus-response* chain works at the basic level (which is not to say it is easy to escape), it also influences our more complex emotions, thoughts and actions. For example:

- The world is changing, so I put my head in the sand.
- I keep checking my inbox, Facebook and Tinder, even though it disrupts my work, keeps me from achieving my goals and makes me restless.
- I let my kids play games on the computer because I am tired or it allows me to get around to doing what I want to do.
- When people around me don't do as I say, I get aggressive and overbearing because I fear I am losing control.

Without the appropriate executive skills, the relationship between stimulus and response is usually direct and so automatic that, assuming you know the other or yourself, you can predict exactly what response will follow a particular stimulus. I will show you how simple this is.

Math problems

Solve the following problems and then immediately respond to the command at the end.

17 + 8 = ______
15 × 3 = ______
93 + 17 = ______
57 + 12 = ______
21 × 8 = ______
24 + 47 = ______
18 + 81 = ______
and the final one, 24 + 27 = ______

Name a tool: ______

I have included the response you just gave to this question at the end of this chapter in order to show you how reflexively you act.

Without the appropriate executive skills, the relationship between stimulus and response is usually simple and stereotypical, as the basic chain below shows:

S ⟶ sR

Stimulus — stereotypical Response

In other words, if the stimuli are calculations and you are focusing on those and are suddenly asked to respond to the command 'Name a tool', your stereotypical response is 'hammer'.

Flexible response

Executive skills make another chain possible, however. These give you room to create more options so you have more than one way to respond. They create a space between stimulus and response, as it were. In that space, all sorts of things can happen, and you can respond in a way that differs from the standard reaction, from what everyone expects, or from whatever you are field-dependently programmed to do. You are able to do what is most conducive to your situation or plans. It allows you to interpret the stimulus in several ways; that fact alone multiplies your possible responses. This makes a new chain possible:

S ⟶ fR

Stimulus — flexible Response

Given a little more time and attention, your response to the command 'Name a tool' might be 'spirit level' or 'miter box' (if you happen to be a professional carpenter), and in that sense your reply would become unpredictable.

This new chain clearly demonstrates the power of executive skills. These skills enable you to transcend short-term stimuli and do what is necessary to reach long-term goals. They turn a reactive person into a proactive person or as the axiom that graces the beginning of this chapter put it: "Between stimulus and response there is a space. In that space is our power to choose our response. In our response lies our growth and our freedom."

SELF-KNOWLEDGE

Your personal stimulus-response chains

Now I will ask you to come up with a series of basic and complex S → sR chains, using stimuli that are relevant to you personally. Describe your response to the stimuli in terms of thoughts, actions or feelings. Take your time to reflect on this and characterize your responses to both basic and complex stimuli.

This task is intended for you to gain insight into the stereotypes that determine your thoughts, feelings and actions. This self-knowledge will help you identify and change the stereotypical responses you want to break out of.

To get you going, I have supplied a few when-then sentences for you to complete. A word of warning is in order: this exercise might push you out of your comfort zone. So, take extra care not to dig in your heels.

Complete	**Thought/Action/Feeling**
S *When I am tired,*	**R** *I am more prone to lose my temper.*
S *When I feel stressed,*	**R** *I drink more alcohol and tell myself I've earned it.*
S When I feel good,	**R** ______
S When I feel disappointed,	**R** ______
S When you yell at me,	**R** ______
S When I feel appreciated,	**R** ______
S When the kids are going berserk,	**R** ______
S When I'm busy,	**R** ______

Now come up with your own set of basic **S → sR**-chains, using stimuli that pertain to you.

Complete	**Thought/Action/Feeling**
S *When I don't immediately achieve my goal,*	***R*** *I blame someone else*
S ______	**R** ______
S ______	**R** ______
S ______	**R** ______
S ______	**R** ______
S ______	**R** ______
S ______	**R** ______

Now define the complex **S → sR**-chains with stimuli that are relevant to you.

Complete	**Thought/Action/Feeling**
S *When I have to leave my comfort zone,*	***R*** *I drag my feet by joking around*
S *When I am given information I don't grasp,*	**R** ______
S ______	**R** ______
S ______	**R** ______
S ______	**R** ______
S ______	**R** ______
S ______	**R** ______

Wise response

Executive skills enable you to respond with more flexibility, because they allow you to see that you have more options at your disposal. However, it is not enough to simply have more random options to choose from. Rather, we want to choose the best or most appropriate option from all those available, based on our goals and the environmental variables. We want to choose wisely. In that sense, you might say we want to evolve toward the following chain:

Wisdom and Success List

In my earlier book *Passies van het brein* I wrote about Thomas Meeks and Dilip Jeste's research at the University of California in San Diego. Meeks and Jeste analyzed a collection of texts about wisdom and came to the conclusion that no matter where or how wisdom was defined, it actually was invariably associated with executive skills. In a more recent follow-up study, they compared a large number of definitions of wisdom and distilled its nine most frequently mentioned components:

1. Pragmatic knowledge of life and social decision-making
2. Prosocial attitudes and behaviors
3. Reflection and self-understanding
4. Acknowledgement of and dealing effectively with uncertainty and ambiguity
5. Emotional homeostasis (the ability to maintain emotional balance)
6. Appreciation of relativism and tolerance
7. Openness to new experiences
8. Spirituality
9. A sense of humor

Aside from these sub-components of wisdom, there is another very informative list you need to see, which is based on an impressive body of research. In their book *Character Strengths and Virtues: A Handbook and Classification*, Martin Seligman and Christopher Peterson studied a wide variety of sources (literally from Confucius to Pokémon) to explore the ingredients of 'character', as in: 'that shows real character'. Using practical applicability as a criterion, they came up with a list of 24 character strengths and virtues that they claim to be universal.

Seligman and Peterson concluded that possessing, developing and expressing these character traits made people most likely to succeed in life. Those who devote themselves to developing these traits, are forging a path to a good life. Such a life brings not just personal happiness; it also contributes to the happiness of those around them and to the greater good.

Later research helped reduce Seligman and Peterson's list of 24 character strengths and virtues to a more manageable list of the seven most critical traits and skills for achieving success:

1. Grit (devotion/perseverance)
2. Self-control

3 Energy/zest for life
4 Social intelligence
5 Gratitude
6 Optimism
7 Curiosity

Again, these qualities tend to call on our executive skills and the prefrontal cortex, a clear sign that it's important to develop these.

For our purposes, it makes sense to merge these lists – the sub-components of wisdom and the success-related character traits – and to remove any overlaps. Pragmatic knowledge of life and social decision making overlap with social intelligence, for instance; just as curiosity overlaps with openness to new experiences, and an ability to maintain emotional balance overlaps with self-control. If we eliminate these overlaps, we end up with a list of skills/traits that are conducive to wisdom and success. Let's see how well you think you score on it.

SELF-KNOWLEDGE

Assess your wisdom- and success-related traits

First rate yourself for the traits related to wisdom and success, and after that, try to give concrete examples (starting on the next page) which support your self-scores, ranging from 'none' to 'a little,' 'sufficient,' and 'a lot.'

Trait/skill	None	A little	Sufficient	A lot
1 Grit (dedication)	☐	☐	☐	☐
2 Willpower	☐	☐	☐	☐
3 Energy/zest for life	☐	☐	☐	☐
4 Social intelligence	☐	☐	☐	☐
5 Gratitude	☐	☐	☐	☐
6 Optimism	☐	☐	☐	☐
7 Curiosity	☐	☐	☐	☐
8 Prosocial attitudes and behaviors	☐	☐	☐	☐
9 Self-reflection and self-knowledge	☐	☐	☐	☐
10 Recognizing and coping with uncertainty	☐	☐	☐	☐
11 Tolerance	☐	☐	☐	☐
12 Spirituality	☐	☐	☐	☐
13 Sense of humor	☐	☐	☐	☐

Supply a number of personal examples. For instance, under 'grit' you might fill in: I followed through with the introduction of that system that I knew most employees would benefit from, even though it cost me blood, sweat and tears. Or: I helped my child overcome his performance anxiety, even though it took me five years to see him through it.

Grit (dedication)

Willpower

Energy/zest for life

Social intelligence

Gratitude

Optimism

As it turns out, wisdom and success-related traits are executive skills associated with the prefrontal cortex.

Curiosity

Prosocial attitudes and behaviors

Self-reflection and self-knowledge

Recognizing and coping with uncertainty

Tolerance

Spirituality

Sense of humor ....

Depending on how easy or difficult it is to come up with examples of the various traits, adjust your earlier scores on the wisdom/success list.

Performance character and moral character

In the US, there is a non-profit organization whose aim is to inspire young adults to engage in ethical behavior and social participation. This organization, the Character Education Partnership, divides character into performance and moral components. In their definition, performance character encompasses traits based on willpower and endurance/perseverance, such as not giving up when there is a setback. Moral character is all about traits based on norms and values, such as being honest, unselfish, and considerate of other people's interests. If we now collate the executive skills, wisdom and success lists, we end up with a list that contains both performance character traits and moral character traits. You can now assess whether you have primarily developed a strong moral or a strong performance character. You might even conclude that you are equally strong in both areas, or that both areas still need a lot of work.

Grit

SELF-KNOWLEDGE

As I said before, the tests and questionnaires included in this book are not official or empirically tested. They are primarily intended to make you think and give you some insight into your personal skills and character traits and various aspects of your behavior. You can determine your score on grit, one of the most critical predictors of success, by taking an official test that was developed by Angela Duckworth and Chris Peterson. If you take this test online, you will be taking part in and contributing to their research, and of course you'll also gain insight into how much grit you possess (for the web address, see note [13]).

After you have taken the test, please write down your score below. You will need it later on in the book.

Grit test score: ....

13 https://sasupenn.qualtrics.com/SE/?SID=SV_06f6QSOS2pZW9qR

By now, you should have some idea of how proficient you are at the various wisdom and success-related skills, at least in your own estimation. The lists you filled out in the previous chapter will have given you some insight into your executive skills level and which ones you need to work on. Together, these two lists provide you with the powerful ingredients of a recipe for success. The list of executive skills is, as the name suggests, compiled of competences, while the variables on the wisdom/success list tend toward character traits. There is some overlap between the two lists, but together they provide you with a reasonably complete picture of what you are good at and what you need to develop to become successful.

Now that we have all this knowledge, we can also apply it in reverse: what missing skills and traits have caused problems in your life?

SELF-KNOWLEDGE

Identifying missing skills

Describe a problem you experienced in the past. Then check the boxes next to the unmastered skills and traits that caused the problem. You can assess each problem separately.

Problem: ....

(For example, dropping out of college or a failed relationship)

1 Grit (dedication) ☐
2 Willpower ☐
3 Energy/zest for life ☐
4 Social intelligence ☐
5 Gratitude ☐
6 Optimism ☐
7 Curiosity ☐
8 Prosocial attitudes and behaviors ☐
9 Self-reflection and self-knowledge ☐
10 Recognizing and coping with uncertainty ☐
11 Tolerance ☐
12 Spirituality ☐
13 Sense of humor ☐
14 Attention: focusing, sustaining, dividing, releasing ☐
15 Emotion regulation (includes coping with stress) ☐
16 Flexibility (ability to deal with change) ☐
17 Inhibitory control ☐

18 Task initiation ☐
19 Organization ☐
20 Planning ☐
21 Self-monitoring ☐
22 Working memory ☐
23 Realistic self-image ☐
24 Capacity for theory of mind ☐

If you have come to the conclusion that you are missing all or most of the skills and character traits needed for success, there is no need to despair. These can all be developed.

Neuroplasticity

The great thing about Seligman and Peterson's list is that, as they say, these skills or traits are not set in stone, but trainable. The same is true of executive skills. Angela Duckworth calls these traits habits, no more and no less.[14] Of course, there is room for you to develop them, within certain genetically defined limits. If you practice and expose yourself to certain traits or skills every day, you can develop a default mode in your brain that triggers you to automatically do the right thing without expending extra energy. You are able to develop this default mode because your brain has a special property known as neuroplasticity, which is what gives us our ability to develop and adjust.

New connections[15]

As we know, our brain steers our thoughts, feelings and actions, but the opposite is also true: everything we think, do and feel directly affects the structure and functioning of our brain. Contrary to what many people think, our brain is continually making new cells (neurogenesis) and creating new connections between cells (synaptogenesis). These processes are influenced in part by the things you experience, think, do and feel. The creation of new cells and connections, and the fact that brain cells communicate with each other and can change how they communicate, means that your brain structure and functioning continues to change as long as you live. I mean this very literally. The networks in your brain are changing in physical shape, creating new pathways, shutting down existing pathways and forming new networks. The way these networks function depends on your experiences, thoughts, feelings and actions. Because the networks' shape

14 Tough, P. (2013). *How Childeren Succeed: Grit, Curiosity and the Hidden Power of Character*. London: Random House. Tough quotes Duckworth, who in turn credits American philosopher/psychologist William James.

15 For an in-depth discussion of this topic, see M.M. Sitskoorn, *Het maakbare brein* 2006, [The Mutable Brain].

and functioning changes, we are able to feel, think, and act differently. And because we think, feel and act differently, our brains will in turn change again. Let this sink in for a minute.

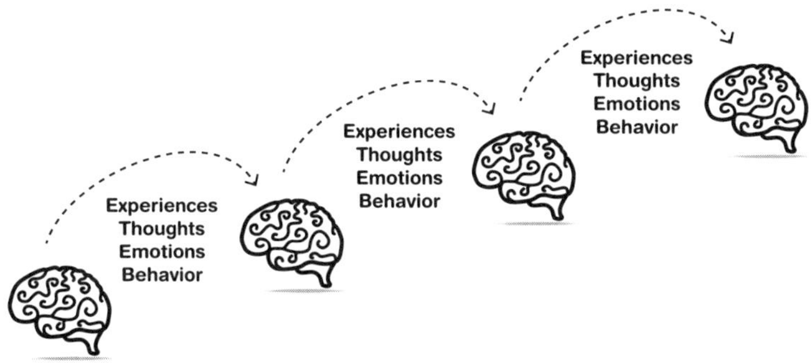

Brain and behavior are continually shaping each other

The emergence of new networks in our brains and the changing communication within and between those networks means we are continuously evolving and becoming. You are someone with all your emotions, character traits and skills; and all these emotions, character traits and skills evolve on the basis of what you are exposed to and what you expose yourself to. In other words, you are one thing, but you are also becoming another. We are not static, but dynamic, just like the world around us. And it is the continuous interaction between us and the world that causes continuous mutual impact and continuous change.

Developing your brain

It's simple: everything you do and are exposed to, develops certain networks in your brain. Under the influence of these evolving networks, your skills, thoughts and feelings change, which in turn changes your interaction with the world. This exposes you to new events, triggering new developments in your brain. Make no mistake: this applies to both positive and negative developments. When I speak in public I sometimes say: 'If you nag all day, you are developing perfect nagging networks in your brain and nagging will come more and more naturally to you. That which you do a lot, that which you expose yourself to a lot, will develop. This applies to skills like playing football or the violin; to feelings such as fear or empathy; to thoughts like 'foreign people are dangerous' or 'I must have an order of fries', and to logical thinking.

The extent to which you develop a characteristic depends on the interaction between your genes and your character traits, and on the extent (duration and intensity) to which you expose yourself to a given stimulus in your environment. Those of us who spend a great deal of time raising kids, develop their pedagogical skills and help their children develop. Those who spend a lot of time on

Once you understand how your brain works, you can no longer fool yourself with excuses like 'I was never any good at that' or 'It runs in the family'.

interpersonal relations, develop their social skills, and those who spend most of their time playing World of Warcraft or watching reality shows, develop ..... (I'll let you fill in the blank). In *Het maakbare brein*, I put it like this: your brain shapes who you are, and who you are shapes your brain.

Our capacity for neuroplasticity explains why our brain continues to change. Time and again, our brain has tried to adapt to the demands of its environment and that is one of the reasons why our brain is different from that of a Neanderthal or even that of someone who lived a century ago. Due to frequent exposure to online experiences and a lack of other types of input digital natives have developed other skills and feelings than earlier generations, as Nicholas Carr and Richard Restak have shown in their books on the brain's adaptation to the digital age. The fact that our environment plays such a key role in developing our brain and hence our skills, thoughts and feelings, is something many people are not aware (enough) of.

Capacity for change

It is crucial to realize we are not born with a fixed set of executive skills and success-related traits, but rather that we are born with the ability to develop such skills and traits, though some of us have more potential than others. We can adapt to the VUCA world and develop our success-related skills and traits, and in so doing effect change in the world. But that does require time, knowledge and energy.

Developing skills requires exposure, practice and performance. Learning a new skill initially takes a lot of energy, but eventually becomes a habit that you perform almost on autopilot. Can you even teach an old dog new tricks? Doesn't neuroplasticity diminish over time? The answer is yes and yes. Yes, it's possible to teach an old dog new tricks. And yes, it's true, brain plasticity is greatest when you are young. However, it is also true that the older you get, the better able you become at deciding what you want to develop and how. In other words, as you age, you learn to take full advantage of your brain's plasticity. So, to develop our brain and our abilities, we need an awareness of the principle of plasticity, selectiveness in what we want to develop, the right practice and/or exposure to the right information, focus, and commitment. Once you understand how your brain works, you can no longer fool yourself with excuses like 'I was never any good at that' or 'It runs in the family.'

Because development requires exposure and time, you should push your boundaries a little every day. Put effort into what has priority and, with the right method and information, gradually develop the skills you need. Doing nothing means deciding to change nothing. That's fine if you are happy and do no harm. But if you want to change, or have to change, then you know it's possible and you know how. As I put it in *Het maakbare brein*, you can choose to be an architect rather than a resident in your brain, a manufacturer rather than a consumer. I will explain this in greater detail in Part II of this book, How to train your CEO brain: the EFFECT Program. This program will enable you to influence the structure and performance of your prefrontal cortex and to develop your executive skills.

Three key components

In Chapter 1 'A Goal to Set Your Sights on', you learned about the three key components that can help you achieve your goals:

- Realistic goal-setting
- Motivation
- Skills

Now that we are a couple of chapters in, you have made great strides and you understand more clearly how these variables relate to you personally. You have set yourself realistic goals and defined a roadmap to achieve them; you have assessed your motivation and evaluated the skills you need to succeed. In the next section of this book, How to train your CEO Brain: the EFFECT Program, you will learn which methods are conducive to developing your prefrontal cortex and how to develop the attendant success-related skills.

Before you actually get started on that, it is useful to take a closer look at some of the factors that commonly undermine your goals, motivation and skills. The next chapter provides some tips and tricks to help you avoid these pitfalls.

Solution to 'Name a tool'

Your response to 'Name a tool' was 'hammer'. How do I know that? Well, the majority of people respond in exactly the same way. Because you were first asked to focus your full attention on those math problems and then suddenly had to respond to that command, the result was a stereotypical, predictable response. And the most stereotypical response is hammer, although drill and saw are sometimes also mentioned. Other responses tend to occur only if the person responding happens to be a professional carpenter or construction worker.

‘Big, sweeping life changes really boil down to small, everyday decisions.’

Ali Vincent

Believe it, be it: How being the biggest loser won me back my life (2009)

Chapter 5 **Pitfalls**

This chapter is about the type of pitfalls that can prevent us from achieving our goals. The knowledge you will gain here will help you avoid or prevent these pitfalls.

Cheap television

Read the following story carefully.

Three students walk into a thrift shop to buy a cheap second-hand television set for their shared apartment. They find one that they like and ask the salesman what it costs. The salesman says the price is 25 Euros, and the students decide to buy the TV and split the cost. They each take a 10-Euro banknote out of their pocket and give it to the salesman, who takes the money and walks to the back of the store to get change. On his way to the cash register, he realizes he can make a little extra money on the TV if he tells the students he made a mistake: that the price is not 25 Euros, but 27. This won't make much of a difference to them, he reasons, and it will allow him to make a little extra on the side. He puts the three tens in the cash register and takes out five 1-Euro coins. He pockets two of the coins and walks back to the students. He apologizes and says the TV actually costs 27 Euros. The students still think it's a good deal and the salesman gives each of them a 1-Euro coin.

The three students happily leave the store with their cheap TV and the salesman is happy too, because he scammed the students and made a little extra money. Everybody is happy, so everything's fine, right?

Or is it? Let's review what happened.

Each of the three students gave the salesman 10 Euros, so they gave him a total of 30 Euros. The salesman came back with five 1-Euro coins from the cash register. He pocketed two and gave each student a 1-Euro coin as change for their 10. So each student ended up paying 9 Euros.

3 × € 9 = € 27 + € 2 that the salesman pocketed = € 29.

But wait a minute, this means we come up 1 Euro short! How is this possible?

Try to solve this riddle without reading any further.

Explanation

I came across this problem in Kevin Dutton's *Split-Second Persuasion*. Do you see what's going on? You might after some time, but don't be embarrassed if you don't get it right away, because many people fail to understand what's wrong, even though they rack their brains. In this story, our brain is tricked into searching for a solution in the wrong direction. The way in which the information is presented cues us to focus on the wrong thing, namely 3 × € 9 = € 27 + € 2 = € 29 instead of twenty-five plus two plus three equals thirty. By the way, I consciously wrote these last numbers in full rather than as numerals, so they would not jump out at you from the sea of words. In this way, I prevented them from attracting your attention and giving the answer away while you were reading the story.

This anecdote illustrates how your thoughts, actions and emotions are steered by that which attracts your attention and by the way information is presented to you. This can create quite a few pitfalls, as we shall see in this chapter.

In the previous chapters you learned that our rapidly changing world, combined with our desires and obligations, can create a lot of pressure and negativity. In order to successfully feel, think and act, we will need to make changes. We will need to learn some skills and unlearn others. That sounds logical, but there is a problem. Knowing that we have to change is only the beginning. Even though we want to, and sometimes have to, change, we often don't. That's because there are many aspects of our thoughts, emotions and actions that prevent us from changing. I will now discuss some of these obstacles, which I am quite sure you're going to run into as you attempt to change. You might even be using them as an excuse – consciously or unconsciously – not to change into someone better.

Pitfall: 'Short-term gain, long-term pain'

Let me start with a personal favorite: 'short-term gain, long-term pain'. In my book *Passies van het brein*, I describe three forces that are crucial to steering your own behavior:

- Pleasure
- Pain
- Wisdom

Pain and pleasure can create quite a few pitfalls. To understand how that works we will link particular pain and pleasure forces with the goals you set at the beginning of this book. Let's focus on that for a minute.

Take a minute to envision the goal you want to achieve. Write it down again.

Goal: ....

....

(I'm having you write down your goal again to stimulate your working memory and your commitment to this goal, which will help you achieve it.)

Short-term gain, long-term pain.

Now, there is a big problem with goals that cannot be reached instantly. It seems as if the path toward those long-term goals is continually crossed by all sorts of short-term goals, such as spending money on lots of little things even though you resolved to save up for something, or grinding that axe anyway despite the fact that you fully intended to remain cool, or eating an entire container of ice cream while watching TV even though your goal was to get in shape. These are all short-term goals and things we really crave at the time, but giving in to them gets in the way of reaching our long-term goals.

This is probably not new to you. You know, in general terms, that you have to suffer short-term pain in order to achieve real long-term gain. Yet, somehow this knowledge is insufficient to make you act accordingly. We often say we want one thing, but slip into satisfying our short-term wants and ignore our long-term goals, making it harder and harder, if not impossible, to ever reach them. Why is this? The reason is that our brain – even though it theoretically has the ability to focus on the long term – also tends to steer us in the direction of our short-term goals. Our brain does this because this has historically proven to be a successful strategy. Success is very simple to define in this case: it is all about survival (note: our lifespans used to be much shorter than now) and procreation. In order to survive and reproduce we needed to eat, drink, gather things, have sex, learn skills, be safe and belong to the group, to name just the most basic things.

Pain and pleasure

Over time, two powerful forces developed in our brain to steer us toward all these necessities: pain and pleasure. These forces developed eons ago, in the early evolution of our species, and they still rule our brains today. The pleasure centers in our brain are stimulated when we're exposed to the things we need to survive and reproduce (food, objects, sex). The pain centers in our brain are stimulated when we're faced with a shortage of necessities or with situations that jeopardize our survival, like fire. So it's pretty simple, really. Eating, drinking, having sex or gathering things stimulates the pleasure center in our brain, which gives us a good feeling (obviously). It is highly motivating to continue to eat, drink, have sex and collect stuff. These things are good for our survival and reproduction. The same goes for pain. Experiences that are detrimental to our survival, such as fire, going hungry or thirsty, exhaustion, or losing possessions, stimulate the pain center in our brain. This causes a degree of pain, which is a great motivator to avoid or alleviate these stimuli (fire, hunger).

As Lieberman and Eisenberger describe, what is so special about the pleasure and pain centers in our brain is that they are not only triggered by physical things like sex, new shoes, and fried chicken (all of them pleasure-related) or a punch in the gut, fire, or a theft (pain-related), but also by social stimuli such as collaboration, trust and friendship (pleasure), or discrimination, bullying, fraud and the loss of loved ones (pain). This is hardly surprising, as social stimuli contribute to our survival and procreation as much as physical stimuli. It is a wonderful mechanism that strongly motivates you to do what is necessary to survive and reproduce.

But there's a problem. This mechanism worked perfectly in times of scarcity (the millions of years during which the mechanism developed), in a relatively simple society and for relatively short lifespans. However, we no longer live in times of scarcity, our existence has become far more complex (just think of your tax forms or mortgage application), and our life expectancy has increased dramatically. Drinks, food, consumer goods, sex: they're cheap, abundant and available anywhere, anytime. In a world as complex as ours – as I described in Chapter 2, 'The VUCA World' – and with a life expectancy that makes long-term planning an ever greater necessity, the pleasure/pain mechanism isn't always our best friend anymore.

The contradictory forces you often experience can be summarized as 'what I really want to achieve is incompatible with what I want right now'. Suddenly this makes sense. Today's world asks for long-term planning in order to achieve our main goals (let's call this the 'ultimately I want' force or the 'actually I want' force), while your brain – honed for millennia in an era when our lives were a simple, short struggle to survive – tends to send you in a different direction (causing the 'I want it now' force). Your brain is conflicted, steering you toward both short-term pleasure and long-term pain. Which is why we often succumb to that glass of wine, or that double cheeseburger, or the guy next door, and end up addicted, overweight and divorced. And no, please don't condense this into 'I want to, but I can't'. Because the truth is: 'I want to, but it's not easy'.

So you probably see where I am going with all this: it's time for some hard work, because those contradictory forces are not going to resolve themselves spontaneously. In the short run, it feels almost unnatural to say no to that cupcake or the woman next door. In other words, you feel a strong craving because your brain steers you toward fat, salt and sugar (or the woman next door, i.e. sex). These tasty bits (and I'm talking about the cupcakes here) used to be scarce, but they were key to our survival and are therefore linked to our pleasure center. They seem to scream: 'Eat me, eat me!' In today's world, however, with its abundance of fat, sugar and salt, these cravings are no longer useful for survival but detrimental. They conflict with the long-term goals that are more suited to this complex world and our own longevity: staying thin and healthy, in other words, passing up that cupcake. In order to achieve these new goals, we will need to develop our prefrontal lobe, our CEO brain. I will explain how you can do this in the 'development' section of this book. And even if a cupcake (or sex) is not your pitfall, or if staying healthy (or married) is not your personal long-term goal, I'm sure you still get the general idea. Just see cupcakes as a metaphor for your own, personal sabotaging 'I want it now' force.

SCARF model

I am about to ask you to explore your main 'I want it now' forces or pitfalls. I will in effect be asking you to specify the exact nature of the obstacles and temptations you expect to face on the path to your goal. Bear in mind that those 'I want it now' forces can also be lurking in the domain of social interaction. As I said before, survival and reproduction is about more than goods, food, drink and sex. It also involves key social variables. David Rock has neatly summarized the most important of these in his SCARF model. SCARF is an acronym for Status, Certainty, Autonomy, Relatedness and Fairness.

- *Status*: How important are you in relation to others, where are you in the pecking order?
- *Certainty*: To what extent are you able to predict the future?
- *Autonomy*: Do you feel able to control events? Do you have options?
- *Relatedness*: To what extent do you feel accepted by others and at home in the group?
- *Fairness*: To what extent do you feel you and others are treated fairly?

Rock relates these five social domains to your pleasure and pain systems. The higher an action's score on the SCARF scale, the more your pleasure center is stimulated and the more motivated you will be to continue doing the thing that provides you with Status, Certainty, Autonomy, Relatedness or Fairness. The lower an action's score on the SCARF scale, the more motivated you will be to discontinue or avoid this action or behavior. The five elements of the SCARF model explain quite well why someone does or does not want to do something. They also provide a good explanation for many human conflicts. After all, if someone does something that weakens your SCARF elements, you will most likely dig in your heels. If someone does or asks you something that boosts your SCARF elements, you will be more than happy to cooperate. Just think back to a conflict you've had with someone. Whatever the ostensible reason, one or both of you probably felt your status was being threatened, your certainty or autonomy undermined, or that you were being excluded or treated unfairly.

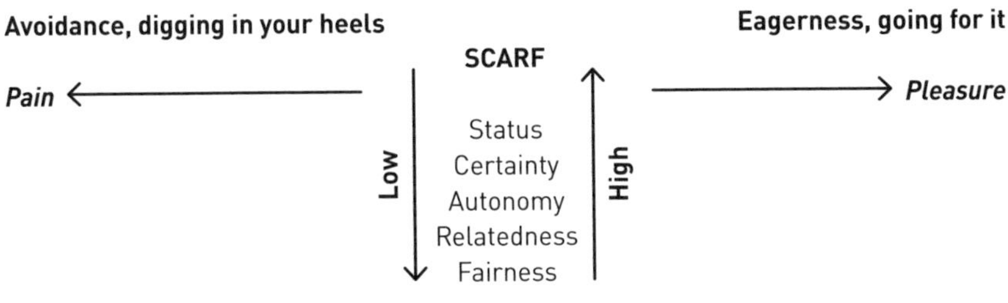

The SCARF model and its relationship to pain and pleasure

Your personal pitfalls

SELF-KNOWLEDGE

To help you become more aware of your 'short-term gain, but long-term pain' pitfalls, I would like you to define the most powerful 'I want it now' pitfalls for yourself. Make sure you include not only the most primary forces like food and sex, but also elements from the SCARF model, like the things you do to gain status or to feel you belong. Don't forget to include other social variables that may come to mind. Ask yourself, and answer truthfully, whether your short-term actions tend to be driven by Status, Certainty, Autonomy, Relatedness and/or Fairness and how this might get in the way of your long-term goals. For example, your decision to have another beer might be based on peer pressure, but conflict with your goal to drink less. Or maybe you resist quitting a job that makes you unhappy and unhealthy because you are not prepared to give up the status and certainty that comes with it, even though your ultimate goal is to create a happier life for yourself. There are countless examples of this kind of dilemma.

While defining your pitfalls, also take into account your stereotypical responses (as laid out in Chapter 4). These are the marshmallows we talked about earlier, but specified in more detail and with more subtlety. It is important to keep your eye on these, because they can make you stumble into an 'I want it now' pitfall in the blink of an eye.

My long-term goals are ______________________________

My 'I want it now' pitfalls in relation to these goals are ______________________________

Pitfall: Potential pleasure

The short-term power of pleasure is amplified many times by the misleading power of potential pleasure, as Kelly McGonigal illustrates so well in her book *The Willpower Instinct*. Potential pleasure seems to outstrip pleasure itself. We know how this works from studies conducted in the 1950s by James Olds and Peter Milner at McGill University. Olds and Milner were interested in steering rat behavior by punishment. Rather than denying rats their favorite food, they punished the rats by administering small electric shocks through electrodes placed directly in the rats' brains. One time, Olds and Milner put an electrode in a rat's brain because they expected stimulation of that spot to trigger fear in the rat. But much to their surprise, the rat did not try to avoid the stimulus as they had expected, but rather tried everything it could to recreate the stimulus. It continued to return to the place where it first received the stimulus. This craving was so strong that Olds and Milner found they could use brain stimulation to control the rat like a drone. If they wanted the rat in corner A of a box, they stimulated it when it walked in that direction, and if they wanted it in corner B, they likewise stimulated the rat's brain when it happened to wander toward that corner. The rat simply repeated the behavior coupled with the brain stimulation.

Olds and Milner were at a loss to explain this. What was going on? Why would a rat repeat behavior that invoked fear? At first, the researchers thought the brain stimulation might have unwittingly invoked the rat's curiosity, but after some investigation they discovered they had mistakenly placed the electrode in an area of the rat's brain that, when stimulated, triggered a kind of reward instead of fear. They tried to corroborate this discovery by doing additional research. They put a very hungry rat with an electrode in its reward center in a T-shaped maze that contained food on either end of the crossbar. Normally, a hungry rat would run toward the food and start eating, but now the researchers discovered that if they stimulated the rat's brain before it reached the food, it would stop in its tracks, preferring the electronically stimulated reward over the actual food.

Olds and Milner's findings were reinforced by follow-up research in which rats were given the opportunity to stimulate themselves by activating a lever. The rats turned out to love the stimulation so much that they continued to press the lever, even to the point of exhaustion. Another study showed that they were even prepared to brave an electric shock so strong it scorched their feet in order to get to the lever that allowed them to stimulate their pleasure center. Olds and Milner had clearly discovered something important: brain stimulation so pleasurable that a rat was willing to give up every other reward it would normally go for (there are interesting videos about this research on YouTube[16]).

---

16 See for example, www.youtube.com/watch?v=aNXhyPj-RsM

The expectation of pleasure

Several years later, psychiatrist Robert Heath repeated Olds and Milner's research on human patients. Electrodes were implanted in these patients' brains, and they were given a self-stimulation button. And sure enough, the psychiatric patients behaved exactly like the rats. They continued to stimulate themselves, refused to stop and preferred to stimulate their pleasure centers rather than feed their hungry bodies. But did all this apparent pleasure make the patients happy? It certainly did not look that way. They actually looked more like addicts who were trying to satisfy a craving than blissfully content people.

Many more studies followed, and all the research pointed toward what we now know: that Olds and Milner had discovered part of the brain's reward system. This system, in which septal nuclei and the nucleus accumbens play a major role, does not actually give us pleasure, but triggers the expectation of pleasure. This expectation involves the release of dopamine[17], which causes a craving and motivates us to pursue whatever we expect is going to give us pleasure. Stimulation of the reward system by external stimuli, such as the sight of gadgets, a Facebook or Whatsapp notification, or a scantily clad woman on the hood of a car, focuses our attention on the potential for pleasure and prompts us to take an action that we expect to deliver this pleasure. This response is connected mainly to things that provide instant gratification, such as food, objects, sex and drink. That is hardly surprising. As I said before, all these necessities are associated with survival and reproduction and by linking pleasure and the potential for pleasure to these key elements, our brain has evolved in a way that ensures we want to leap into action when exposed to triggers that will help us survive or reproduce. Having satisfied our craving, we no longer need to experience pleasure because the thing we needed to do to survive or reproduce has already happened. The goal has been achieved. So, pleasure (or potential pleasure) is a means to an end, not an end in itself, even though we tend to perceive this very differently.

Times have changed

Here's what we should take away from this: what we crave does not always equal pleasure, but the craving happens to be an incredibly powerful steering influence. It makes us dream and anticipate; it makes us willing to work for it, but it does not always guarantee real pleasure. Even if you experience the expected pleasure only intermittently, or not all, you will keep seeking pleasure. This craving system is triggered by any of our primary needs: food, drink, sex, safety, a sense of belonging, you name it. This was our brain's surreptitious way of ensuring that, in times of scarcity, we would focus on that which would help us survive and actually work to acquire those necessities. This mechanism is still deeply entrenched in our brains. Anytime we see something linked to food, drink, sex, safety or

17 Dopamine is a neurotransmitter, that is, a substance in the brain that enables cells to communicate with each other.

belonging, we get a dopamine shot that guarantees our short-term goal will seem far more important than our long-term interests.

A long, long time ago it was expedient to respond instantly if you finally came across fat, salt and sugar, or an opportunity for sex, as seizing these opportunities would help you survive or procreate. For most of us, those days are long gone. Practically everything we come across nowadays holds some opportunity to eat, drink, have sex, feel safe and feel like we belong. Wherever we go, we are confronted with fatty, salty, sweet food, semi-nude bodies, beautiful objects, great deals and other dopamine-stimulating attention getters. We see them in the supermarket, on billboards, online, on TV, on our phones, and so on. This ensures that we, like Olds and Milners' rats and Heath's psychiatric patients, are continually in a position to self-stimulate and give our reward system a dopamine shot. Often we don't even realize that we are endlessly, obsessively, mindlessly pressing that lever like an addict. We work around the clock because we could potentially earn more money, buy more stuff and earn more status. We continually eat and drink too much because of the potential pleasure that every bite or sip affords. We stay glued to our computer screens because we might reach another level in a game, get sex, get attention, or find a great deal. It holds out the illusion of bringing happiness within reach. Of course, none of this actually makes us happy, and we would realize this, if we thought about it. If we dwelled on it for more than a minute, it would probably dawn on us that this endless chase is actually quite stressful. After all, it never stops. When have you reached your goal in this perpetual pursuit? And what do you lose in the attempt? Think about that.

I am not naive enough to think that this new awareness is enough to make you quit your addictions and ditch your bad habits. After all, many of us stubbornly deny that we are addicted at all. But I dare you to keep track of how often you check your phone for new emails and notifications from Whatsapp, Snapchat, Twitter or Tinder, and how often you eat or drink something you shouldn't, or how many hours you spend on your computer while real life is clamoring for your attention. What I do know, however, is that being aware of this powerful mechanism will enable you to recognize it, and that recognition enables you to do something about it. And I know that this, in turn, will enable you to get closer to your ultimate goals – the goals that give you real pleasure and that help you to stay away from the temptations that will ultimately harm you. Part II of this book, How to train your CEO brain: the EFFECT Program, will teach you how you can effectively withstand those dopamine shots.

We often think that satisfying our instant wants is going to bring us pleasure and even happiness, making it a worthwhile endeavor. Worse yet, we tend to think that chasing our desires equals pursuing happiness. Unfortunately, this is false, and our confusion between giving in to cravings and behavior that leads to health and happiness causes big problems.

Alternative dopamine shot

This exercise will give you more insight into what triggers the release of dopamine in your brain. Every time you feel an irresistible short-term urge, you should try to find out what is causing it:
- Does it have to do with work, sex, computers, your smartphone?
- Is the urge so strong that you have to act upon it immediately, or can you avert it and focus your behavior on something else?

A good way to focus your activity on something else is to replace the dopamine shot you want to avoid with a different dopamine shot. So rather than buying the fatty food you are craving, take a leisurely bath, call a friend or go dancing. Mark down what mood you were in when this happened and what rewards your alternative actions brought you.

Craving?	**Replaced by?**	**What mood were you in?**	**What did you gain from your actions?**

Pitfall: Now is harder than later

The short-term forces of pain and pleasure also seem to influence your thinking when it comes to the things you want now. If you think about all the things you'll need to do in the future to achieve your long-term goal, those thoughts, and the long-term rewards they promise, are easy to come up with. For example, if my goal is to live healthier, I am better off cooking from scratch with fresh ingredients than heating up a frozen dinner or ordering a pizza. The food will not only be tastier, but also healthier, more varied and cheaper. These are all very logical and positive outcomes. Yet, at dinnertime, when you've just come home from a long day at work, your thoughts are suddenly drastically different. You're no longer concerned with a varied, healthy, cheap diet, but find yourself thinking thoughts like: 'Cooking from scratch is very tiring.' 'All that vegetable prep takes so much time', 'I'm hungry and it is going to take much longer, because I'm going to have to wait for the potatoes to get done', and 'I deserve a quick bite after such a long day'.

Your ultimate goal, a healthier lifestyle, and the things you need to do to get there, seemed quite easy when the moment of action was still in the future, yet now, at the moment of truth, those choices seem almost impossible or at least undesirable. Traci Mann, Denise de Ridder and Kentaro Fujita wrote about this mechanism in a paper entitled *Self-Regulation of Health Behavior*. They also wrote about research that showed how we can safeguard against this. If the temptations that are going to keep you from achieving your goal are staring you in the face, it is best to describe them in abstract language. For example, those French fries do not contain any vegetables; they do not even look like they were cut from a potato, but like some prefab mush poured into a mold; and those fries with mayonnaise and curry sauce are full of fat and salt. Such a dispassionate approach is better than the highly charged language we tend to think in: those fries look really yummy and mouth-wateringly good. Think back to the difference between hot and cold executive skills; describing the thing that you crave in cold terms (without emotion) instead of hot terms (full of emotion) makes it easier to resist the craving. This technique is known as cognitive reframing.

Unfortunately, we tend toward the opposite. In other words, we usually fan our pain and pleasure systems by emphasizing the pleasurable aspects of temptations and the pain-inducing aspects of the things we would have to do instead. What we should be doing is cognitively linking these better behaviors to our long-term goals. So think, 'Exercise helps me to live a healthier life, sleep better and look better and I have just 30 minutes to get some in' rather than 'Exercise makes me tired, I don't feel like getting changed, and that bag of potato chips and beer are within reach'. So next time you feel those long-term goal-undermining forces of pain and pleasure kick in, try to take a step back and use language to reframe those feelings. I know, this is incredibly hard, but give it a try and keep trying. It will get easier.

Pitfall: Moral licensing

As if the short-term forces of craving and actual pain and pleasure are not enough to keep you from your goals, we also need to take into account another strong, deceptive force that undermines our long-term resolve. You might even have unwittingly applied this force when you were reading about the dopamine mechanism; perhaps you thought to yourself, 'surely this dopamine mechanism does not apply to me'. The force I'm talking about is called moral licensing or moral justification. Kelly McGonigal writes about this force in a chapter of *The Willpower Instinct* entitled 'The Right to Sin'. Allow me to name a few examples and I'm sure you will understand exactly what I am talking about, without me even needing to provide a scientific definition of the term moral licensing.

Moral licensing works as follows:

- 'No, I don't actually need to separate my garbage, because the waste treatment center just chucks it all together anyway'.
- 'I don't need to put any energy into checking my kids homework, or playing a board game with them or taking them to the museum, because they're happy using the Xbox and even if they do this for several hours every day, they seem to be enjoying it'.
- 'I have barely eaten anything all day, so some greasy takeaway tonight won't hurt'.
- 'I refuse to give to charity, because I've heard most of the money goes to some CEO's salary anyway'.

You get the picture: moral licensing is a justification for not doing something you ought to do, or for doing something you ought not to do, because you believe you have already done something good, or because you can think of a reason that appears to outweigh doing the right thing. Research also shows there needn't even be a connection between the good you've already done and the thing you're now morally licensing yourself to do or not do. For example, 'I can feel perfectly justified in not going to the gym because I have worked hard all day, even though I know that my job contributes nothing to a healthy lifestyle or my need for exercise and that exercising will actually make me feel better than sitting on the couch'.

Even the progress you make toward a goal, say losing weight or finishing a job, can be used for moral licensing. For example, 'I have already lost 6 pounds, so I deserve that double cheeseburger with fries'. This is partly caused by a process that Ayelet Fishbach and Ravi Dhar call goal liberation. You are moving toward your goal by achieving sub-goals, but you have not achieved your ultimate goal yet. Goal liberation is based on something we have discussed before, namely the tension between your ultimate goals and your short-term desires. Like, 'I want to lose weight, but I also want to eat that brownie'. If you are effectively working toward your long-term goal (losing weight), the tension associated with that goal diminishes while the tension associated with your short-term goal (eating that brownie) grows. Temptation is waxing, while your real goal is waning.

Fishbach and Dhar's research shows that people who define success in terms of their subgoals are more likely to give in to temptations once they have achieved a subgoal. People who see a subgoal as a step toward their ultimate goal are better able to keep their sights on their long-term goal and less likely to give in to temptation after achieving a subgoal. So, don't tell yourself that giving in to temptation now is a reward for everything you've already done to achieve your end goal, but ask yourself why you have done those things. This will help you keep the ultimate goal foremost in your mind and make you less prone to succumb to temptation.

Just a thought will do

There's yet another mechanism that makes it harder to achieve your long-term goals and easier to give in to your short-term desires, McGonigal writes. Based on her research, she argues that you needn't even have done something good to justify subsequent bad behavior. Just thinking about some good you might do – for example, donating to a charity or volunteering to help organize a tournament – is moral license enough to indulge in behavior you would be better off avoiding, or to give up on something you ought to do.

From now on, pay close attention when you decide not to do something you ought to do or when you do something you shouldn't. Are you relying on moral license? Are you so happy with yourself that you are automatically sanctioning yourself for something short-term that conflicts with a long-term goal? If you find yourself thinking in phrases like 'It's okay this time, because....' alarm bells should be ringing. If you think you are seeing signs of moral licensing in yourself, take a few seconds to think about it and then try to make the decision again on better grounds. Be aware that moral licensing is a very powerful agent that can undermine your long-term goals. It is a force you need to actively resist in order to get where you want to go.

SELF-KNOWLEDGE

Know thyself

Try to identify for a day (or more) when you give yourself a moral license. Write down when you do it, and indicate each time whether you are justifying doing something you shouldn't do (I rode my bike this morning, so now I can eat whatever I want) or not doing what you ought to do (I helped a co-worker today, so now I don't have the energy to spend time with my family). Remember that the contented feeling you are experiencing because you've already done something good may have absolutely nothing to do with the goal-undermining behavior you are about to engage in.

Used moral license	Didn't do what I had to	Did what I shouldn't have

Pitfall: Force of habit

The last pitfall I want to describe is force of habit. Often, when we fail to achieve our goals, it is not because we have failed to behave in the right ways, but because we're creatures of habit who keep doing what we've always done. You've resolved to stop snacking between meals, but your hand is already in that bag of chips; you need to save money, but you keep spending it on non-essentials; or you've decided to be honest from now on, but you find yourself telling another white lie.

When we say force of habit, we're actually talking about the stereotypical stimulus-response chains I described in Chapter 4, which are deeply ingrained through years of repetition but no longer serve your purposes. This mechanism is simple. If you continue to do more of the same, you will get more of the same. In fact, it's even worse; it gets harder and harder not to repeat that particular behavior, whether you like it or not. As Saint Augustine wrote, *Habitus non restitué facta est necessitas*, or 'Habit that goes unresisted soon becomes necessity'. It is key to break with old habits that get in your way, but this is easier said than done because you've reinforced the networks underlying your habitual thought, feeling or behavior through repetition. This is why habits seem to 'come naturally'. Your environment also plays a big part in this. For example, seeing a particular friend may trigger your desire for alcohol, or smelling fried fish at the market can give you a seemingly irresistible urge to buy fish and chips.

So the trick is to expose yourself to environments and learn thoughts, feelings and behaviors that are conducive to achieving your goals and attaining success. As I explained in the previous chapter, this is possible, because our brains are mutable. Understanding how force of habit works and realizing that you have the power to change habits is extremely useful. So let's return to your list of stereotypical stimulus-response chains from Chapter 4 and add any new stereotypical responses or habits you can think of that could become obstacles to change. For a little head start on the development section of this book, try the following apps: Coach.me and Habit Streak Pro. Both can help you start new habits.[18]

Force of habit

SELF-KNOWLEDGE

Write down the habits that could get in the way of your goals.

For example, when I get home from work and feel hungry, my eyes are drawn to the kitchen cupboard and I make a beeline for some salty and sweet snacks. Or, as soon as

18 www.coach.me
https://play.google.com/store/apps/details?id=uk.amimetic.habitspro

I get into my car, I start thinking of that cool glass of beer and how drinking will take the edge off. Or, I know that if I drive home and cook and eat first, I will not feel like leaving the house again to go to the gym, but I'm tired so I'm going home first anyway.

Goal-undermining habits ....

....

....

....

....

....

....

Before we start on Part II, I want to talk a little about the conditions that reinforce our tendency to go for instant gratification, avoid pain, give ourselves moral license and continue old habits. These comprise practically every situation that saps your energy. For example, situations that cause stress, fear, depression, guilt or an unappreciated feeling. And conditions like: multitasking, being overburdened, uncertainty, being under pressure to perform, being belittled or discriminated against, worrying and not sleeping well. When you are low on energy, your prefrontal cortex, an energy-consuming part of your brain, performs more poorly. You start finding you can't see the forest for the trees, your emotions boil over and you make short-term rather than long-term decisions.

You are no doubt familiar with the effect of alcohol use, but I want to mention it anyway. Alcohol instantly diminishes executive skills such as inhibitory control and keeping your eye on long-term goals. Alcohol also decreases the prefrontal cortex's influence on the reward and emotion centers of your brain, giving those areas more sway over your behavior. Needless to say, this has undesirable repercussions. What I am saying is neatly summed up by a sign I saw recently in a bar: 'Alcohol can lead to unwanted pregnancies'.

Using our executive abilities to suppress undesirable behavior and to keep our sights on our long-term goals takes up loads of energy. If we are already low on energy, it gets even harder to carry out such tasks. And this energy dwindles further when we feel too much, or have to think, remember or do too much. In other words, when we are overloaded with work and emotions. So keep in mind that when you feel angry, scared, sad, embarrassed, tired, stressed or sick, you're more vulnerable to short-term temptations, excuses and bad habits that undermine your long-term goals.

No more excuses

To be honest, there are many more pitfalls I could name. Instead I have boiled them down to the few pitfalls I consider most important to avoid. What it comes down to is that there are many forces steering us toward short-term pleasure and long-term pain. Having strong executive skills ensures that you can decide at certain junctures to act or not to act rather than allow various old forces to decide for you. Based on all this, you might conclude that executive skills suck the joy out of life. 'I'm not allowed to drink or smoke anymore, I can't enjoy food, I can't spend money anymore, I can't have sex with the neighbor, I can't work long hours anymore and I can't leave my kids at their computers for hours either!'

If this is your reaction, then perhaps I haven't made myself clear enough. So let me try again:

Executive skills don't suck the joy out of your life. They remove the drama, the conflicts with yourself and others, the failures and the sick-making habits from your life.

This creates room for success, health, ideas and happiness. I am not going to make you do or not do anything, especially if you're content, happy and not harming anyone. Do as you please. But at least ask yourself whether you are really doing what you want to do. Or whether you are actually being manipulated like a puppet on a string even if you camouflage this with ex post facto justifications and excuses.

If you want to change things, or if you want to achieve some goal for yourself or others, but you find it hard, then developing your prefrontal cortex and the executive skills it controls will help you. Executive skills help you to adapt to your environment and get ahead. They assist you when you are experiencing chaos and doubt, and they bolster your ability to deal with forces that elicit a stereotypical, but not necessarily functional, response. In daily life, there is often no one right response or appropriate reaction. What is appropriate depends on your internal goals and your environment, and usually neither of these are completely unambiguous (not even your own goals). Both your goals and the environment are subject to change. Executive skills help you deal with uncertainty and situation-dependent truths. They help you make decisions and commit to them, but also to adjust them if necessary. To put it in more psychological terms, executive skills help you to counteract field-dependent behavior (completely dependent on the stimuli in your environment) and perseverative behavior (repetitive behavior, thoughts and feelings). These skills help you move toward adaptive decision-making (responding competently to change and making appropriate, situation-dependent decisions). In other words, executive skills help you do what's best in a particular situation, both in the short run and in the long run.

Executive skills are what make humans an extraordinary species. We not only have the ability to carry the past with us and experience the present, but we can also envision and even determine the future. This mix of past, present and future, combined with well-developed executive skills, enables us to become better educated and live healthier lives, to maintain better business and private relations, to raise our children more effectively, and in short to enjoy happier and more successful lives in which we contribute more to the world. Executive skills unlock your full potential and that of the world around you. Developing your executive skills enables you to become the best version of yourself.

'The illiterate of the 21st century will not be those that cannot read or write, but those that cannot learn, unlearn and relearn.'

Alvin Toffler

goodreads.com

PART II **Introduction**

In the previous section, I explained why it is important to develop the prefrontal parts of the brain and the executive skills associated with these areas. In this section, I will deal with methods that are scientifically proven to develop the prefrontal cortex and executive skills. Some scientific studies look mainly at the development of the prefrontal cortex and related structures, while others focus primarily on how executive skills are enhanced. I have used both kinds of studies in my research for this book. I elected to deal with the methods that are likely to yield the best results: those that have a generally positive effect on the development of both the prefrontal cortex and the executive skills rather than those that train executive skills in isolation. For now the aim is to create a better default mode in your brain and your behavior.

Because this book is meant for practical use, this section will focus on the conditions you can influence: Environmental Enrichment, Flow Focus, Fixed Sleeping Pattern, Exercise, Connecting Today with Tomorrow, and Time. As a whole, the methods to create these conditions comprise a coherent program known by its acronym, EFFECT. In each chapter, you will find exercises called PFC Exercises (PFC = PreFrontal Cortex). Doing these exercises will have a positive influence on the development of your prefrontal cortex and/or its associated executive tasks.

Some of my methods may leave you wondering how they could possibly help you develop executive skills and the brain. You may feel some resistance to them. Try not to let yourself be inhibited by this feeling. Try, as you practiced in Chapter 2, to recognize this resistance and overcome the feeling. If you deny yourself methods that can improve your life, you aren't doing yourself any favors.

PART II
HOW TO TRAIN YOUR CEO BRAIN: THE EFFECT PROGRAM

How to develop your prefrontal cortex and the executive skills that will help you achieve your goals and be successful.

‘Man’s mind once stretched by a new idea, never regains its original dimension.’

Oliver Wendell Holmes

goodreads.com

Chapter 6 **Environmental Enrichment – Challenging Your Brain**

In this chapter you'll learn why stimulating your brain is key, and how training your prefrontal cortex will encourage you to do what you've always wanted to do.

SELF-KNOWLEDGE

Ping-pong balls

This experiment requires a bit of preparation and a conscious decision. You will need:
- A ping-pong ball,
- Masking tape or Scotch tape,
- A sharp knife,
- A radio or a smartphone.

Cut the ping-pong ball in half and tune the radio to white noise (or use your smartphone for this purpose).[19] Find a quiet place, tape the halves of the ping-pong balls over both your eyes, so that you're looking at the inside of the halves, and then lie down and listen to the white noise. Now wait patiently. It is definitely worth waiting, because after a minute or two you'll start experiencing something bizarre. Pink elephants, chocolate fountains and dancing criminals are just a few of the things people have reported seeing when doing this experiment. So, before you begin, think about whether you are sure you want to try this. You never know what you might see. I will explain why this happens after you've tried it.

19 For example, www.youtube.com/watch?v=ldlh7OLIdV8

This experiment makes use of what is known as the *Ganzfeld* effect (German for complete field). Putting the ping-pong ball halves over your eyes creates a homogenous field of vision, a blankness. This, combined with the white noise, deprives your brain of all meaningful sensory stimulation. And that is something your brain can't stand. So, it starts generating information on its own. And as you just found out, it can induce visions of practically anything.

I came across the ping-pong ball experiment in *The Boston Globe* and it really made me think. The point is to show you that your brain craves new experiences and information. The experiment is geared to that. Deprive your brain of new input and you'll lose touch with reality and start to hallucinate. Now that you understand how this works, you'll begin to see why people who never do anything new or only take in one-sided information sometimes have such strange ideas, but also why solitary confinement and sensory deprivation are so terrible and are used as a torture method.

Experience-dependent plasticity

At the end of Chapter 4, 'A Recipe for Success', you read about neuroplasticity, the brain's ability to continue to develop and adapt when exposed to new stimuli. There are different types of neuroplasticity. One key type is experience-dependent plasticity.

Experience-dependent neuroplasticity is the brain's unique ability to adapt to its environment. The importance of this cannot be overestimated; it's one of the reasons why there are so many of differences between people. To give one example: all healthy brains have an innate capacity to develop language, but which language you learn depends on the one you're exposed to. Exposure to a specific language causes specific changes in the brain, which in turn ensure that you learn to speak and understand that specific language, say Chinese rather than French. In the same vein, a football player's brain develops differently than a ballet dancer's, and a cook's differently than a stock broker's.[20]

We used to think – and unfortunately, some people still do – that the brain cannot change its structure and functioning, or can only do so during a 'critical period' in our youth. But we now know this is untrue and that our brains continue to change in response to our environment and the stimuli we deliberately expose it to. The brain can change because it continues to form new cells (neurogenesis), because cell tentacles (dendrites) and shoots (axons) continue to grow and branch out, and because the brain keeps making new connections between

20 For a more detailed discussion of this topic, see M.M. Sitskoorn, *Het maakbare brein*, 2006, [The Mutable Brain].

cells (synaptogenesis). But that's not all. For instance, an insulating substance (myelin) forms around the dendrites and axons, improving intercellular impulse transmission; some connections are cut off (pruning); and the substances that facilitate intercellular communications, called neurotransmitters, also change. Signals grow stronger or weaker, and various cells and groups of cells strengthen, weaken or stop their collaboration. The brain can even create new blood vessels in a process we call angiogenesis. The effects of all this can be good or bad, as I explained earlier. What develops, and how, depends partly on what you expose your brain to. It's quite simple really. The things you do, think, or feel a lot, will develop and get easier to do, so you'll do these things more readily and frequently, whether this is yelling at people, singing, thinking of your loved ones, or eating cupcakes.

Many studies provide evidence for experience-dependent neuroplasticity in humans. Eleanor Maguire and co-authors (2000) showed that London cab drivers, who have excellent knowledge of the streets of their city, have enlarged posterior hippocampi – a part of the brain that facilitates memory, the ability to make connections and visual spatial skills. Furthermore, the size of their posterior hippocampi is proportional to the amount of cab-driving experience they have. Another well-known study, by Bogdan Draganski (2004), shows that the areas of the brain involved in processing and storing complex visual movements are larger in people who've spent three months learning how to juggle than in people who have not done so. When a juggler stops juggling, these expanded brain regions gradually shrink again. The same effect probably applies to all new motor skills, as other studies on people learning to play golf or do aerobics have shown. Other studies have demonstrated changes in the brain areas involved in somatosensory and auditory perception in professional musicians. On the downside, however, neuroplasticity can also lead to negative adaptations. Writer's cramp (focal hand dystonia) results from repetitive finger movements that have caused negative adaptations in the somatosensory and motor areas of the brain.

Negative feelings

Fear and addiction are also associated with plasticity-related changes. These changes seem mainly to affect the prefrontal cortex and the areas most closely associated with emotions. On the other hand, we also know that consciously influencing negative feelings and thoughts, for instance with the help of cognitive behavioral therapy, reinforces the prefrontal cortex in regulating the areas of the brain associated with emotion. This makes you increasingly better at neutralizing negative emotions and regulating your mood. Of course, this is not a one-off thing you apply when a negative thought hits you, but it is good to realize you do have the option – with the help of a cognitive behavioral therapist, for instance – to rewire your brain by consistently thinking and acting differently. This helps you to develop yourself in the direction of who you want to be, how you want to feel and how you want to behave.

Studies proving experience-driven plasticity are too numerous to mention, but what they reveal is that a wide range of activities can reshape your brain. Such activities include: learning to name colors, training your spatial skills and memory, memorizing abstract information, acquiring a new language, training your working memory, meditating, learning to mirror read, and learning to decipher Morse code. The rule of thumb is that whatever you do and expose your brain to, develops. What you don't do and don't expose your brain to, stagnates or even decays. How much time and training you need to change your brain structure and performance and learn a new skill depends on various factors: the task, the type of training involved, the knowledge and skills you already possess and your learning ability. These variables make it hard to approximate how long it will take to acquire a new skill.

General and specific environmental enrichment

As we now know, primarily from research on rodents, the brain thrives in surroundings that are conducive to physical movement and social interaction and that are full of things to explore – as long as these surroundings aren't overwhelming. This is called an enriched environment. Environmental enrichment and neuroplasticity go hand in hand. Humans are built to discover new things. Discovery activates and develops the brain. What you are, that is to say what you do and the environment you seek out, determine the shape of your brain. Your brain, in turn, determines what you are: your behavior and the environment you put yourself in. This is a lifelong process that you can exert a strong influence on. What you are and what you're becoming are partly shaped by the environment you create and use.

Exposing yourself to an environment that offers a combination of *physical, social* and *cognitive* stimuli is called *general environmental enrichment.* Exposing yourself to very specific cognitive, social or physical challenges to develop particular preselected skills is known as *specific environmental enrichment.* If you would like to enrich your environment to develop your prefrontal cortex, I can offer you some suggestions. A few particularly good ways to challenge the prefrontal cortex are gaining new insights, grasping new ideas, practicing logic and exposing yourself to abstract information. Other ways are reflecting on your own behavior and initiating and maintaining social contact. In fact, every game we play, every outing or physical activity that requires us to use our twelve executive skills (see Chapter 3, p. 61) are activities that stimulate and develop our prefrontal cortex.

It's important to note that learning new things, challenging yourself and raising the bar not only develops your brain and your skills, it also increases neural plasticity in general by engendering molecular changes. It appears to boost a protein found in the brain (brain-derived neurotrophic factor) that greatly enhances

Enriching your environment enables you to improve your executive skills, protects you from brain degeneration and can even increase your neural plasticity.

brain cells, their synapses and neuroplasticity. Exposing yourself to new information and developing new skills also activates cells known as spindle cells. Large concentrations of these cells are found in our cingulate cortex. Spindle cells form connections between the prefrontal cortex and the areas in the brain that process emotions. They bridge the gap between thoughts and emotions and as such enable you to make rapid, well-founded decisions in complex, emotionally charged situations. They help develop your hot executive skills. In short, environmental enrichment seems to induce positive structural and biochemical changes in your brain that result from neuroplasticity and help you to function better. So, while environmental enrichment relies on neuroplasticity to develop your brain, it enhances neural plasticity too.

This is an incredibly important finding, but it gets even better. We now know that environmental enrichment also acts as an antidote to age-induced brain degeneration. Studies have shown that people who continue to challenge themselves cognitively through education, work, social relations or leisure activities (or a combination thereof) are less prone to cognitive degeneration and various brain disorders. This is known as cognitive reserve.

To recap, environmental enrichment ensures that:

- you develop your brain and your behavior;
- your neural plasticity is enhanced;
- you're more resistant to brain degeneration;
- you're less likely to develop other age-related brain disorders.

Building your cognitive reserve

Cognitive reserve requires active building and maintenance. It's not something you either have or don't have, but a quantity that can be enhanced or kept up to par by enriching your environment. The Prefrontal Cortex (PFC) exercise below will help you do just that. This might be the single most enjoyable exercise in the whole book, because you're asked to do something you've always wanted to do, but never got around to.

PFC exercise: Challenge yourself

PFC

Take the following steps.

1 Think of something that:
   - you've always wanted to do (use your intrinsic motivation);
   - is cognitively challenging and diverse;
   - and is feasible (so, you think you'll be able to do);

I don't really care what you choose, as long as it meets these three conditions. It could be learning to play chess or speak Arabic, planning and taking that trip you've always dreamed of, researching a new market opportunity, mastering a computer program, developing a new product, meeting interesting people or reading more in-depth news and current affairs analyses. As long as it teaches you something new, sparks your interest, requires intellectual work, and seems feasible.

2 Find out where and how you can achieve this goal. If it's a learning goal, you can take lessons online, from a private tutor, in a classroom or from a book. How you do it doesn't matter. Join a club, take out a subscription or buy the book. Just do it.

3 Spend one hour three times a week (or half a day once a week) working toward your goal. Choose whatever schedule suits you and is sufficient. Spending more time is fine too. I can already hear you think, 'Wow, that's a lot of time. I'll never be able to spend that many hours. I'm not going to manage that.' If you're indeed asking yourself where you'll find the time, spend a week keeping track of how much time per day you watch TV, play computer games, use Facebook or other social media, and have meaningless chats, meetings and so on. Now subtract 3 hours from this; it will make you feel better right away!

Tip: Keep in mind that the best ways to challenge your prefrontal cortex are: acquiring new insight, absorbing new ideas, practicing your logical abilities, exposing yourself to abstract information, reflecting on yourself and initiating and maintaining social relations.

I've always wanted to learn how to ______________________________

I'm now actually going to do this, in the following way: ______________________________
____
____
____
____

(Optional) Average number of hours per day spent watching TV, playing online games, on Facebook, etc.

Monday ___ hours
Tuesday ___ hours
Wednesday ___ hours
Thursday ___ hours
Friday ___ hours
Saturday ___ hours
Sunday ___ hours

-3 hours

4 Assess the amount of frontal lobe training you'll get from the activities you selected and to what extent these activities engage the 13 wisdom- and success-related traits (from Chapter 4, p. 86) and the 12 executive skills (from Chapter 3, p. 61).

Activity: ______________________ ,

engages the following trait/skill:

	Trait/skill	**Not**	**A little**	**Sufficiently**	**A lot**
1	Grit (dedication)	☐	☐	☐	☐
2	Willpower	☐	☐	☐	☐
3	Energy/zest for life	☐	☐	☐	☐
4	Social intelligence	☐	☐	☐	☐
5	Gratitude	☐	☐	☐	☐
6	Optimism	☐	☐	☐	☐
7	Curiosity	☐	☐	☐	☐
8	Prosocial attitudes and behaviors	☐	☐	☐	☐
9	Self-reflection and self-knowledge	☐	☐	☐	☐
10	Recognizing and coping with uncertainty	☐	☐	☐	☐
11	Tolerance	☐	☐	☐	☐
12	Spirituality	☐	☐	☐	☐
13	Sense of humor	☐	☐	☐	☐
14	Attention: focusing, sustaining, dividing, releasing	☐	☐	☐	☐
15	Emotion regulation (includes coping with stress)	☐	☐	☐	☐
16	Flexibility (ability to deal with change)	☐	☐	☐	☐
17	Inhibitory control	☐	☐	☐	☐
18	Task initiation	☐	☐	☐	☐
19	Organization	☐	☐	☐	☐
20	Planning	☐	☐	☐	☐
21	Self-monitoring	☐	☐	☐	☐
22	Working memory	☐	☐	☐	☐
23	Realistic self-image	☐	☐	☐	☐
24	Capacity for theory of mind	☐	☐	☐	☐

To enrich your environment even more, you could use some educational apps. I have listed some examples below. These are merely suggestions and if none of them appeal to you, feel free to look for an app you like better. If you find one, I hope you'll also share it with me. Suggestions are always welcome!

- Google Arts & Culture: information on museums and art collections all over the world
- Daily Art: daily dose of art history stories
- Drops: language learning
- Anki: flashcard app
- Wattpad: free, user-generated e-books
- A local public library app
- Audible: audio book app
- Birdsounds Europe: birding app
- News apps: The Guardian (free), NY Times (paid)
- Chess apps
- Mastermind apps

The benefits of enriching your environment are enormous. Everyone should know this and put it to use. On the other hand, not enriching your environment has big negative consequences. Just think back to the ping-pong ball experiment. The brain was telling us it can't stand being deprived of input. Or, think of what happens when you lead a sedentary life. If you don't move, you're letting your body down. It gets more and more susceptible to disease and other physical setbacks. Similarly, if you're intellectually inactive, you're letting your brain down. And letting your brain down means letting yourself down. This applies to both the present and the future, because if you stop developing yourself, you stop building up cognitive reserve and start losing touch with reality.

Enriching your environment enables you to improve your executive skills, protects you from brain degeneration and can even increase your neural plasticity. You could describe environmental enrichment as a cocktail of environmental drugs for your brain. The best thing about environmental enrichment is that it's simple, happiness inducing and instantly applicable. After all, we already live in an enriched environment. All we need to do is be selective and practice moderation. The next chapter, dealing with Flow Focus, will explain how to be more selective about outside influences.

‘Any man who can drive safely while kissing a pretty girl is simply not giving the kiss the attention it deserves.’

Albert Einstein

brainyquote.com

Chapter 7 **Flow Focus – Directing the Plasticity of Your Brain**

In this chapter you will discover how important it is to focus. You'll learn to use various focusing techniques to strengthen your prefrontal cortex and executive skills. You'll discover how to focus without experiencing stress, so you can perform well when you need to most. I call this Flow Focus.

Word list

Take 10 seconds to look at the words below.

SUGAR LOLLIPOP CUTE TASTE COOKIE

CHOCOLATE COCA-COLA CARROT DELICIOUS

GOOD SYRUP PLATE ICE CREAM CAKE

Now cover the words with a piece of paper so you can't see them. Which word or words were not in the list: SUGAR, TASTE, SWEET, or WEAPON?

Most people will know that WEAPON was not included in the list. But who noticed that SWEET wasn't there either? Well it wasn't. This test shows you one of the ways in which attention works.

I based this exercise on an exercise in Kevin Dutton's *Split-Second Persuasion*. It shows that the things that attract your attention steer your thinking, your memory, your actions, and much more. Attention makes you think you remember seeing the word SWEET in the list. Deciding what to focus on is a skill regulated partly by the prefrontal cortex; it is an important factor in shaping your life. It's a key capability, but few people realize this. I will explain this in greater detail in the pages ahead.

Focusing your attention

To learn new skills and develop your brain, you need to focus. Although everyone knows what focusing is, many fail to realize how strongly it factors in what you absorb, feel, think, do and develop. Focusing your attention does miracles. It nourishes your being (or what you think, feel, and do) and your becoming (or your growth, so what you are going to think, feel and do in the future). The saying 'everything you pay attention to grows' is really true. That's because the act of paying attention directs brain plasticity. It sends a kind of signal to the brain that says: this is important, be prepared. By doing this, we are priming the brain to do something with whatever we are focusing on.

Again, this goes for both positive and negative things. Focusing on something you fear, like the possibility that you'll choke on a presentation, increases the fear and allows it to take up more room in your head, heart and actions. As I said earlier, the neural pathways underlying these feelings of fear will be trained. A readiness to be afraid will literally occupy more space and gain strength in your head. Feeling fear will become easier. Focusing instead on preparing your presentation or on relaxing will develop more positive tendencies (though that will take a lot of effort at first). As you progress, fear will diminish while the activity that you have deliberately focused on will take up more room and gain strength. In this chapter, I will provide techniques to help you achieve this.

Focusing activates your prefrontal cortex and lays the foundations for change and development in your brain. This makes it possible to change your feelings, thinking, skills and behavior. Every day, there are thousands of things you could pay attention to. It is impossible to focus on everything, so you have to be selective.

Focusing your attention is like using a flashlight. By keeping your attention fixed on something, you direct the plasticity of your brain and your development. Jeffrey Schwartz calls this *self-directed neuroplasticity*. Plasticity in and of itself has no orientation, so it allows you to develop in any direction, positive or negative. It's your focus that guides plasticity in a particular direction. The more attention you focus on something (or better yet, the more you decide to focus on something), the more it will develop and the easier you will find it is to change. Note that I emphasize the word 'decide.' Focusing your attention is such a powerful tool that it would be a shame not to gain control of it, so remember:

Actively focusing attention on something
directs neuroplasticity and shapes your brain,
feelings and skills in the direction you want.

PFC exercise: Focus and distraction

PFC

Try to become aware of what you pay attention to over the course of a day. Do this at night too, if you find yourself unable to sleep (from worries, for instance).

- Is your attention drawn by stimuli from your own body – sensations, thoughts and feelings – or rather by stimuli in your surroundings, like images, sounds and smells?
- Do these stimuli hold your attention for long?
- Is this good or bad?

Decide whether you are the master of your attention, focusing on whatever you choose, or more of a marionette that responds to all kinds of internal and external stimuli.

Attention drawn by	Holds your attention yes/no	Positive	Negative

I am the master of my attention yes ☐ no ☐
I focus my attention on what I want to develop or achieve yes ☐ no ☐

What do you want to focus on? Keep track of whether you succeed in doing so.

I want to focus my attention on ....

External stimuli

Attention that is immediately shifted by external stimuli is also known as exogenous attention, automatic attention or stimulus-driven attention. This type of attention is often drawn by a stimulus that directly engages your pleasure or pain system, like the smell of frying bacon or fresh-baked apple pie, the sight of your Xbox or that guy with the six-pack at the gym, or a feeling like the fear of missing out, losing status, getting old or ending up penniless. These distractions often undermine your long-term goals. Earlier, I identified these as the 'I want it now' forces. They tend to be stronger than the 'I actually want' or 'ultimately I want' forces we talked about in Chapter 5, 'Pitfalls'. You need to understand that all those tempting 'I want it now' forces are designed by nature to automatically draw your attention, even when you don't want them to. They stimulate evolutionarily older, more primitive systems deeper in your brain. This is why attention is said to be controlled bottom-up, or directed by stimulation of the lower brain.

Once distracted, you obviously still have the capacity to steer your attention away from these tempting, goal-undermining stimuli by consciously applying your prefrontal cortex. The prefrontal areas of your brain are evolutionarily younger and controlled more consciously than the lower brain. They can also regulate the functioning of the lower areas. That is why this type of attention is known as top-down, conscious, executive, goal-directed or endogenous attention. This type of attention deliberately directs your focus toward activities and information that support your goal, or stimuli that have a relaxing effect without undermining your goal.

You zoom in on your goal, for example improving your marriage and family ties or building a long-term business relationship. You zoom out from distractions like that guy with the six-pack at the gym or the quick profit you could make by selling your clients a subpar financial product. This requires redirection: you ignore that guy at the gym, ask your husband out for a date night, and play football with your kids after work. Or, in the second example, you focus on the long-term damage of selling financial junk and explore how a better, more ethical product will benefit you, your client and, ultimately, the world. If you fail to redirect your attention from the 'marshmallow' to your long-term goal, the temptation – i.e. the gym guy or the quick profit – will only grow, making it ever harder to resist.

Wilhelm Hofmann calls the practice of disregarding the forces of temptation and focusing on your goal an "action-oriented mindset". The process of redirecting attention in this way is called goal shielding. We tend to do the opposite, of course. We focus on the quick win, or the quick lay, and in the process help to undermine the very goals we set.

A particularly pernicious vulnerability of ours is that we don't even have to be physically exposed to a tempting stimulus, because just thinking of it can weaken

‘Heavy multitaskers are suckers for irrelevancy.’

Clifford Nass

http://news.stanford.edu/2009/08/24/multitask-research-study-082409

our resolve. Incidentally, it makes no sense to feel guilty or angry about such intrusive thoughts. Trying to suppress them is pointless too. Doing so merely makes it more difficult to focus your attention and will cause the intrusive thoughts to surface more often rather than less. Instead, you must accept that such tempting thoughts surface from time to time, and that you need to deliberately direct your attention away from them to break their spell.

Multitasking

Unfortunately, the world we live in is not exactly conducive to focusing on things that are good for your brain and personal development. We are bombarded with stimuli that promise short-term gain and long-term pain. Temptations like unhealthy food, alcohol, games, media and sex are inescapable. At the same time, we are overloaded by stimuli that require us to divide our attention and energy. We may try to give this a positive spin and call it multitasking, but the downside is that we're losing the ability to stay focused on any one thing for a protracted period of time. We're learning only to divide our attention.

Although multitasking has been hailed as a key competence in our society, it comes at a cost. I have to explain this quite frequently, because many people are unaware of this or don't want to believe it. The truth is, our brains are not very good at parallel information processing. They're great at serial information processing. So even if you think you're doing various things at the same time, in reality your brain is not processing all the information simultaneously, but switching between different tasks. And in all those moments of transition, your brain does not process information. In other words, by multitasking you become less efficient in executing tasks and absorbing information, which means it takes a multitasker more time than a serial-tasker to perform the various tasks well. Communication professor Clifford Nass at Stanford University put it nicely when he said that "[h]eavy multitaskers are suckers for irrelevancy". Frequent mulitaskers' brains focus on practically every scrap of information in their environment and lose the ability to ignore unimportant information in favor of what is relevant.

I am sure you remember the 'Overtaxing the brain' exercise from the beginning of Chapter 2. I asked you to draw a figure 9 in the air while turning your ankle the other way. That was pretty much impossible. The explanation for this phenomenon is quite simple. When you overtax your brain, the quality of one of the tasks you're trying to perform diminishes. With a lot of practice, you can of course learn to perform these two tasks simultaneously – thanks to neural plasticity. But the question is whether you really want to do this. You only live once, and maybe your time could be spent better. My point is that your brain has real trouble doing multiple things simultaneously; it can hardly draw a circle and a figure 9, let alone some far more complex combination of tasks. Just imagine how severely you must be overtaxing your brain when you're driving in heavy traffic while trying to conduct a meaningful phone conversation.

Actively focusing your attention directs neuroplasticity and shapes your brain, feelings and skills.

There is another drawback to multitasking, as Robert Sapolsky explains in his book *Why Zebras Don't Get Ulcers*. The endless to-do list of menial tasks that new technologies are forcing us to deal with is creating major stress in our brains. We are constantly battling a feeling of 'not being done', 'I still have to do x' and 'this is important, this is urgent!' This is causing unrelenting stress, which is something our brains are not equipped to deal with. Our stress systems are meant to respond effectively to short-term, acute stress, like an attack by predators or a rapidly spreading wildfire. When faced with such an emergency, our stress network kicks in and signals us to run, fight, watch out, hide, or respond with all our energy, and to do so now. As soon as this kind of danger has subsided, we can relax again. These days, however, we're kept in a continuous state of alertness.

Chronic stress

Numerous studies have shown that this constant alertness caused by the ongoing stimulation of our stress system is bad for our health. It brings about several physiological, neurological and psychological changes. Not only does it have short-term consequences, like raising your heart rate and respiration, it also has long-term harmful effects such as killing cells in your hippocampus (a brain structure that facilitates memory and is part of the emotion network). This is why people who suffer from chronic stress often suffer from memory problems and moodiness.

Chronic stress makes the amygdala hypersensitive. This brain structure is associated with emotional reactions such as fear. Amygdala hypersensitivity makes people more nervous and fearful. They often take offense at the slightest thing and are hypervigilant and ready to attack or defend. A current manifestation of this condition is hyperawareness and the feeling that we have to be prepared to deal with something important that could be about to happen at any moment. PING. As you know, of course, most notifications your phone receives from Facebook, Instagram and other social media are of no consequence. Sure, somebody has posted something, but that post seldom contains any urgent or even mildly important information. Daniel Levitin calls it the "ultimate empty calorie candy for the brain". But it doesn't feel that way. You still think something major might happen. Because it could. Your attention keeps getting drawn by new notifications from whatever platform and before long, you indeed turn into a sucker for irrelevancy and you increasingly lose the all-important power to steer your own attention.

Despite these serious drawbacks, I'm not saying multitasking is all bad. Sometimes it comes in handy, but only when it pertains to tasks that do not require your full attention. Then it's practical. But try not to multitask exclusively. Continue to focus your attention on a goal, because without this skill you will lose control over your life.

PFC exercise: No smartphone

Try to go for a day – or if you can't face that, half a day – without your smartphone, or at least without Whatsapp, Snapchat, Facebook and so on. So, only use your phone as a telephone and see how this affects your attention and focus.

When you take away social media and other short-term distractions, it gets easier to focus your attention for a sustained period, a skill associated with your prefrontal cortex. Once you get used to this change, you'll notice that you get calmer, your focus and memory improve, and you gain greater self-control.

This is a very powerful exercise, so try to not reject it outright because you feel resistance or don't want to be pushed out of your comfort zone. It may help to refer back to the 'Out of your comfort zone' exercise at the end of Chapter 2 (p. 45). See what you filled in there and check whether you are experiencing these feelings now too.

Internal stimuli

Your attention is drawn not only by external stimuli (exogenous attention), but also internal distractions. Hunger and pain are common types of internal stimuli, but thoughts and emotions can have the same effect. Worse yet, thoughts and emotions often form not just fleeting distractions, but persistent ones that we can't let go of. So, we continue to mull over the same thought, or we get stuck in worries or negativity, unable to focus on information that could jar those persistent thoughts and emotions loose.

Falsify

English psychologist Peter Cathcart Wason came up with a simple test that shows why we get stuck and only see evidence that justifies and supports our preconceived notions, even notions that worry us. The test is based on Austrian philosopher Karl Popper's falsification process. Popper argued that you can only test whether something is true by trying to prove it false. Strongly influenced by Popper, Wason knew that humans are not very good at falsification, that we tend to search for proof of what we already believe rather than proof that we are wrong. And this is exactly what Wason's test was designed to demonstrate, journalist Paul Tough writes in his book *How Children Succeed.*

Number sequence

SELF-KNOWLEDGE

Below, you will a see a series of three numbers. Your task will be to find out what the rule is that governs the sequence. You can do this by providing me with a second series of three numbers and then I will reveal whether this sequence follows the rule you were asked to uncover.

2-4-6- ....

1 Write down the first sequence of three numbers that comes to mind to test which rule governs this sequence. ....

If you wrote down a series along the lines of 4-8-12 or 8-10-12, then my answer would be, 'Yes, your sequence follows the rule'.

2 Now write down another sequence of three numbers that you think continues the pattern or fits the pattern further along in the sequence. ....

If you have written down a sequence along the lines of 20-22-24, then you were right again.

3 What do you think the rule governing this sequence is? ....

Most people will answer that the rule must be: add two to the previous number, or that it is a series of ascending, even numbers. Did you think so too? And did you also think that my answers confirmed your guess? If so, you will be sorely disappointed when I tell you that neither rule applies. The rule was simply: an ascending sequence of numbers. So it would have been fine to suggest 3-5-7, or 13-18-29, or even 321-712-988.

Perhaps you think this is a silly example, but in fact it isn't. I just showed that you tested your rule by merely looking for evidence that would prove you right. You could easily have discovered the right rule by trying out a sequence that did not fit the rule you had in mind, that is, by writing down a sequence that did not add two or was not an ascending sequence of even numbers. Or, to put it in Popper's words, by trying to falsify your hypothesis.

As you can see, falsification does not come naturally to us. We tend to look for confirmation. Everywhere we look, we try to find proof that what we think and feel is true and justifiable. This is how we end up stuck, with our eyes and ears shut off to new information that could help us discard erroneous thoughts. As a result, we often stunt our own development and remain entrenched in our own little world. If I had to summarize this tendency, I would repeat the words I once overheard on a bus: 'If you look left, you don't see what's happening on the right.' Let me qualify this somewhat. If you continue to look left, you'll never see any of the interesting things passing you by on the right, and you'll base your thoughts, ideas, feelings and actions on only a small portion of the information that's available. Next time, try to consciously look for information that proves the opposite of what you think and feel. This can liberate you from a rut in which you endlessly repeat the same thoughts and feelings. It gives you room to see other perspectives and freedom to act accordingly.

I included this little test to make a point: what's in your head determines your focus, and that little spotlight we call focus prevents you from seeing other options. As I explained before, anything that gets attention grows. So, if you continue to worry about something without taking action, or to fret about some event in the past that made you feel bad, you're increasing your inability to let these worries and stress go. As this continues, these negative feelings will seem increasingly real and important. Also, if your attention is focused only on that which worries you, you'll no longer see other information that might help you solve the problem at the root of your worries. Again, just like what happens when faced with those tempting, exogenous distractions, you will have lost control of your attention and your focus will be controlling you, as it were. Under the banner 'Let's not only look left, but also right', the next exercise is a simple way to train yourself to notice more than that which you usually see. It is based on an exercise in John Arden's *Rewire Your Brain*.

PFC exercise: Daily routine

Take a routine behavior, like walking your kids to school or getting coffee at Starbucks, and try to focus your attention on what you see while on the way. How many things did you notice that you had never seen before? Be safe, so don't do this exercise while driving a car.

By consciously focusing on daily routines or on things that seem to contradict your typical thoughts, you activate your prefrontal cortex and train yourself to deliberately focus your attention. In this way, you learn to notice things you didn't see before. This will help you absorb information that could be important – and not just information that others consider important or that you already had at your disposal.

Meditation

I've given you some idea of the power of focus and a few easy guidelines that can help you direct your attention better. But there's more you can do. Many studies have shown that meditation trains people to focus. In truth, I'm always a little hesitant to bring up meditation. Although many people have at some point tried some kind of meditation, many others are skeptical because of its New Age image. If this describes your attitude, it's worthwhile to try to get past your initial embarrassment, because mindfulness and other meditation techniques benefit not only our general sense of well-being, but also our executive skills and prefrontal cortex. And this has been scientifically proven, as you'll soon find out.

Meditation is an umbrella term for a variety of techniques with different objectives. In this chapter, we focus first on meditation techniques that foster *selective attention*. Such techniques teach you to narrow your focus to a specific object, so you learn to target your attention at the things that matter. Later, we will look at meditation techniques that foster broader, *open attention*, such as mindfulness. Instead of teaching you to focus on a single object, these techniques train you to consciously, yet non-responsively monitor what is happening from one moment to the next. Open attention meditation can help you become more aware of what's going on and teach you not to get stuck in certain emotions or thoughts. Finally, we'll see some meditation techniques that combine both types of focus.

Selective attention

Meditation techniques geared toward selective attention are known as focused attention meditation. In 2008, cognitive neuroscientist Antoine Lutz and co-authors published a literature review of selective attention and open attention training. The authors argue that selectively directing, or focusing, your attention is key to goal-directed behavior and that there are clear similarities between focused attention meditation and what cognitive neuroscientists call 'attention regulation'. To reach your goals, you need to be able to focus your attention, maintain it, be aware when you get distracted, and be able to release your attention from the distraction and refocus it on the target of your choice.

All these skills call upon the prefrontal network and other areas of the brain it is connected to. Studies show that people who practice focusing their attention get better at focusing on a specific target, even when there are distractions around.

Meditation is directly related to the development of your executive skills.

Their brains show changes in activation in various areas, including the dorsolateral prefrontal cortex and the superior frontal sulcus. It appears that this type of meditation initially activates certain areas of the brain more. With longer-term practice, however, these areas are activated less, because the brain no longer needs to work as hard. This is known as *effortless selective, or focused, attention.* Experienced focused attention meditators also appear to respond less sharply to emotional stimuli that could break their concentration. Lutz and co-authors call this "inhibition of automatic responses", an ability that is conducive to staying on track toward a goal, particularly when that path is strewn with marshmallows.

The essence of selective attention meditation, as Lutz and co-authors describe it, is:

- being able to focus and sustain attention on a target of choice (e.g. your breathing, but ultimately anything you consider worth focusing on and staying focused on);
- being aware of when your thoughts start to wander and when other distractions draw your attention; this improves your monitoring skills, enhancing your ability to check whether you're still doing the right things to achieve your goals;
- being able to release your attention from the distracting stimulus and redirect it toward the target of your choice; ultimately, this will ensure you're less prone to give in to temptation, impulsive behavior, intrusive thought patterns and negative memories; you'll also be less affected by stimuli that trigger negative emotions and less likely to get stuck in those emotions once they're triggered;
- being able to cognitively reframe the distraction (e.g. 'it's just a thought', or 'it's okay to get distracted, as long as I can refocus').

All these elements are essential for moving toward the type of long-term goals you set at the beginning of this book. The following PFC exercise, based on an exercise in David Harp's *3 Minuten Meditaties* [3-Minute Meditations], trains all four elements.

PFC exercise: Just count

Sit on a chair in a quiet spot. Put your feet flat on the ground, put your hands in your lap and straighten your back. Make sure you are comfortable. Now start silently counting every time you inhale, while concentrating on the sensation of breathing, that is: how you inhale the air through your nose and how your belly expands. So, inhale 1... and exhale; inhale again 2... and exhale. Inhale 3... and exhale, inhale 4... inhale 5.... and so on.

Try to do this at a relaxed pace and to focus only on your breathing. Do not try to control your breathing, so don't start breathing faster or slower. Just count. Start over at 1 every time you lose count or when you notice your mind has drifted to something else. Try not to judge yourself, by telling yourself that you are doing well or not so well. The first time I tried this, I didn't get beyond 2. Just start over again.

Every time you get distracted and start over, you're strengthening your skill, because redirecting your attention to 1 is the perfect way to learn to let go of distractions. You're also training your self-monitoring skills and your working memory, because you're keeping your sights on a goal. In other words, you're training your prefrontal cortex and various executive skills. If you're bothered by thoughts, desires, feelings of restlessness and the wish to escape, trade these in for an inhalation. Inhale 1 and exhale, inhale 2..., inhale 3..., and so on.

When trying to focus, don't get discouraged if your attention is drawn by thoughts you'd rather not think, or feelings you wish you didn't have (cake, porn, a deadline, mistakes you've made, anger, envy, sadness, you name it). Research has shown that attempts to suppress such thoughts are generally counter-productive. No doubt, you've experienced that the more you try not to think of something, the more it continues to pop up in your mind and have a negative impact on your behavior. Instead, just let those unwelcome thoughts and feelings well up, but try not to get hung up on them. Just keep focusing your attention on your breathing. Don't condemn yourself for having intrusive thoughts or emotions, but try to accept them and then move on to your real goals. This will eventually reduce the power of those thoughts and feelings.

You can substitute pretty much any other target for your breathing. Personally, I do this exercise every morning and every evening when I brush my hair. Stroke 1, stroke 2, stroke 3, and so on. At first, I found it very hard not to get distracted, but I have to admit that it now takes barely any effort at all. I've even started to expand this exercise to various other activities, such as the sensation of taking bites from an apple, my co-worker's breathing during some endless meeting, my own breathing during a root canal, or the grout between the bricks on the wall behind the person delivering that boring presentation. Select your own focal point and expand this exercise to other times of day. You'll find that it keeps getting easier and that you'll gain more and more control over your selective attention, distractions and emotions. This can help you understand, learn and achieve things in a way that makes life more fulfilling.

The previous exercise is just one example of the many types of training available. There are many apps that can help you practice focused attention meditation. Just have a look in the app store.

You can use selective attention to gain control over the marshmallows in your life. If you redirect your attention, the marshmallows will lose some of their allure and have less effect on your brain. It will be hard at first, but the more you do it, the easier it will get.

PFC exercise: Redirecting your attention

Write down what kind of marshmallows, or temptations, you expect to come across on the way to your goal. Every time you feel you're about to succumb to one of them, which you don't want to do because this will interfere with your long-term goals, you need to consciously think 'I'M GOING TO REDIRECT MY ATTENTION'. Then, focus on something else, such as your long-term goal, or a book, a meditation exercise or a phone call with a friend. Write these things down.

Marshmallows	⟶	Attention redirected to
	I'M GOING TO REDIRECT MY ATTENTION	

Open attention: mindfulness

We have seen that it is useful to be able to control your selective attention, but being able to apply open attention also comes in handy. One of the techniques that foster open attention is mindfulness. For this reason, this technique is also known as *open monitoring training*. Mindfulness can be defined as:

- Paying attention to the here and now by monitoring your experience from moment to moment without judging. In that sense, we shouldn't speak of mindfulness as something you can train, because a non-judgmental attitude implies that you can't improve on anything.

Mindfulness requires you to apply your monitoring skills. It helps you become aware of sensations, traits, thoughts and feelings, and to accept these things without getting caught up in them. Mindfulness practice often starts with selective attention meditation to calm the mind and quell the urge to give in to distractions. These meditations are then expanded to an open attention meditation that teaches you to progress toward simply monitoring what is going on without attaching all sorts of emotions to it and without turning your attention to any individual experience you become aware of. For example, an irritating noise won't prevent you from getting your work done; you can notice it and quietly continue what you were doing. Or, worries won't keep you awake at night; you'll simply note that they are there, but you'll be able to let them go and fall asleep.

Mindfulness enables you to notice what's going on, like a co-worker loudly talking on the phone while you're trying to write an email; worries about how your children are doing in school; or the dread you feel about approaching someone. It teaches you to accept these feelings without judging them, reducing the stress you feel. This "clear reflexive awareness" of what is going on inside, as Lutz and co-authors describe it, is the primary goal of mindfulness meditation. In other words, mindfulness helps you develop self-reflection. According to Lutz and co-authors, it's generally accepted that awareness of what's going on in your mind will improve your ability to break old habits.

Proven effectiveness

Mindfulness is an ancient type of attention meditation rooted in Buddhism. Modern science has confirmed that it is an excellent way to improve your executive skills. Mindfulness targets thoughts, bodily sensations and emotions. Meditation is always beneficial and there is definitely some meditation technique that will appeal to you. Let me offer you some more scientific findings to convince you, and then ask you to try some simple exercises whose effects are bound to win you over.

Research in the field of selective attention and open attention meditation has been summarized in several literature reviews, including those of Alberto Chiesa and Martin Dresler and their respective co-authors. Research shows that people experienced in these types of meditation:

- have greater cognitive flexibility;
- are quick to respond to their mistakes without feeling a lot of stress;
- are better at adaptive, goal-directed behavior;
- have a better working memory;
- are more creative;
- are better able to regulate their emotions;
- are generally better at self-control.

So, clearly meditation is directly related to the development of your executive skills, but it does more, because those who meditate regularly are also better at dealing with relationship problems, are less fatigued, and may even have a later onset of the cognitive degeneration that comes with age. I'm sure this list of benefits includes at least one you would personally like to have.

Brain scans of people who meditate show that meditating has a positive effect on the structure and performance of the prefrontal cortex, and specifically on areas involved in metacognition and self-reflexivity. We also see changes in other areas in the brain, such as the anterior cingulate cortex, the basal ganglia and the hippocampus, and in the connections between the various areas of the brain. Parts of the prefrontal cortex, the hippocampus, the temporal lobe and the insula grow larger. Meditation training also benefits the connections between various parts of the brain and the anterior cingulate, an area deeply involved in our ability to identify errors and exert self-control; this results in a more efficient network. Meditation even improves how the brain regulates pain and emotion, so that we feel less when we receive a painful stimulus and we find it easier to stay on an even keel emotionally. As I said before, some areas of the brain start collaborating better and responding simultaneously to a particular stimulus (a phenomenon we call coupling), while other areas cease to be triggered simultaneously (de-coupling). 'So what?' you might be wondering. But these last two effects can decrease the triggering of urges or stress when you're exposed to a particular stimulus, like fatty food, cigarettes or standing in front of an audience.

People who practice integrative body-mind training (IBMT), which includes mindfulness, show more alpha activity (8-13 Hertz) in their brain when they are resting. This effect is visible, particularly in the frontal lobe, after as few as five days of training. Many scientists associate an increase in alpha activity during rest with better cognitive performance, relaxation, lower anxiety and more positivity. Meditation can sometimes also lead to an increase in theta waves (4-8 Hertz), which are associated with relaxation. The effects of mindfulness are similar to those found after IBMT. Mindfulness practice creates Flow Focus: a relaxed state coupled with supreme alertness.

Experiencing the effects of meditation

You don't need to be an expert or practice for years to experience the benefits of meditation. A few months of practicing can be quite effective, while even a few isolated attempts can be beneficial. Fadel Zeidan at Wake Forest School of Medicine showed that even a four-day meditation course can reduce fatigue and improve your mood, your ability to regulate fear and your executive functioning. As few as three days were enough to increase your ability to withstand pain. Although brief periods of practice can be effective, it appears that the longer you practice the more benefits you will reap.

Alberto Chiesa and co-authors assert that in healthy people, short-term mindfulness training is associated with top-down emotion regulation, while long-term mindfulness practitioners learn to regulate their emotions bottom-up. At first, you appear to primarily use your prefrontal cortex to consciously influence your lower brain structures to regulate your emotions. If you practice enough, the lower brain structures involved in experiencing emotions, like the limbic system, appear to be activated less, so less emotion regulation by the prefrontal cortex is required. This is a plausible hypothesis, but more detailed research is needed.

Mindfulness courses generally require about eight weeks of practice for several hours a day. You gradually become more aware of everything that's going on around you and inside you. You learn to monitor your state of being without judging it. Some mindfulness courses teach you to do this practically automatically, which enables you to monitor more, and to more easily ascertain the causes and effects of your thoughts and feelings. This is also what some anxiety and addiction therapies are based on.

At first, practicing mindfulness will tax your brain. But the more you practice, the easier and more beneficial it will become, both at the level of behavior, thoughts and emotions and at the level of brain structure and performance. Obviously, these levels are related. Now we're going to do some exercises that let you start experiencing the benefits of mindfulness.

The great thing about mindfulness is that you can do it anytime and anywhere, even when reading a book or watching TV. Personally, I use an app to practice mindfulness for about ten minutes every morning. The following PFC exercise is based on one of John Arden's short mindfulness exercises from his book *Rewire Your Brain*.

PFC exercise: Observing

Start by reading the two paragraphs below. Read them fully before you do the exercise.

Sit down with this book in your hands and relax. Focus on what you feel. Do you feel the weight of the book in your hands? The texture of the cover? Breathe in and out slowly and deeply. What else do you notice? Sounds from outside? A smell perhaps? Are you aware of your back against the back of your chair? Your hands in your lap? Your buttocks on the seat? Your feet on the ground?

You might find all sorts of thoughts flitting through your mind. That's okay. Let them approach, fill your mind and then pass by, like traffic on a road. Don't try to stop these thoughts and feelings, just let them pass through you. They're giving you the perfect opportunity to observe them and then let them go. Monitor what is going on, label the things you notice (identify what they are) and try not to judge.

Now do the exercise.

By labeling your thoughts and emotions without judging them, you learn that they don't define you, but can pass through you without controlling you. In their books, John Arden and Jeffrey Schwartz describe how identifying and labeling your thoughts and emotions helps to control the negative influence of the amygdala, an area in the brain associated with emotions, including anxiety. Simply observing and labeling the emotion you feel ('I am scared', for example), will help you avoid being consumed by it, reducing its intensity.

This type of exercise trains your prefrontal cortex and helps you develop an open focus. Mindfulness reduces pain, stress, anxiety, cravings, irritations and depression because it increases the prefrontal cortex's control over pain- and emotion-related areas; in so doing, it helps make you less of a puppet on a string. In short, mindfulness reinforces your prefrontal cortex, related structures and your executive skills.

There are various ways to master the art of mindfulness. You can take classes, read books about it, or, like me, use an app on your smartphone to practice mindfulness daily. I use the Headspace app, but I've also heard good things about Buddhify. If you're still resisting the idea of mindfulness, the 'F*ck That: An Honest Meditation' video[21] on YouTube might be right for you (it's full of expletives, but funny and relaxing too). For other ideas, check out these websites.[22]

If we look at all the effects of open attention meditation, we see right away that there's a close connection between these effects and the executive skills associated with the prefrontal cortex (and success). The list below shows you which executive skills mindfulness helps to develop:

1	Focusing, sustaining, dividing and releasing attention	☑
2	Regulating emotions	☑
3	Flexibility in the face of change	☑
4	Inhibitory control	☑
5	Task initiation	☑
6	Organization	☑
7	Planning	☐
8	Self-monitoring	☑
9	Using your working memory	☑
10	A realistic self-image	☑
11	The capacity for theory of mind	☐
12	Prosocial behavior (altruism)	☐

Flow Focus

The title of this chapter is Flow Focus. The term 'flow' mainly gained popularity through the work of Hungarian psychologist and author Mihaly Csikszentmihalyi. Flow is based on ideas and techniques from Eastern religions and philosophies. Also known as 'being in the zone', flow entails complete absorption in a particular activity. Your attention is fully focused on this activity and this gives

21 www.youtube.com/watch?v=92i5m3tV5XY
22 www.theguardian.com/technology/2016/may/26/five-of-the-best-meditation-apps
www.mindful.org/free-mindfulness-apps-worthy-of-your-attention/
www.healthline.com/health/mental-health/top-meditation-iphone-android-apps#5

you a pleasant, energetic feeling. You can get so focused that you become oblivious to things you are normally aware of: the passage of time, your worries, the presence of other people, etc. Your whole being and all your energy are focused on the one thing that induces that state of flow.

My definition of the term Flow Focus is not entirely in line with Csikszentmihalyi's concept and description of flow. If you'd like to learn more about his ideas on flow and creativity, I can wholeheartedly recommend his books. I have opted instead for the term Flow Focus because this combines two key elements I've dealt with so far: focus (attention) and relaxation. This combination is sometimes also referred to as flow, so that's why I came up with the term Flow Focus. Let me qualify that, however. Learning to relax more and cope with stress improves the performance of your prefrontal cortex. But, as we saw in Chapter 6, 'Environmental Enrichment', you can't be zen all the time. You need a little bit of tension along the way. It goes hand in hand with discovering new things and raising the bar. A bit of stress helps you make decisions, stay on your toes, develop and change. Never being exposed to stress leads to boredom and understimulation of your brain, and hence underdevelopment. When I talk about Flow Focus, I'm talking about avoiding prolonged stress. Unlike the healthy challenges that temporarily raise your stress level, lengthy periods of stress are bad for the brain; it is therefore important that you avoid these and regulate daily levels of stress.

The exercises I've included here can help you make great strides in developing your prefrontal cortex and executive skills. The next chapter will focus on another essential requirement for reinforcing your prefrontal cortex: sleep.

'If sleep does not serve an absolutely vital function, then it is the biggest mistake the evolutionary process has ever made.'

Allan Rechtschaffen

University of Chicago Sleep Laboratory, 1978

Chapter 8 **Fixed Sleeping Pattern – Unleashing the Power of Sleep**

This chapter will show you how a good night's sleep and the occasional catnap can dramatically improve your prefrontal cortex and executive skills.

Catnap

SELF-KNOWLEDGE

You can only do this experiment when the time is right. Wait for a day when, around 3 or 4 p.m., your thoughts start feeling stuck. Find a quiet spot to lie down for a while or put your head on your arms on your desk. Close your eyes for 20 minutes or so. It's fine if you fall asleep, but if you think your nap might last longer than 30 minutes, set an alarm. After your nap, open your eyes, take some time to fully wake up and then try to assess what this catnap did for you.

My guess is that you'll feel refreshed and ready to tackle whatever you were working on before your nap. I will come back to the subject of napping a bit later on.

We spend about a third of our lives asleep. That's a lot of time. And while we sleep, we're extra vulnerable because we don't perceive what's going on around us. In emergencies, we're unable to respond quickly and appropriately.

Sleep deprivation

Most of us consider life a hectic experience. For some of us, the familiar pattern is that we get to bed too late, but have to wake up early the next morning for work or to get the kids to school. After several days like this, we end up sleep-deprived and tired during the day. Others find it hard to fall asleep because of worries and stress. Many people wake up at least once, but often several times a night and can never get in enough hours of uninterrupted sleep. All these problems generate a lot of concern; at my speaking engagements, I'm asked countless questions about how much sleep we should get and what constitutes a healthy sleeping pattern. But I also encounter another group of people: those who boast that they only need a few of hours sleep per night. In response, I explain how important it is to get enough sleep, and emphasize that sleep deprivation has proven negative consequences.

Research has shown that sleep deprivation has a wide range of negative effects on the skills and behaviors regulated by the prefrontal cortex. It decreases your self-control, attention span, memory and judgment. It increases perseveration and slows your reaction time. It affects your hot executive skills in particular. Your mental resilience falters, so you have a harder time handling everyday stress. Stress hormone levels soar and your heart rate variability declines. You readily slip into a fight or flee reflex. At the cellular level, sleep deprivation reduces your body's ability to absorb glucose, the main fuel for the brain. Your prefrontal cortex needs a lot of this fuel, which might explain why your executive skills diminish so fast when you've had too little sleep. Another effect is a reduction of your neural plasticity. In short, sleep deprivation causes mild prefrontal dysfunction, which is an apt description considering the consequences, which is exactly what we're trying to correct!

The high pace and never-ending demands of the VUCA world lead us to systematically underestimate the importance and benefits of sleep. A great many people have no idea anymore what it feels like to be fully rested, because even on vacation our mobile phones and laptops continue to bombard us with the same demands we face during our working week. What's more, we disrupt our natural sleeping pattern by drinking coffee, alcohol and energy drinks. We expose ourselves to artificial lighting. What many of us don't realize is that sleep is just as crucial to our well-being as nutrition. It's indispensable, not just for getting rest, but also for boosting cognitive functions, particularly attention, memory and executive skills. It also increases our brain plasticity. Getting enough sleep helps you memorize whatever you learned before you went to bed. It also helps you remember what you still need to learn when you wake up. Moreover, a good night's sleep increases your understanding and judgment. And it makes you more creative as well.

Siesta

Sleep researchers have not only studied the effects of nighttime sleep; they've also explored whether daytime naps improve cognitive skills. And sure enough, they do. Long live the siesta! However, naps are only beneficial if they are short and not taken every day. A brief nap, less than 30 minutes, enhances some aspects of your cognitive performance and improves your mood too. Some studies even show that a 6-minute nap is enough to boost your memory, but 10 minutes is the generally recommended minimum naptime. Sleep experts also recommend that you limit your midday nap to 30 minutes at most, as longer naps can diminish your cognitive skills and health. Long naps can also disrupt your nighttime sleeping pattern. Apparently, Winston Churchill and Albert Einstein were big on taking afternoon naps because this helped them think more clearly and get more done. Their experiences are supported by current research.

If you find that a 20-minute siesta is too short for you, you might not be getting enough sleep at night. It would be a good idea to start monitoring that. Other factors that apparently have an impact on the benefits of an afternoon nap are your general state of health, your sex, and for women, where you are in your menstrual cycle. For example, napping appears to improve memory in men and in women who are in mid-menstrual cycle. In general, it appears to be the case that the healthier you are, the more benefits you reap from napping.

PFC exercise: Taking more catnaps

This exercise expands on the Catnap exercise.

For one month, take twice-weekly naps of 10 to 30 minutes. Use an alarm clock to ensure you don't oversleep. This will train your brain to wake up from a short nap instead of falling into a deep sleep from which it's harder to wake up.

How many hours of sleep you need per night depends on various factors, including your age and lifestyle. The chart below shows how many hours of sleep are recommended for your age group (and for your children). Above and below the recommended range, you will see the number of hours that may be right for individuals who may need slightly more or slightly less sleep. These recommendations from the U.S.-based National Sleep Foundation are based on a large body of sleep research, so I believe they should be taken seriously.

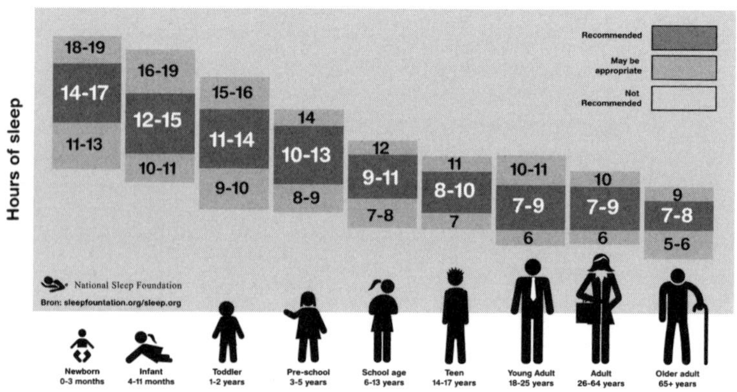

Recommended hours of sleep per night[23]

Sleeping pattern

The National Sleep Foundation also recommends monitoring how you feel after different amounts of sleep per night. By experimenting with different sleeping

23 M. Hirshkowitz, The National Sleep Foundation's sleep time duration recommendations: methodology and results summary, *Sleep Health* (2015), http://dx.doi.org/10.1016/j.sleh.2014.12.010.

patterns within the recommended bandwidth for your age group, you can find the number of hours that is right for you.

PFC exercise: Discovering your ideal sleeping pattern

Experiment for a couple of weeks with different bedtimes and wake up times.

- Do you feel unhappy, less productive or tired?
- Are you stressed out? Do you have a short fuse?
- Do you fall asleep on the couch early in the evening?
- Do you get drowsy behind the wheel?

If you answered any of the last three questions affirmatively, you probably need more hours of sleep per night and need to adjust your sleeping pattern. Five hours of quality sleep is considered the absolute biological minimum. If you regularly get less sleep, you are bound to feel the consequences, physically, emotionally and cognitively.

There are sleep diaries that can help you keep track of, and understand, your sleeping habits. You can find one on The National Sleep Foundation's website. Others are available from the AASM and the NHS.[24]

If you feel the need to do this more quickly, just use the following diary for two weeks to log how you feel after a short night's sleep and after a long night's sleep. Filling in the list below will take no more than a minute or two every morning and will provide you with some insight into your sleeping habits.

Sleep diary

DAY 1				
	Hours of sleep			
	Mood	☐ good	☐ okay	☐ bad
	Energy level	☐ high	☐ normal	☐ low
	Patience	☐ little	☐ normal	☐ a lot
	Stress level	☐ high	☐ normal	☐ absent
	Daytime drowsiness	☐ not at all	☐ a few times	☐ a lot
	Alcohol use	☐ Type		Units ....
	Caffeine use	☐		
	I feel like I had a good night's sleep	☐ yes ☐ no		

24 http://yoursleep.aasmnet.org/pdf/sleepdiary.pdf, http://www.nhs.uk/Livewell/insomnia/Documents/sleepdiary.pdf
http://healthyhabitstoolkit.com/wp-content/uploads/Printable-Sleep-Diary.pdf

DAY 2

Hours of sleep ______

Mood	☐ good	☐ okay	☐ bad
Energy level	☐ high	☐ normal	☐ low
Patience	☐ little	☐ normal	☐ a lot
Stress level	☐ high	☐ normal	☐ absent
Daytime drowsiness	☐ not at all	☐ a few times	☐ a lot
Alcohol use	☐ Type ______		Units ______
Caffeine use	☐		
I feel like I had a good night's sleep	☐ yes ☐ no		

DAY 3

Hours of sleep ______

Mood	☐ good	☐ okay	☐ bad
Energy level	☐ high	☐ normal	☐ low
Patience	☐ little	☐ normal	☐ a lot
Stress level	☐ high	☐ normal	☐ absent
Daytime drowsiness	☐ not at all	☐ a few times	☐ a lot
Alcohol use	☐ Type ______		Units ______
Caffeine use	☐		
I feel like I had a good night's sleep	☐ yes ☐ no		

DAY 4

Hours of sleep ______

Mood	☐ good	☐ okay	☐ bad
Energy level	☐ high	☐ normal	☐ low
Patience	☐ little	☐ normal	☐ a lot
Stress level	☐ high	☐ normal	☐ absent
Daytime drowsiness	☐ not at all	☐ a few times	☐ a lot
Alcohol use	☐ Type ______		Units ______
Caffeine use	☐		
I feel like I had a good night's sleep	☐ yes ☐ no		

DAY 5

Hours of sleep ______

Mood	☐ good	☐ okay	☐ bad
Energy level	☐ high	☐ normal	☐ low
Patience	☐ little	☐ normal	☐ a lot
Stress level	☐ high	☐ normal	☐ absent
Daytime drowsiness	☐ not at all	☐ a few times	☐ a lot
Alcohol use	☐ Type ______		Units ______
Caffeine use	☐		
I feel like I had a good night's sleep	☐ yes ☐ no		

DAY 6

Hours of sleep			
Mood	☐ good	☐ okay	☐ bad
Energy level	☐ high	☐ normal	☐ low
Patience	☐ little	☐ normal	☐ a lot
Stress level	☐ high	☐ normal	☐ absent
Daytime drowsiness	☐ not at all	☐ a few times	☐ a lot
Alcohol use	☐ Type		Units ....
Caffeine use	☐		
I feel like I had a good night's sleep	☐ yes ☐ no		

DAY 7

Hours of sleep			
Mood	☐ good	☐ okay	☐ bad
Energy level	☐ high	☐ normal	☐ low
Patience	☐ little	☐ normal	☐ a lot
Stress level	☐ high	☐ normal	☐ absent
Daytime drowsiness	☐ not at all	☐ a few times	☐ a lot
Alcohol use	☐ Type		Units ....
Caffeine use	☐		
I feel like I had a good night's sleep	☐ yes ☐ no		

DAY 8

Hours of sleep			
Mood	☐ good	☐ okay	☐ bad
Energy level	☐ high	☐ normal	☐ low
Patience	☐ little	☐ normal	☐ a lot
Stress level	☐ high	☐ normal	☐ absent
Daytime drowsiness	☐ not at all	☐ a few times	☐ a lot
Alcohol use	☐ Type		Units ....
Caffeine use	☐		
I feel like I had a good night's sleep	☐ yes ☐ no		

DAY 9

Hours of sleep			
Mood	☐ good	☐ okay	☐ bad
Energy level	☐ high	☐ normal	☐ low
Patience	☐ little	☐ normal	☐ a lot
Stress level	☐ high	☐ normal	☐ absent
Daytime drowsiness	☐ not at all	☐ a few times	☐ a lot
Alcohol use	☐ Type		Units ....
Caffeine use	☐		
I feel like I had a good night's sleep	☐ yes ☐ no		

Getting a good night's sleep should be high on your priority list.

DAY 10

Hours of sleep ....

Mood	☐ good	☐ okay	☐ bad
Energy level	☐ high	☐ normal	☐ low
Patience	☐ little	☐ normal	☐ a lot
Stress level	☐ high	☐ normal	☐ absent
Daytime drowsiness	☐ not at all	☐ a few times	☐ a lot
Alcohol use	☐ Type		Units ....
Caffeine use	☐		
I feel like I had a good night's sleep	☐ yes ☐ no		

DAY 11

Hours of sleep ....

Mood	☐ good	☐ okay	☐ bad
Energy level	☐ high	☐ normal	☐ low
Patience	☐ little	☐ normal	☐ a lot
Stress level	☐ high	☐ normal	☐ absent
Daytime drowsiness	☐ not at all	☐ a few times	☐ a lot
Alcohol use	☐ Type		Units ....
Caffeine use	☐		
I feel like I had a good night's sleep	☐ yes ☐ no		

DAY 12

Hours of sleep ....

Mood	☐ good	☐ okay	☐ bad
Energy level	☐ high	☐ normal	☐ low
Patience	☐ little	☐ normal	☐ a lot
Stress level	☐ high	☐ normal	☐ absent
Daytime drowsiness	☐ not at all	☐ a few times	☐ a lot
Alcohol use	☐ Type		Units ....
Caffeine use	☐		
I feel like I had a good night's sleep	☐ yes ☐ no		

DAY 13

Hours of sleep ....

Mood	☐ good	☐ okay	☐ bad
Energy level	☐ high	☐ normal	☐ low
Patience	☐ little	☐ normal	☐ a lot
Stress level	☐ high	☐ normal	☐ absent
Daytime drowsiness	☐ not at all	☐ a few times	☐ a lot
Alcohol use	☐ Type		Units ....
Caffeine use	☐		
I feel like I had a good night's sleep	☐ yes ☐ no		

DAY 14

Hours of sleep			
Mood	☐ good	☐ okay	☐ bad
Energy level	☐ high	☐ normal	☐ low
Patience	☐ little	☐ normal	☐ a lot
Stress level	☐ high	☐ normal	☐ absent
Daytime drowsiness	☐ not at all	☐ a few times	☐ a lot
Alcohol use	☐ Type		Units ....
Caffeine use	☐		
I feel like I had a good night's sleep	☐ yes ☐ no		

You can also download apps to monitor your sleeping patterns. These are available on Azumio.com, sleepcycle.com and other sites.

Healthy sleeping habits

To improve your sleeping habits, I have devised a PFC exercise using tips drawn from the National Sleep Foundation and several Dutch organizations.[25] These tips offer you healthier, more sustainable solutions for sleeping problems than sleeping pills.

Sleeping pills are habit-forming, which means that if you keep using them, you will need an increasing number of pills to produce the same effect. It also means you will suffer from withdrawal symptoms whenever you stop taking them. Such symptoms include daytime drowsiness and persistent surface sleep at night. If you are using sleeping pills now, I would strongly advise you to phase them out. For more information, refer to sleeping websites or consult your doctor. A visit to the doctor is also advisable if you are a long-term insomniac or have other worries that interfere with healthy sleep.

Healthy sleeping habits

SELF-KNOWLEDGE

- Stick to a *fixed sleeping schedule*, with the same bedtime and wake up time every day. The National Sleep Foundation emphasizes how important it is to stick to this schedule even on weekends, even if that's hard to do. A fixed sleeping schedule regulates your biological clock, while deviating from it disrupts the clock. You can sleep

25 http://sleepfoundation.org/how-sleep-works/how-much-sleep-do-we-really-need
https://sleep.org/
http://educatie.ntr.nl/beterslapen/index.jsp?nr=574728
www.dokterdokter.nl/gezond-leven/psyche/10-redenen-om-meer-te-slapen/

late as an exception, but only for 1.5 hours at the most. Disrupting your biological clock too often and too sharply may cause sleeping disorders.
- Introduce a relaxing *bedtime ritual*. It doesn't really matter what you do, as long as it relaxes you. You could do a 3-minute meditation, or one of the exercises you will find at the end of this chapter.
- Try to get some *exercise every day*, but not right before going to sleep. Exercise three to six hours before bedtime, so your body has enough time to recover. I will return to the importance of exercise in the next chapter.
- Make sure your *bedroom is quiet* (wear good earplugs if necessary). Avoid unfamiliar, non-repetitive noises. These immediately draw your brain's attention and put you in a state of alertness, which is undesirable when you're trying to get some sleep.
- Sleep in a *cool, dark room*. Light and temperature affect your circadian rhythm. Normally, it gets darker and the temperature drops when it's time for bed. If you get enough exercise during the day, your body will be better at regulating your body temperature around bedtime. This improves the quality of your sleep.
- Make sure you are *comfortable*, so sleep on a good mattress and pillow. If necessary, seek advice on this.
- *Stop drinking coffee and alcohol* several hours before bedtime. Although alcohol may help you fall asleep, it will also cause you to wake up during the night. This is because alcohol inhibits REM sleep in favor of surface sleep. Likewise, drinking tea or water right before bed may disrupt your sleep, because you may need to get up to urinate.
- Do not eat a *heavy meal* right before going to bed, but don't go to bed hungry either. A large meal can cause discomfort and raise your energy level. But being hungry doesn't feel good either and may keep you awake.
- Take care *not to sleep too much during the day*, as this may interfere with how sleepy you feel at bedtime.
- *Do not use your phone, tablet or laptop* right before going to bed. The light, especially the blue light that is similar to sunlight, affects your biological clock. Also, playing online games or chatting with people activates your brain and causes alertness and restlessness.
- If you are tense, try a few *relaxation exercises* from Chapter 7, 'Flow Focus'. Sports can also help you to relax (but not right before bedtime), and a hot bath can do the same. A bath has the added advantage that your body temperature will drop when you get out of the tub.
- Use your bed for sleeping, sex and reading a relaxing book. Never use your bed as an ersatz office or living room. Make sure you *associate your bed with rest, relaxation and sleep*. Your brain needs to make the same connection.

Usually, trying to fall asleep doesn't help. If you can't sleep, get up and walk around to make your body temperature go down. Pacing can also help you avoid brooding. If you find yourself worrying anyway, try to apply a mindfulness technique. If you have intrusive thoughts, write them down instead of keeping them in your mind. Worrying about not being able to sleep will only make it harder to fall asleep. Realize that it's not the

Are you one of those people who think they perform just fine after sleeping only a few hours a night? Just imagine how much better you would perform, how much better you would feel, if you got enough sleep.

end of the world. You will probably sleep better the next night. There are plenty of ideas in this book that can help you sleep better. And as my granddad used to say: 'Even if you don' t sleep, you're still getting rested.' This wise saying has helped me not to lose sleep over losing a night of sleep.

If you've had a bad night, stick to your sleeping schedule anyway. Trying to 'catch up' by sleeping during the day will ultimately disrupt your rhythm.

PFC exercise: Sleep meditation

I'm going to give you a simple, effective sleep-inducing exercise I came across on the Art of Manliness site.[26] Please read through the entire exercise before you try it.

Sit down on a chair. Relax. Put your hands in your lap and your feet on the ground. Close your eyes and imagine you are a hollow tree trunk lying on a green bed of moss in a beautiful, remote and quiet forest.

Try to maintain this thought for a couple of minutes and then go to bed.

This visualization should make you relaxed and sleepy.

If this visualization does not appeal to you, there are plenty of other sleep meditations and sleep improvement exercises to choose from on YouTube. One of them is bound to appeal to you.

Success in life depends partly on whether you're skilled at absorbing pertinent information and disregarding what is irrelevant. It also requires an ability to make informed decisions once you have filtered out useless information. But if you aren't getting enough sleep, your performance on these skills will decrease. If you do get enough sleep (see the chart on p. 156) and take the occasional catnap, you will improve on these crucial skills. It's hard to imagine a more relaxing, pleasant and affordable technique! Just make sure you get enough hours of nighttime sleep and take an occasional 10-minute nap after lunch if you feel the need. You will benefit hugely. I never cease to be amazed at the results I get from a 10-minute nap after lunch. And if you're one of those people who think they perform just fine after sleeping only a few hours a night, try to imagine how much better you would perform, how much better you would feel, if you got enough sleep.

---

26 www.artofmanliness.com/2012/08/08/12-concentration-exercises-from-1918/

More and more health experts are acknowledging how important sleep is for our overall health. Getting a good night's sleep should be high on your priority list. Make it a habit. You're going to need the energy. The next chapter deals with some pretty high-energy activities, as we're going to discover how exercise can help you develop your prefrontal cortex.

‘A healthy mind in a healthy body’

Presocratic axiom

Chapter 9 **Exercise – Shaping and Training Your Brain**

This chapter shows you how physical exercise enhances the development of your prefrontal cortex. As you do your favorite kind of exercise, you are automatically training your brain and reinforcing your executive skills.

SELF-KNOWLEDGE

Riddle

You're in a room with a door. There's a table with some weights and a book on it and there are two ropes hanging from the ceiling, some distance apart. You have to try to get hold of both ropes at the same time, but you find that if you grab hold of one and try to reach the other, the rope is not long enough. How are you going to get hold of both ropes at the same time?

1 If you don't understand exactly what to do, watch an online video about the problem by clicking the 'Stretch-group participant attempting solution' link on the page 'internal.psychology.illinois.edu'.[27]

If you can't figure out the solution and need a hint, read on.

2 Make swinging motions with your arms and count backwards in 3s from 667 as follows: 667, 664, 661 and so on, until you've found the solution.

If you're unsure of what to do, click the 'Participant during a Swinging Exercise break' link on the same website.

3 Did you manage to find the solution?

To watch the solution, click on the 'Swing-group participant attempting solution' link.

The exercise you just did is based on a study by Laura Thomas and Alejandro Lleras. As the videos show, they asked their subjects to do the same. It turns out, you need to be quite inventive to solve the two-rope problem. Thomas and Lleras demonstrated that the type of movements you make can determine whether you solve a given problem. Of the two groups – those who were asked to stretch their arms and those who were asked to swing them – it was the swingers who more

27 http://internal.psychology.illinois.edu/~alleras/videos.htm

often found a solution to the rope problem.[28] This supports a theory known as *embodied cognition.*

Embodied cognition means that it's not just the mind that influences the body, but also the body that influences the mind. In other words, the movements you make affect your thoughts and emotions just like your thoughts and emotions have an effect on your body. So, swinging your arms triggers the thought of making the ropes swing, so you can grab both at the same time. This example demonstrates very clearly how your physical movements can specifically influence executive skills such as logic and creativity. But exercise effectively helps you improve your executive skills and enhance the performance of the prefrontal cortex.

Endurance

We all know that physical exercise is good for your physical health. In our body-obsessed society, many people also exercise to increase their physical attractiveness. We normally associate exercise with building muscle and decreasing the risks of cardiovascular disease and diabetes, but seldom consider the fact that it benefits our sleep, state of mind and brain. But it's true: physical exercise sharpens your executive skills and enhances the prefrontal cortex. Recently, a meta-study on a large body of exercise research concluded that regular exercise appears to improve various executive skills. It has been shown to improve concentration, working memory (capacity), inhibitory control and task-switching abilities. It can even accelerate your information-processing speed. Some studies, however, showed that during exercise, certain executive skills like redirecting your attention diminished. More research is needed to explain these contradictory results, the meta-study concluded.

Most exercise research has focused on endurance training, also referred to as cardiovascular or aerobic exercise. Endurance training causes metabolic, respiratory and cardiovascular changes in the human body, as Claudia Voelcker-Rehage and Claudia Niemann's literature review clearly demonstrates. Such training involves repetitive, automatic activities that require no thinking, like jogging, biking or swimming. Studies show that endurance training not only improves cognitive skills, but also induces various structural and functional changes in the prefrontal cortex and other areas of the brain. For example, during tasks that involve executive skills, the grey matter in the prefrontal cortex expands and the activation patterns in this area change, according to several studies. Sometimes, the prefrontal cortex functions more efficiently, while in other cases, it compensates for the diminished performance of other areas of the brain, ensuring that a task is carried out well anyway.

---

28 I also used this example in *Ik wil iets van jou, jij wil iets van mij*, 2012, [I Want Something from You, You Want Something from Me].

Endurance and neuroplasticity

Some evidence suggests that endurance training activates the generation of new blood vessels and might thus enhance blood flow to the prefrontal cortex and the hippocampus, supplying these areas with more oxygen and nutrients. Endurance training also appears to enhance the connections between these areas and other areas of the brain. Researchers have additionally found that endurance training increases the serum concentrations of brain-derived-neurotrophic factor. This is a protein that affects the generation of new cells in the hippocampus and is involved in plasticity-supporting processes. In short, endurance training not only noticeably influences our executive skills, it also has a clearly visible impact on the structure and functioning of our brain.

Another great thing about endurance training is that it doesn't just benefit the young. So far, most studies into exercise and cognitive skills have been conducted with older subjects; they show that exercise counteracts cognitive degeneration in seniors. They also reveal that grey matter-containing areas that usually degenerate with age, such as the prefrontal cortex and the hippocampus, stay intact longer. These studies, too, show that exercise mainly affects the skills associated with the prefrontal cortex and the hippocampus. Some researchers have shown that there is a correlation between the degree of fitness, the level of particular executive skills like spatial working memory and inhibitory control, and grey matter volume in the prefrontal cortex. These are important findings because the prefrontal cortex and its attendant executive skills are among the first 'victims' of aging. That this degeneration can to some extent be delayed, prevented or compensated for by exercise, is good news.

Other types of exercise

Research shows that other types of exercise can be beneficial, too. For instance, Voelcker-Rehage and Niemann explore the effects of training the movements necessary for hand-eye coordination, such as reacting to fast-moving objects. Examples of this kind of movement are learning to tend goal, shoot, balance or do yoga. Such training requires the use of higher cognitive skills: attention, anticipation and integration of complex movements. According to the research, doing this kind of training also improves executive skills and the ability to filter out distracting information and process information effectively.

Initial studies in this area show that just like aerobic exercise, such coordinated movement exercise expands areas that contain grey matter, including the hippocampus and the frontoparietal network. Because such exercise requires the use of various higher cognitive skills, Voelcker-Rehage and Niemann hypothesize that these effects are due to environmental enrichment rather than improved fitness (which is not what such exercise is aimed at anyway). This hypothesis is in line with findings from animal studies. Therefore, there is reason to believe that aerobic exercises combined with either coordinated movement exercises, environmental enrichment or cognitive exercises has a far greater effect on our brain and skills than aerobic exercise in isolation. It appears that physical exercise primes the brain to respond better to an enriched environment and cognitive training.

Based on all the current research, it's clear that endurance training on its own is not enough, argues Adele Diamond, Professor of Developmental Cognitive Neuroscience at the University of British Columbia. She asserts that physical exercise needs to be accompanied by a requirement to think at the same time. Her advice is to add on a game element, or to practice a type of coordinated movement such as dance or a martial art like taekwondo. Diamond even argues that you get the best results from physical exercise that you enjoy doing, that engenders self-confidence and pride, and that involves positive social interaction. She rightfully points out that exercise improves your sleep and your mood, and that these effects alone improve your executive skills, so that aerobic exercises always enhance your executive skills, if only indirectly. Although more research is needed to determine the exact effects of exercise on your executive skills and their underlying mechanisms, it is indisputable that exercise benefits your brain.

So, what should you do? First of all, find a type of exercise that you like: something that makes you feel good. It could be as straightforward as basketball or football, but perhaps you'd rather learn how to walk a tightrope or do acrobatics. If you need ideas or information about a particular type of sport, check the olympisize_me quiz, the NHS's dedicated webpage, topendsports.com or an explanation of the rules of 42 different sports on YouTube.[29] Secondly, the social interaction inherent to certain sports seems to enhance your executive skills. You might want to take this into account when making your choice.

Exercise intensity guidelines

If you have selected some form of endurance training, there are additional guidelines you should consider. It is well known that you don't need to exercise at maximum heart rate. You will achieve the greatest possible effect when training at a moderate heart rate, so 60-70% of your maximum. You can estimate this percentage by using the Karvonen formula (see p. 173). If you are out of shape, it might be better to start at 50% of your maximum heart rate and slowly build up to 70%. This will help you to stick to your exercise regimen and prevent lactic acidosis.

Although there are no exact guidelines, you are certain to benefit if you exercise at least 3 times a week, for 30-60 minutes at a moderate heart rate, for a period of 6-12 months. Obviously, it's best to exercise regularly on a permanent basis.

---

29 www2.open.ac.uk/openlearn/olympisize_html/?state=0, http://www.nhs.uk/LiveWell/Fitness/Pages/Fitnesshome.aspx
www.topendsports.com/fitness/sportspecific.htm
www.youtube.com/playlist?list=PL9NYvjxBy6SOxm8UjvbqXmpBDsvJLDClw

Exercise is a potent drug. It appears to improve neuroplasticity, executive skills, and your ability to adapt to a changing environment.

Accentuate the positive. Remind yourself every time you've exercised that it was worthwhile and that it did you good: not just your executive skills, but also your brain, sleep, mood and overall health. Many factors determine how much effect your exercising will have, including age, sex, stress levels, hormonal changes, genetic variables, initial fitness level, and the type, duration and intensity of exercise you do. However, properly executed exercise is always good for mind and body. If you're not sure how to properly exercise or play sports, start slowly and do it only under supervision. Check with a doctor beforehand to be sure you're not running any health risks.

Karvonen Formula

The Karvonen formula is based on your maximum heart rate (MHR) and your resting heart rate (RHR). Determining your resting heart rate is easy. Every day for three days, monitor your heart rate for one minute before you get out of bed in the morning. After three days, you can calculate the average. This is your resting heart rate.

However, determining your maximum heart rate takes a lot of effort and can be risky, so you're better off estimating it, as follows:

— If you are female, subtract your age from 226. The resulting number is your estimated MHR.

— If you are male, subtract your age from 220. The resulting number is your estimated MHR.

Then calculate your heart rate reserve (HRR) by subtracting your RHR from your MHR.

In order to calculate your target training heart rate for exercising (THR), apply Karvonen's formula, as follows:

THR = RHR + (training rate (%) × HRR)

Example
Suppose you are a 48-year old woman. Your MHR is estimated at 226 – 48 = 178. Let's say we've established that your resting heart rate is 70. Then the Karvonen formula tells us that your heart rate reserve (HRR) = 178 – 70 = 108 beats per minute.

If you want to exercise at 70%, your target heart rate is calculated as follows:

THR = RHR (70) + (target rate (70%) × HRR (108)) = 70 + (0.7 x 108) = 70 + 75.6 = approx. 145 beats per minute.

If you find these calculations too complicated, you can also use a Karvonen-app or an online Karvonen calculator.[30]

Estimating your maximum heart rate is not very accurate. If you want to know the actual rate, you need to have your heart rate monitored while you are exerting yourself physically at maximum level. The best way to do this is to have a full sports medical examination at a sports medicine facility. The examination involves cycling on a stationary bike that gets progressively harder to bike while you try to maintain the same speed (Cardio Pulmonary Exercise Test; CPET). Your heart rate is measured and your breath gas is analyzed as well. This will tell you what your maximal oxygen intake (VO_2max) is, which is the best measure of cardiorespiratory physical fitness. You will find out your maximum heart rate at the same time. An added advantage of doing this is that it can also reveal any additional health risks that you were unaware of.

Then, once you start your cardiovascular exercise routine, and you wear a heart rate monitor, you know what target heart rate to aim for in order to train at 70% of your maximum heart rate, or 70% of your VO_2max.

Children benefit from 45 minutes of exercise per day. The benefits of this extend well into the future. Research shows that starting to exercise at a young age is very good for the general development of executive skills. We know that seniors benefit too. If you exercise twice a week from the age of 50, your grey matter (i.e. your brain cells) in your prefrontal cortex remain healthy longer when you're in the 70+ range. Research findings do suggest, however, that you need to keep exercising to maintain the cognitive effects your sweat has earned you.

Let's not beat around the bush. Exercise is good, for young and old, for now and later, for many reasons. If you're not exercising regularly yet, it's time to start. Let me try to get you started. Let's begin by estimating how much exercise you're currently getting and how willing you are to change this for the better. This is a pretty accurate indicator of whether you'll actually increase your exercise level and keep it up.

SELF-KNOWLEDGE

Do you get enough exercise?

There's a quiz you can take to determine your activity level and your willingness to increase your activity or exercise level. I have included this quiz – known as the PACE questionnaire (PACE stands for Physician-based Assessment and Counseling for Exercise) – below.[31]

30 www.topendsports.com/fitness/karvonen-formula.htm

31 http://onlinelibrary.wiley.com/doi/10.1038/oby.2002.193/full

1 Determine your current physical activity level. Before you fill in the questionnaire, read the list of sample activities below to get some idea of what vigorous and moderate exercise entails.

Examples of vigorous exercise (raising your heart rate):
- Jogging
- Running
- Speed cycling
- Aerobics
- Swimming laps (for speed)
- Singles tennis

Examples of moderate exercise:
- Walking
- Biking
- Gardening (like mowing the lawn and pruning trees)
- Doubles tennis
- Dancing
- Household chores

2 Which one of the 8 statements below best describes your CURRENT level of activity or your readiness to do physical activity? This excludes job-related activity.

Current activity level

1 I don't do regular vigorous or moderate exercise now, and I don't intend to start in the next 6 months.
2 I don't do regular vigorous or moderate exercise now, but I have been thinking of starting in the next 6 months.
3 I'm trying to start doing vigorous or moderate exercise, but I don't do it regularly.
4 I'm doing vigorous exercise less than 3 times per week (or) moderate exercise less than 5 times per week.
5 I've been doing 30 minutes a day of moderate exercise 5 or more days per week for the last 1-5 months.
6 I've been doing 30 minutes a day of moderate exercise 5 or more days per week for the last 6 months or more.
7 I've been doing vigorous exercise 3 or more days per week for the last 1-5 months.
8 I've been doing vigorous exercise 3 or more days per week for the last 6 months or more.

If you checked item 1, you are not physically active and you are not ready to change.

If you checked item 2-4, you are indicating that you are willing to become physically active.

If you checked item 5-8, you have a regular and active lifestyle.

3 So what is your activity level? Is it lower or higher than you had anticipated or did you know exactly how active you are?

If you checked item 1, you are not getting any exercise and you have no intention of changing that either.

4 If you're interested in getting physically active, fill in what sport or type of exercise you would like to do:

Sport / exercise of choice: ______________________________

If you're unable to find a type of exercise that appeals to you – even after doing some online research – then I would recommend that you try taekwondo or another martial art, as this type of exercise has all the ingredients that can enhance your executive skills.

PFC exercise: Sticking to your plan

Use the weekly schedule below to mark the times you think you might have time to exercise. Doing this will help you get motivated. Keep in mind that you should not exercise late at night, because if it is too close to your bedtime it might be harder to fall asleep.

	Sunday	Monday	Tuesday	Wednesday	Thursday	Friday	Saturday
6:00 AM							
7:00 AM							
8:00 AM							
9:00 AM							
10:00 AM							
11:00 AM							
12:00 noon							
13:00 PM							
14:00 PM							
15:00 PM							
16:00 PM							
17:00 PM							
18:00 PM							
19:00 PM							
20:00 PM							

Next, assess whether you think you can actually stick to your plans. According to biological psychology experts Kirsten Hötting and Brigitte Röder, the more convinced you are that you can stick to your exercise schedule, the more likely you are to actually do so.

Rate your ability to stick to your plans on the line below:

Not at all	Perhaps	Probably	Likely	For sure

If you rated your ability at 'not at all' or 'perhaps', you need to ask yourself why you think you won't see your plans through. Then try to rephrase those reasons as goals and then try to work on achieving those goals, if necessary with the help of other people, or online tips.

I think I won't really start exercising, because ....

....

....

....

....

....

....

....

Most people indicate that they want to exercise. The problem is that working out, like regularly getting a good night's sleep, meditating, and so many other things that are good for you, is at the bottom of the list. Yet it is very important to make exercising a part of your day and to make it part of your non-negotiable plans, like brushing your teeth and going to school or work. If you are really dead set against exercising, at least start monitoring the number of steps you take. This might motivate you to increase your daily activity.

Apps that can help you to get regular exercise:

- Fitnessbuddy
- Argus
- Myfitnesspal
- Runkeeper
- Joggy coach

Exercise is a potent drug. It appears to improve neuroplasticity, executive skills, and your ability to adapt to a changing environment.

So, get moving. And not just to get toned and improve your health, but also to improve the skills you need for success in this rapidly changing world. The next chapter will show you how to get better at connecting the present with the future and why this is crucial for achieving your goals.

‘What you do today can improve all your tomorrows.’

Ralph Marston

brainyquote.com

Chapter 10 **Connecting Today with Tomorrow – Start Changing the Future**

Yesterday, today and tomorrow are connected with success and failure, and what connects them is choices. Your choices. In this chapter, you will learn how to keep your sights on tomorrow and incorporate the future into your behavior today.

SELF-KNOWLEDGE

Iowa Gambling Task

Play the Iowa Gambling Task on your tablet or smartphone.[32] If you don't have either kind of device, watch a YouTube video about this task on your laptop or desktop.[33]

The Iowa Gambling Task asks you to gamble and engages your hot executive skills, as described in Chapter 3, 'The CEO Brain'. After you've played the game, continue to read below.

Delayed gratification

Remember the marshmallow test from Chapter 3, 'The CEO Brain'? Kids were left alone with a marshmallow, after being told that they could eat it, but that they'd get an extra one if they held out until the experimenter returned to the room. So, the choice was between one marshmallow right now, or – with some patience and self-control – two marshmallows later. This mechanism of suppressing your desire for instant pleasure in favor of something bigger and better at some point in the future is known as delayed or deferred gratification.

You might remember that this marshmallow test turned out to be a pretty good predictor of success in all areas of life thirty years on. Not that you should jump to conclusions if your children have trouble delaying gratification. Thanks to brain plasticity, there is time to help develop their ability to defer gratification. Nonetheless, the test is quite revealing. It makes life seem simple and predictable. People wonder whether there is a marshmallow test for adults too. Obviously, you are best qualified to describe your own personal marshmallow test and you probably did just that in Chapter 3, 'The CEO Brain' and in more detail in Chapter 5, 'Pitfalls'.

---

32 iPad: https://itunes.apple.com/nl/app/iowa-gambling-task/id807409936?mt=8
Android phone: https://play.google.com/store/apps/details?id=com.zsimolabs.iowa&hl=en

33 www.youtube.com/watch?v=39A3z3S6aY0, or read on

You could also see the Iowa Gambling Task as a sort of marshmallow test. This task was originally developed by Antoine Bechara and Antonio Damasio, but now has countless variations. The idea behind all of them is the same: there are four stacks of cards and you are asked to take a card from one of them. Each card tells you how much you win or lose. Two of the stacks are high stakes cards: you win big, but you also lose big and you gradually lose more than you win. The other two stacks are low stakes: you make small wins and small losses. If you play your cards right, you can gradually increase your winnings. How did you do when you played the game? Which stacks did you choose? Did you catch on to the hidden rules of the game? Did you go for the quick win and the inevitable loss, or did you resist temptation and end up with a modest win?

To achieve success, you need to set goals, define a roadmap, and stick to it. You have to do what needs doing and when. Just as importantly, you have to avoid doing what you shouldn't do. This requires executive skills. Let's refresh your memory. The three core executive skills consist of the ability to suppress urges (inhibition), cognitive and mental flexibility, and working memory:

1. *The ability to suppress urges and resist temptation* (inhibitory control) is a skill that enables us to break out of habits that hold us back. I discussed this skill in depth in Chapter 4, 'A Recipe for Success'. You learned about your personal S-sR chains, stimuli that evoke stereotypical responses from you. You also learned what it takes to develop S-wR chains: wise responses to stimuli. Inhibitory control enables us to transcend our short-term urges and to resist whatever strong stimulus happens to catch our attention. It enables us to focus on the long term and live our lives to the best of our ability.
2. *Cognitive and mental flexibility* enables us to get unstuck from the things we once did, thought or learned, and to adapt smoothly to our changing environment with its shifting demands, priorities, rules and concepts. We no longer need to feel like a victim of our past, present or future. Rather, it allows us to keep pace with or even anticipate changes, so we can be happy and successful regardless of the changes in our environment. Possibly, we can even create conditions in which we flourish.
3. *Working memory* is the ability to retain information over a period of time and put it to use. Your working memory enables you to have information at the ready for a particular goal. It keeps track of what has happened and links this to what still needs to happen. In other words, it links your past to your present and your future. It's crystal clear that this is a skill you can't do without if you want to achieve your goals.

If you look closely at these three core executive skills, you'll see they have something in common: the aspect of time. Possessing these skills ensures that time becomes a constant, and that past, present and future remain connected. This may sound obvious, but if you look at your own conduct and the behavior of others, you'll see that this connection is often strangely absent. Many of us feel that we are at the mercy of the negative forces in our lives and that bad things just happen out of nowhere. Obviously, that's true in some cases, but it's equally untrue in many others. The latter includes things like running out of money because you've spent it on the wrong things, seeing your marriage fall apart because you're having an affair, being stuck in a job you hate because you don't bother to get retrained, or losing your clients because you took them for a ride. A lot of bad things that happen to us are a direct consequence of bad choices in the past and bad choices today.

In short, today is when you reap the benefits of yesterday's choices and plant the seeds for tomorrow's harvest. This applies to every day of the week. Past, present and future are never completely separated. Each day carries both past and future in it. This concept was neatly summed up in *The Counselor*. In this movie, the protagonist, who's made so many bad decisions that they've cost him (and his wife) everything, asks what he can do to change the situation. The answer is nothing. It's too late. If he'd wanted to end up in a different place, he should have taken a different path. Having taken the path he's taken, he has to face the consequences. Real life need not be as dramatic as life on the big screen, but the movie does get the message across: to prevent big trouble ahead, you'd better master that skill of keeping your sights on the future. Let's start with the basics: how to keep sight of the fact that you have to do certain things to achieve your goal.

Prospective memory

In Chapter 3, I introduced the phrase 'memory of the future', coined some 30 years ago by Swedish neuroscientist David Ingvar. Ingvar used this term to denote our ability to remember our plans for the future and the actions we must take to see them through. This capacity allows us to imagine, anticipate and create a future. The ability to remember that you need to carry out some task in the future is also known as *prospective memory*.

Our lives are full of tasks, goals and other things that call on our prospective memory. Let's take an average day. Whether you spend it at home, at the office, or both, you need to remember all the things you need to do: pack your bag, reschedule meetings, make changes in some report, run specific errands, be back by 5:30 p.m. to bring your son to football practice, put your daughter's sheet music in her backpack so she's ready for her piano lesson after school, and so on. You get the picture.

Theoretically speaking, we distinguish two types of prospective memory: event-based and time-based.

Event-based prospective memory deals with remembering that you have to do something if a particular event or circumstance occurs. For example, you need to remember to pick up the flash drive you left at the office yesterday if you happen to pass by the office building today.

Time-based prospective memory pertains to remembering that you have to carry out a task at a particular time. For example, you need to remember to pick up your child from school today at 3:30 p.m.

Research suggests event-based memory is a more effective reminder than time-based memory. This is particularly true if you can respond to the triggering event immediately with the right action. For example, you go in and get the flash drive you left at the office when you pass the building instead of waiting until after your meeting. Research also shows that people with a well-developed prospective memory are better at setting and achieving goals.

Implementation intention (if-then plan)

Our prospective memory, and how to improve it, are the subject of many studies. One way to improve it is called implementation intention, which is best described as 'if A happens, then I'll do B'. Actually, this is similar to a stimulus-response chain, much like the S-R chain from Chapter 4, 'A Recipe for Success'. Except this is an intentional chain, so more of a S-wR chain. Implementation intention consists of two components:

1 Anticipating a situation or event that prompts particular intentional behavior. This is the IF part of the plan.
2 Articulating a response that will help you attain your goal. This is the THEN part of the plan.

A recent paper by Xing-jie Chen and co-authors collates various studies of the effects of implementation intention on prospective memory. This literature review reveals that implementation intention is an effective method for healthy subjects in different age groups. The following PFC exercise instructs you to put implementation intention to use in your everyday life as a means of furthering your personal goals..

PFC exercise: Implementation intention

This PFC exercise will help you stick to your intentions and reach your goals because it bridges the gap between your goal and the behavior required to reach it. In other words, this PFC exercise connects today with tomorrow.

Write down the goal you are trying to achieve.

Goal:

What do you need to do to reach your goal? What obstacles do you expect to encounter along the way? These are the things you wrote down in Chapter 1, 'A Goal to Set Your Sights on', when I asked you to articulate your goal and roadmap (p. 26). You can copy it down here, and add to it, if you'd like.

What do I need to do to achieve my goal?

Step 1

Step 2

Step 3

Step 4

Step 5

Step 6

Step 7

Step 8

Step 9

Step 10

Step 11

Step 12

What obstacles/temptations do I expect to run into along the way?

Obstacle 1

Obstacle 2

Obstacle 3

Obstacle 4

Obstacle 5

Obstacle 6

Obstacle 7

Obstacle 8 ______________________________

____

____

____

Obstacle 9 ______________________________

____

____

____

Obstacle 10 ______________________________

____

____

____

Obstacle 11 ______________________________

____

____

____

Obstacle 12 ______________________________

____

____

____

Next, define the situations in which you need to take the steps (actions) you defined to reach your goal. For example:

- My goal is to eat more healthily.
- Step 1. Buy healthy foods so I only have healthy foods to choose from at home.
- Action 1. If I go to the supermarket, I will head to the fruit and vegetable aisle first and buy healthy foods.

Implementation intention: What do I need to do to achieve my goal and how do I incorporate this into my everyday life?

Goal: ______________________________

____

Action 1 If ______________________________
Then ______________________________
Action 2 If ______________________________
Then ______________________________
Action 3 If ______________________________
Then ______________________________
Action 4 If ______________________________
Then ______________________________
Action 5 If ______________________________
Then ______________________________
Action 6 If ______________________________
Then ______________________________

Action 7 If ....
Then ....
Action 8 If ....
Then ....
Action 9 If ....
Then ....
Action 10 If ....
Then ....
Action 11 If ....
Then ....
Action 12 If ....
Then ....

Do the same for the obstacles you foresee. For example:

- Obstacle 1. I always buy unhealthy snacks if I go shopping when I'm hungry.
- Action 1. If I need to go shopping, I'll make sure I eat a salad first, so I won't feel hungry when I'm at the supermarket.

Implementation intention: How can I avoid likely obstacles and temptations?

Obstacle 1 If ....
Then ....
Obstacle 2 If ....
Then ....
Obstacle 3 If ....
Then ....
Obstacle 4 If ....
Then ....
Obstacle 5 If ....
Then ....
Obstacle 6 If ....
Then ....
Obstacle 7 If ....
Then ....
Obstacle 8 If ....
Then ....
Obstacle 9 If ....
Then ....
Obstacle 10 If ....
Then ....
Obstacle 11 If ....
Then ....
Obstacle 12 If ....
Then ....

I would not be surprised if you were feeling some resistance to this, along the lines of what you described in the 'Out of your comfort zone' exercise in Chapter 2 (p. 45). Try to keep in mind, however, that this exercise is excellent for training your prefrontal cortex. Give it a try. Visualize and articulate the if-then chains and create a strong mental representation. This will help you implement your intentions when the situations you have defined actually occur. It prepares you for the situations you're going to face and ensures that you won't be taken by surprise. You'll have an S-wR chain ready so you can act in your long-term interests if the situation gets thorny. This takes a lot of energy at first, but gets easier over time. The more often you implement these chains, the more you understand their importance and the more automated they become thanks to neural plasticity.

What you'll be doing is creating a pathway between situation and response. See it as a challenge. Remember that every time you apply the S-wR chains you're actually reinforcing your prefrontal lobe and strengthening your executive skills. This exercise trains you in deferring gratification. It brings you closer to your ultimate goal while bolstering your prefrontal networks. Another exercise that helps you delay gratification is 'Redirecting your attention' in Chapter 7 (p. 147). The great thing about implementation intention is that it not only helps you preempt temptation, but also makes you take concrete steps toward your end goal.

Some people have a hard time committing to their goals, even though they are the ones who set them. They might say they want to get into shape, or create room for innovation, or do volunteer work, but time and again they choose to act in ways that are not conducive to achieving their goal. It's almost as if they see whatever they need to do to achieve their goal – start jogging, adjust their management principles, or make time for nonprofit work – as something negative or something they're being forced to do. If you're honest, this might also apply to you and your goals. Am I right?

If so, you need to redefine your goals, or make a concerted effort to commit to them. Your objective should be reflected in the choices you make, the way you behave and your willpower in the face of temptation. Implementation intention can help you stick to your roadmap. Every time an event or situation – the IF part of implementation intention – invokes the same premeditated response – the THEN part – your brain is repeating and hence reinforcing your intention. People who have trouble committing to, or identifying with, their intentions can benefit from this neuroplasticity effect, which literally increases the room their intentions take up in their brain. Still, this is more of a band-aid than a real solution. Ask yourself in all honesty whether you truly identify with the goals you've set, because that's where real motivation comes from.

Implementation intention enhances your prospective memory and helps you hold on to your intentions and reach your goals. There is another tool that can give your prospective memory a helping hand: your smartphone. You can have your phone send you GPS-based reminders to do something when you are in a particular location. Do this, and you're actually creating an external event-based prospective memory. To find out how to program such reminders, look online.[34]

You can also lend your time-based prospective memory some assistance by using your phone to set alerts. Keep in mind, however, that these tips and tricks are a tool rather than an exercise that trains your brain. The implementation intention technique has more intrinsic benefits than using your smartphone, as I explained before.

In order to get the most out of implementation intention, you need your working memory. Not only do you have to remember what you need to do if a given event or situation occurs; you also need specific information that ensures you can carry out the actions you defined in the right way and at the right time. Like your prospective memory, your working memory connects your past, present and future. It ensures that you have continued access to the information needed to achieve a particular goal, and that, based on this information, you take certain actions and avoid others.

Training your working memory

Because your working memory steers your attention, it can keep you away from things that interfere with your goals. It can help you take the heat out of a hot executive skills task by applying your cold executive skills (see Chapter 3). For example, your working memory can help you focus on S-wR chains rather than the smell of fried chicken (a metaphor for any temptation that applies to you personally). This makes it easier to stick to your roadmap and keep working toward your goal. People with a good working memory are skilled at de-emphasizing distractions early on by focusing on what is conducive to achieving their goal. What's more, they're better at regulating the negative emotions they feel when confronted with temptations. People with a weak working memory are prone to go for candy, alcohol, a quick win, while people with a strong working memory are likely to achieve their goals.

Fortunately, various studies show that your working memory is trainable. There's evidence that training makes changes in your frontal and parietal cortex, your basal ganglia, and your brain's sensitivity to dopamine. Currently, scientists are hotly debating whether or not training your working memory also benefits certain types of intelligence and whether it affects only the specific task you're training or related memory tasks as well. The jury is still out on the wider implications

34 For example, https://support.apple.com/en-us/HT205890

of training your working memory, but at least you can train your own working memory, even if the results are mainly limited to getting better at a specific type of task.

PFC exercise: Training your working memory (simple variation)

The following exercise trains your working memory. Read a line of letters. Every time you come across a letter you've seen three positions earlier, cross it out.

l c o o m z m z a a d m n c c n c l v e e h e g h

q b q f f f g x y x q g a o m m o f d e f g v h v

d n o n m d q q w t w d p e q e h w b f f g s g s

p p o p m q m d e f r e r f g k l l t b t d k k l

b d d b d c c f c g f h q i q q k t l t w w t r r

v c o o x z z x q d h d l i k g k h w o w l o l j

l e g a l p a i s k o t m o r w a v e a s s t c o

r e n c l i g l w i e h t o s e e a s b r l y s t

o p s o f r c e s t e p s e l h o u d o w r t e c

o a s t t r i e d k e s a e n h a s f t e t t r n

g r o r b a m o u n u l l n l h o s t e l a v l a

n o s e p u l i s h t e s e n l e g a n b e p r n

h w a h h c t h l o r o w k s s e d t h r o m w a

e d m a t c w e a u p w a l l w s a r s f r g r a

b a s e n e d w n s m a s k c h m a v i n z r e d

o o r m o d e e d e n s t t e n e n e i p j d l r

i e t i e n z n d e n r a i n t e n t t e n m e n

PFC exercise: Training your working memory (complex variation)

The following exercise is a more complex variation of the previous exercise. Read two lines, one with letters and one with numbers, at the same time. Every time you come across a letter or a number you've seen three positions earlier, cross it out.

h	i	w	k	i	w	p	m
6	8	3	6	8	2	9	5
r	a	h	o	a	p	e	n
1	6	4	8	1	7	8	9
l	j	h	a	g	h	a	b
1	8	1	5	1	9	2	1
k	e	j	k	d	j	n	g
1	0	1	6	9	4	1	9
m	v	f	m	u	f	g	i
5	2	5	4	2	3	7	2
f	m	g	f	k	i	e	d
8	8	1	3	5	5	9	3
c	v	c	b	c	v	c	n
2	2	0	3	3	8	9	8
l	f	d	a	h	g	a	j
3	0	5	0	8	4	7	4
g	u	i	d	u	s	b	h
5	7	6	2	7	1	1	8
b	x	c	v	c	c	v	i
6	4	4	0	6	7	7	9
v	m	f	u	e	f	h	h
6	6	1	6	0	5	2	3

These two sample exercises for training your working memory are just the tip of the iceberg. There are many online exercises and tests available, some of which are free:

- www.cogmed.com/working-memory-challenge
- http://cognitivefun.net/test/4
- www.gocognitive.net/demo/working-memory-capacity
- www.lumosity.com/
- http://zap.psy.utwente.nl/zaps/zaps/zaps/sternbergsearch.res/frames.html

If you take these tests, remember to write down your scores. I will come back to these in the last chapter.

Task	Score

There are other ways of enhancing your working memory as well. Elements from the EFFECT program – like Flow Focus and Exercise – have been proven effective at that. The best way to train your working memory in everyday life is to use it as much as possible instead of relying on written or electronic notes for everything. For example, try to read and memorize the recipe you use to cook dinner. Don't keep referring back to the cookbook, but learn it by heart. Little things like that will help you train your working memory on a daily basis, particularly in areas you need in everyday life.

Children's executive skills

This chapter is about connecting today with tomorrow. The ultimate connection between the present and the future is our children, of course. So, it's key to ensure that they develop their prefrontal cortices. Because the prefrontal cortex is so important for success in education, work, physical and mental health, social relations and general happiness, ensuring that our children develop this area of the brain will help create a better future for everyone.

A growing body of research is focusing on the development of executive functions in children. What's clear so far is that good role models, experience and practice have a great impact on the development of the prefrontal cortex, its connections to other areas in the brain and the executive skills that go with them. The National Scientific Council on the Developing Child and the National Forum on Early Childhood Policy and Programs offer various tips on how to foster this development. Integrating certain age-appropriate routines into everyday life, such as brushing your teeth after every meal and setting the table every night, helps children develop their executive skills. Giving cues for certain tasks and splitting up large 'executive' tasks into smaller ones does the same. Parents should do this until their children are capable of exercising these skills and executing these tasks independently. When children show they have mastered this, the parents can move on to more complex tasks. Parents and other caretakers are advised to create a structured, consistent, loving, stable and safe environment and to be sensitive and responsive to children's needs, so as to ensure that children develop these indispensable executive skills.

Growing up with stress

The brain networks related to executive skills have many connections to areas in the brain that regulate the perception of danger and stress. It's therefore no surprise that very stressful events, particularly when experienced early in life, directly affect the development of the prefrontal cortex. In his book *How Children Succeed*, Paul Tough describes how children who grow up in a stressful situation and experience stressful events (adverse childhood experiences) have a harder time developing executive skills. They have trouble concentrating and sitting still, they find it hard to remember and carry out instructions, they are less able to defer gratification in favor of long-term goals, and regulating their emotions presents difficulties too. Based on other studies, Tough also shows how a lack of these skills directly affects future events and aspects of these children's lives, such as education, relationships, health and work.

Because of their connections to the prefrontal cortex, anxiety, stress and other strong negative emotions directly affect the development of the brain system responsible for executive skills. When well developed, these connections also have a beneficial effect. The connections between the prefrontal cortex and the stress system enable the brain's executive skills system to regulate and reduce children's anxiety, stress and other negative emotions. The development of executive skills in children can be retarded by neglect, abuse, violence, insensitivity, and other sources of prolonged or serious stress.[35] On the brighter side, loving parenting and education can make children resilient to the destructive force of adverse childhood experiences and can directly support the development of the prefrontal cortex and all of its connections.

We have known this for a while, actually since British psychiatrist John Bowlby in his attachment studies showed that safe attachment between a mother or sur-

35 For more information on this topic, see Working Paper 11 by the National Scientific Council on the Developing Child/National Forum on Early Childhood Policy and Programs and the Adverse Childhood Experiences Study.

Children adopt their parents' morals and behavior, which, depending on the example their parents set, may either benefit or damage their executive skills.

rogate mother and her child is indispensable to the child's healthy, emotional, exploratory and cognitive development. Harry Harlow did famous experiments with baby monkeys that grew up with sufficient nutrition, but without a mother's warmth and care (their surrogate mother was made of chicken wire). These tests clearly demonstrated how detrimental a lack of love, care, responsiveness and protection are to development. Michael Meaney proved the same with his rat experiments. Meaney and his co-workers showed that rat pups that were licked and groomed more by their mothers were more curious and exploratory, better able to find their way out of a maze (a working memory test), more social and less aggressive, better at self-control and even longer-lived. The same positive effect was observed if the pups were not raised by their biological mothers, but by another, caring doe. The effects of their loving parenting were not only visible in the pups' behavior and development, but also in their brains, particularly the system that processes and regulates stress. The same effects are at work in humans, as follow-up studies with children have demonstrated.

Consistency

In short, children need a loving, structured approach. Such an approach should not only be aimed at avoiding adverse experiences, but also at receptiveness and appropriate, consistent responsiveness to children's emotional needs. Mind you, I'm neither advocating that you always let your children get their way, nor that you as a parent efface yourself. Certainly not. Children also need to experience failure and setbacks if they are to learn to cope, persevere and adjust their plans. But they also need sufficient opportunity to develop the skills and traits that can help them achieve success in later life.

What I'm talking about is a parenting style in which you consistently provide a safe, loving environment with clear rules and guidance, but also encouragement to explore at an appropriate pace. When I say children, I don't just mean 0-12 year olds, I also mean teens and young adults. Sometimes parents take a big step back when their children go to secondary school, particularly in the time they spend with them. Obviously, children are more independent at that age. They know how to eat and shower and dress independently. They bike or take the bus to school and can get to their extracurricular activities without any help. Whatever they can do independently, they should. And yet, in terms of executive skills they're still beginners.

Teenagers and young adults
It is precisely between the ages of 10 and 25 that the prefrontal cortex develops most, creating a great opportunity to further develop children's executive skills. It's empowering to realize that you can still have as big an impact on your kids' development as when they were younger, as long as you invest enough time in

them. Now, of course, the skills they need to learn are not crawling, walking, eating, using the potty, playing, reading, writing and arithmetic, but rather:

- resisting getting distracted (by apps, Xbox, PlayStation, Instagram, Facebook, Snapchat);
- regulating emotions (I'm sure you'll find plenty of opportunity for that one with your teenager);
- staying flexible in the face of change (a key property of the VUCA world);
- suppressing undesirable behavior (prompted by all the temptations in their environment);
- planning, organizing and initiating;
- monitoring their own progress at school (a key step toward independence that relies heavily on their working memory).

I haven't even mentioned issues like morality, prosocial behavior and responsibility. Teaching all these skills is part of bringing up children and preparing them for independence and lifelong happiness and success. These are the building blocks for good cognitive, emotional, social and moral skills that need ongoing maintenance and expansion throughout life. The learning process starts in early childhood, but continues through young adulthood. A key factor is the parents' own behavior, because children copy their parents. Various studies have shown that children adopt their parents' morals and behavior, which, depending on the example their parents set, may either benefit or damage their executive skills. So, let's set a good example and make sure we're role models with high-functioning executive skills.

While writing this section on parenting and frontal lobe development, I was torn. One the one hand, I felt it did not belong in this book, because *Train Your CEO Brain* is about adults' frontal lobe development, but on the other it struck me as highly relevant for us adults as parents of the next generation. In the course of my own research I was so struck by the magnitude of our impact on our children, by the damage caused by adverse childhood experiences and the benefits of loving, consistent and stable parenting, that I decided it was well worth including here. Much more can be said on the topic, but my aim was to acquaint my readers with the basics in the hope that I will inspire as many people as possible to put these principles into action in their own lives. Providing a loving, consistent environment for children – both your own and others' – has an incredibly positive effect on their brains, emotions, behavior and actions, and contributes to a better future. For them, for us, for everyone.

Enough said. Let's move on to the final chapter of Part II of this book, which deals with time.

‘The only place where success comes before work is in a dictionary.’

Vidal Sassoon

Penguin Dictionary of Modern Quotations

Chapter 11 **Time – Giving Your Brain Time to Change**

This chapter re-emphasizes two things you already know and will certainly have experienced while doing the exercises in this book. The first thing is that knowing how to do something is not enough. For knowledge to have effect, you need to put it to use in your life. The second thing is that there is no magic wand you can wave to achieve a goal. It takes time to get from A to B. No, this is nothing new. But read on anyway, because this chapter will help you move from theory to practice.

SELF-KNOWLEDGE

Second hand

For this eye-opener you need an old fashioned analog clock with a second hand. Sit down, make yourself comfortable and then suddenly look at the clock. Did you see something unexpected?

You probably experienced the illusion that the first second took longer to pass than the seconds that ticked away after that. It's as if the second hand got stuck a little before it resumed ticking. For a moment, time seemed to stand still.

This is called the stopped clock illusion, which is a type of chronostasis or a temporal illusion. Let's look at how this illusion occurs. As we suddenly shift our gaze from one point to another, known in scientific jargon as a saccade, we think we are perceiving a continuous stream of input. But that's not the case. During the switch between two focal points, there's a split second when you don't receive any visual information. Our brain tries to gloss over this gap with an illusion of seamless perception. It does so by retroactively 'filling in' the perception gap with the new visual information you are receiving; in this case, the second hand's next stop. That's why that first tick you watch appears to be longer than the seconds that follow: hence, the stopped clock illusion. My point is that even a phenomenon like time, which is something we consider a fixed quantity, can be experienced in different ways. Because it depends on the brain, our perception of time can be manipulated.

So, what role does time play in the development of our prefrontal cortex and executive skills? Let's recap. We are living in a VUCA world where distraction is everywhere and the pace of change is accelerating. We've learned to analyze and dissect this. More than ever before in the evolution of our species, we need our executive skills to reach our goals and succeed. This goes for all areas of life: family, work, health, and social interaction. Executive skills are linked to prefrontal cortex development. We have the power to enhance these skills thanks to neural plasticity, or the malleability of our brain. Research has revealed that we can harness this power by enriching our environment, taking control of our attention, sleeping regularly, exercising more and training our working memory to integrate present and future. Obviously, these adjustments are not something you do at the snap of a finger. They take time. But they also take something called grit.

Grit is like perseverance: the will to put in effort and remain committed for an extended period. Your motivation must be open-ended. You have to be dedicated to do what it takes, for as long as it takes, to reroute and reinforce the ingrained pathways in your brain. Those pathways are the physical structures that facilitate specific counterproductive behaviors and emotions that stand in the way of happiness and success. You can mold and shape your brain's pathways and networks into structures that enable other behaviors and emotions: the kind that foster happiness and success because they help you achieve your goals. But like I said, that takes time and effort. Which means you need grit and resilience. Don't forget, it took you years to reinforce your 'bad' habits and build the networks that turned them into stereotypical responses. Likewise, it takes time to undo those networks and turn more preferable skills into habits. It will take practice, practice, and more practice.

This is why I decided to make Time the last element of the EFFECT program. Give your brain time to change. It is an indispensable part of the program. When I first started incorporating all the EFFECT elements into my own life and felt myself resisting, I found it helpful to think back to some of my travels. I took a lot of low-budget trips in my younger years. I went backpacking, took long hikes and traveled on buses, trains and boats, visiting nomads in Tibet and tribes in the Baliem Valley in Papua New Guinea. I traveled for months on a shoestring budget, with nothing but a mosquito net and a first aid kit in my backpack. Sometimes I felt overwhelmed by tiredness, bugs, violence, hunger or other setbacks, but I couldn't just sit down and give up. I knew that would mean freezing to death or having to sleep somewhere unsafe, so I would tell myself to just keep putting one foot in front of the other. I took it literally step by step. By dividing the road to my end goal into incremental goals and moving from one incremental goal to the next, I always arrived at my (adapted) destination.

You could use the same approach to tackle the various elements of the EFFECT program. If you find it difficult to incorporate all the EFFECT elements into your life, just start with one you like most and find easiest to deal with. Applying the first element will prime your prefrontal cortex and gradually make it easier to eventually incorporate the elements you have a harder time with.

Growth mindset

I have some more helpful tips for you. One comes from Stanford psychology professor Carol Dweck, who's shown that your basic mindset can make a huge difference. Dweck studied intelligence and concluded that there's an important distinction between a fixed mindset and a growth mindset. A fixed mindset represents an attitude of 'not believing that you can change a particular skill or trait'. People with this mindset think skills are innate and immutable. By contrast, people with a growth mindset believe skills and traits can be changed and developed because skills are dynamic in nature. Dweck discovered that students with a growth mindset do better at school and get higher grades than pupils with a fixed mindset. Other studies show that the same pattern applies to other traits and skills, such as empathy.

My hope is that what you've learned about brain plasticity has inspired you to assume a growth mindset, because that alone would be a big step toward incorporating all elements of the EFFECT program into your life and achieving your goals.

I have another tip that can help you persevere and integrate the EFFECT program into your life: train your willpower. There are many books that show you the way, like Kelly McGonigal's *The Willpower Instinct*. One way to summon some willpower when you need it, is by using embodied cognition. As I explained in Chapter 9, 'Exercise', embodied cognition works on the principle that movements influence your thoughts, emotions and actions. As a result, you can also use exercise to steel your willpower. The following PFC exercise, which I also included in *Ik wil iets van jou, jij wil iets van mij*, shows you how.

PFC exercise: Giving up

If there is something you must do to achieve your goal, or you're trying to implement an EFFECT element, but you feel resistance and the urge to give up, find a straight-backed chair and have a seat. Cross your arms.
Believe it or not, you'll find that this gesture alone is enough to give you the willpower to continue doing what you have to do.

This exercise is based on a study by social psychology experts Ron Friedman and Andrew Elliot. In one experiment, they had subjects solve anagrams that had several possible solutions. In another experiment, they asked subjects to solve anagrams for which there was no solution. In both tests, half the subjects were told to find new words from the jumbled letters while crossing their arms, and the other half were asked to do the same while resting their hands on their legs. In both cases, the half-groups that crossed their arms proved more persistent than the other halves. The arm-crossers kept trying to solve the anagrams (even when there was no solution) for much longer than the leg-resters, and also found more solutions. The experimenters ascribed the difference in performance to embodied cognition.

For ages, the human brain has associated crossing the arms with perseverance, because people who are persistent often cross their arms. Because the physical movement and the mindset have become intertwined over time, a reciprocal relationship may have evolved. If that is the case, then persistence not only causes you to cross your arms, but crossing your arms also makes you more persistent. Friedman and Elliot's findings can come in handy in everyday life: when you feel like giving up, cross your arms and stay the course.

Enlisting negative emotions
Another golden tip is the one I borrowed from Michael Inzlicht and co-authors. In their article, they describe how gaining control over your thoughts and actions starts with negative emotions like resistance, anxiety, self-pity and frustration. We normally see these emotions as our enemy, but Inzlicht explains that they're part of the process of gaining self-control. The emotions arise from an inner conflict between what you want, and what you ought to do or not do. The emotions you experience during this conflict are a sign that you need to work harder on regulating your emotions. They are telling you to immediately and deliberately enlist your executive skills to ensure that you will stay on the path toward your ultimate goal. If you fail to enlist your executive skills, you run the risk of being overtaken by stereotypical responses that steer you toward short-term gain, long-term pain.

What this means is that you have a built-in guard dog that warns you when you are in danger of taking a wrong turn. The dog sends a warning signal in the shape of negative emotions. The signal says 'turn around and choose a different path'. The great thing about negative emotions is they're hard to ignore. You do need to learn how to label them, though. They shouldn't become an excuse to give in to temptations and behaviors that sabotage your long-term goal. See them instead as a pushy friend telling you it's time to muster some more executive power.

When we remove the negativity from our internal conflict, it becomes harder to gain self-control, Inzlicht explains. Somehow, the negativity is a key ingredient in activating your executive skills to push back when you face adversity. Mind you, I called it a key ingredient, and not a key element, which is an important distinction. The negativity alone won't make you do what's necessary. You'll still need to spend time and effort on doing the right thing to reach your goal. The thing to remember about negative emotions is that they signal a conflict between what you want to do, and what you ought to do. Just listen to what the signal is telling you, and exert more self-control. The moment you start doing that, you'll be taking steps in the right direction. Your negative emotions will wane and your resolve will get stronger, as will your prefrontal cortex. In other words, when negative emotions arise in the conflict between temptation and long-term goals, don't shun them as your enemy, but enlist their help. And yes, I know that's easier said than done.

Negative emotions

SELF-KNOWLEDGE

Write down which negative emotions bubble up when you experience a conflict between temptation and your long-term goal. This will make it easier to identify the emotions, so your executive skills can come to the rescue.

Negative emotions I experience during conflicts between temptation and long-term goals:

Let me conclude with a few more tips and tricks. You need to keep using the techniques that develop your prefrontal cortex. So to ensure that you stick with them, start by focusing on the elements that you like working on. After all, intrinsic motivation is the best incentive to persevere. It's a way to manipulate time, because time flies when we're having fun. This also keeps you interested longer when it comes to activities like physical exercise. Finding something you like is fairly easy when it comes to enriching your environment, but might be harder in the area of flow focus. And if you have insomnia or feel there aren't enough hours in the day, it can be quite a challenge to build a fixed sleeping pattern into your daily routine. Obviously, you would get maximum benefit if you incorporated all five EFFECT elements into your life right from the start, but if that's too hard, start with the ones that appeal to you most and slowly expand from there.

In her literature review on executive skills, Adele Diamond suggests ways of getting the most out of executive skills exercises. For one thing, she recommends building up the difficulty level of the various elements. It's all about challenging yourself and staving off boredom. The most demanding tasks have the greatest effect, it seems. Perhaps this thought will motivate or comfort you, if at some point you're ready to give up.

Here, I've compiled a list of apps developed to help you persevere when you want to achieve certain goals:

- Dosomethingdifferent
- Strides
- Goalsontrack
- Superbetter
- Beeminder

- Omnifocus
- Sociidot
- Unstuck (helps you make decisions)

It's very simple. To achieve your goals, you'll need to put in effort. Putting in effort requires energy and time. To find out how much time it actually takes to implement the EFFECT program, just keep track of it. Write it down. We'll use this log in the next chapter, when we measure the results of your endeavors.

SELF-KNOWLEDGE

Keeping time

Every week, fill in how many hours you've actually spent on the other five elements of the EFFECT program. In the next chapter, you will use this log to determine the effect of your efforts.

	Monday	Tuesday	Wednesday	Thursday	Friday	Saturday	Sunday
Environmental Enrichment	___	___	___	___	___	___	___
Flow Focus	___	___	___	___	___	___	___
Fixed Sleeping Pattern	___	___	___	___	___	___	___
Exercise	___	___	___	___	___	___	___
Connecting Today with Tomorrow	___	___	___	___	___	___	___

I know, it probably feels like I'm asking a lot. Maybe too much. But if so, that only goes to show how far removed you are from a happy, healthy life. Because all I'm asking you to do is:

- to make your life truly interesting (by enriching your environment);
- to gain control of your attention (flow focus);
- to make sure you get enough sleep (by implementing a fixed sleeping pattern);
- to get sufficient exercise;
- to link the present to the future;
- and to spend enough time to ensure these elements become part of your daily routine.

These are all very straightforward things that will help you develop your prefrontal cortex and executive skills. Doing this can help you stop feeling like a puppet on a string, gain control of your life and achieve your goals.

If you still think this is too much to ask, let me put it more succinctly: All I'm asking you to do is develop yourself and live a happier, healthier, more successful life by doing things that are actually common sense.

So, I'm sorry, but if you feel I'm asking too much of you, you need this book all the more. Trust me, I'm speaking from experience.

I know you're not putting in all that effort just for the fun of it. You want to see results. You want to meet that better version of yourself. So, let's go meet your new and improved self in the third and last part of this book: Part III, Harvesting the fruit of your labor.

‘Being and becoming, that’s what it’s all about.’

Margriet Sitskoorn

goodreads.com

PART III **Introduction**

The last part of this book is meant to help you assess the effects of the time and energy you have invested in developing your prefrontal cortex and executive skills. You will do this mainly by retaking the questionnaires and tests you completed earlier and comparing the results. We will also look at how much progress you've made toward achieving the goals you set at the beginning. Adding new goals to your agenda will start you off on another cycle of growth.

This part of the book, in which we assess the impact of this method, only makes sense if you have actually invested the time it takes to complete (parts of) the EFFECT program. Therefore, you should only begin using this chapter after you've spent at least six months carrying out the EFFECT program detailed in Part II.

PART III
HARVESTING THE FRUIT OF YOUR LABORD

What is the impact of implementing (parts of) the EFFECT program and the self-knowledge I have acquired? Am I closer to attaining my goals and what is the wider objective I have achieved?

’It is good to have an end to journey toward; but it is the journey that matters, in the end.’

Ernest Hemingway

goodreads.com

Chapter 12 **The Effect: Assessing the Impact of the EFFECT Program**

In this chapter, you'll measure some of the effects of your hard work. You'll learn that your efforts haven't just helped you achieve the goal you set in Chapter 1, but all future goals too..

Another look at the maze

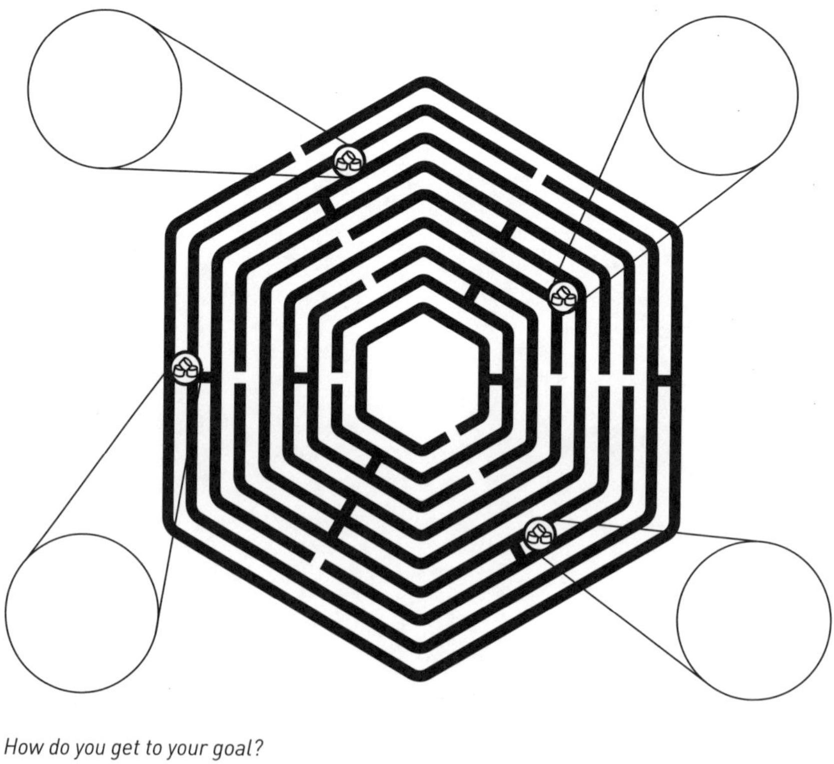

How do you get to your goal?

Write the goal you set in Chapter 1 in the center of the maze. Then use the marshmallow circles to fill in the various obstacles you expected to encounter and the moral licensing temptations you predicted you would succumb to (and probably did). You can find these obstacles and temptations in Chapter 5, where you did the 'Your personal pitfalls' exercise on p. 104). Now try to find a way through the maze with your eyes, in the same way you did in Chapter 1.

As you'll remember from Chapter 1 (p. 18), this is a metaphor for your journey. It's a neat way of visually summing up what you've learned and practiced. In Chapter 1, I explained that this image is based on the Minsky-Papert figures, which are designed to show us the limitations of our observational skills. The maze brings home the fact that we don't always know how to attain our goal beforehand because we simply can't see and know everything. "When you've set yourself a goal, you usually assume you can achieve it. But you don't always know how to get there or whether you have the skills to complete the journey. This could lead you to choose the wrong path, because you either don't see the big picture, base your decisions on the wrong information, or get distracted by whatever you encounter along the way. If this happens, you will invest a lot of energy, but your efforts will fail. All your work will likely lead to more of the same; you'll wind up on dead end streets, frustrated and disappointed, and worse off in terms of health, wealth and well-being. Achieving a goal is like a well-planned vacation. It pays to do more than just get in the car and start driving. You're better off also putting energy into gathering information and preparing for possible problems before charting your route."

That's exactly what we've done in this book. We've gathered information, practiced skills and learned to sidestep our pitfalls. Presumably, the result is that you have brought your goal within reach.

Review

In Part I, 'Gaining self-knowledge' you learned about goal-setting, the VUCA world, the CEO brain, success-related traits and skills, and the pitfalls you could expect on your journey to success. In Part II, you learned about and practiced the 6 elements of the EFFECT program that develop the prefrontal cortex and your executive skills: Environmental Enrichment, Flow Focus, Fixed Sleeping Pattern, Exercise, Connecting Today with Tomorrow and Time. The acronym makes it easy to memorize the various elements:

E = Environmental Enrichment
F = Flow Focus
F = Fixed Sleeping Pattern
E = Exercise
C = Connecting Today with Tomorrow
T = Time

EFFECT

I asked you to keep track of the time you spent on the first five elements of the EFFECT program (see schedule in Chapter 11 (p. 203)).

	Monday	Tuesday	Wednesday	Thursday	Friday	Saturday	Sunday
Environmental Enrichment							
Flow Focus							
Fixed Sleeping Pattern							
Exercise							
Connecting Today with Tomorrow							

As I explained, time is of the essence. It's an important active ingredient in the EFFECT formula. If you don't invest enough of it, the benefits you reap will be small. So, if you've hardly spent any time on the other five elements, it makes more sense to hold off on assessing their impact. First spend some more time incorporating these elements into your everyday life. Then measure their impact.

The results you've achieved by implementing elements of the EFFECT program and making them part of your daily routine can be measured in either subjective or slightly more objective terms. Doing a self-assessment will give you an idea of how you did and what you learned, in your own estimation. Questionnaires with self-reported scores are commonly used for this purpose. An objective assessment takes an outside perspective on your actual skills and often makes use of tests.

Since this book is aimed primarily at self-reflection, self-knowledge and self-help, we're using a self-assessment. You can do a somewhat more objective assessment by retaking the tests you did on the various websites. This will also give you an idea of how well you've mastered the executive skills. If you feel the need for a truly objective assessment, I'd recommend you contact a neuropsychologist.

Of course, the best test of this book's impact is whether you've achieved your goal. Have you accomplished what you set out to do in Chapter 1? Perhaps you haven't yet, because you haven't spent enough time incorporating the EFFECT elements into your life. Maybe you simply haven't progressed enough on the path toward your goal. Remember, give yourself time to gain control of your life and reach your goals.

Assessment time

In Chapter 2, you learned about executive skills and in Chapter 3 about the skills and traits related to wisdom and success. You assessed your own mastery of these skills and traits and also asked someone who knows you well to rate your abilities. Now it is time to fill in that same questionnaire again, and to ask a friend or co-worker to rate you again too. Then compare these scores to your earlier scores.

Assessing your executive skills

Rate your own ability for all twelve executive skills on a scale ranging from 'Incapable' to 'Bad' to 'Pretty good' to 'Good'.

Self-assessment		Incapable	Bad	Pretty good	Good
1	Attention: focusing, sustaining, dividing, releasing	☐	☐	☐	☐
2	Emotion regulation (includes coping with stress)	☐	☐	☐	☐
3	Flexibility (ability to deal with change)	☐	☐	☐	☐
4	Inhibitory control	☐	☐	☐	☐
5	Task initiation	☐	☐	☐	☐
6	Organization	☐	☐	☐	☐
7	Planning	☐	☐	☐	☐
8	Self-monitoring	☐	☐	☐	☐
9	Working memory	☐	☐	☐	☐
10	Realistic self-image	☐	☐	☐	☐
11	Capacity for theory of mind	☐	☐	☐	☐
12	Prosocial behavior (keeping others' interests in mind)	☐	☐	☐	☐

In order to test your self-knowledge (because opinions tend to differ), ask someone you trust and who knows you well to score you again on these 12 executive skills. Ask this person to assess how well you've generally mastered these skills.

Check whether these scores match your own, and whether you agree with the other person's assessment of you. Adjust your own scores if you find the other person's assessment more accurate.

Assessment by someone else		Incapable	Bad	Pretty good	Good
1	Attention: focusing, sustaining, dividing, releasing	☐	☐	☐	☐
2	Emotion regulation (includes coping with stress)	☐	☐	☐	☐
3	Flexibility (ability to deal with change)	☐	☐	☐	☐
4	Inhibitory control	☐	☐	☐	☐
5	Task initiation	☐	☐	☐	☐
6	Organization	☐	☐	☐	☐
7	Planning	☐	☐	☐	☐

8	Self-monitoring	☐	☐	☐	☐
9	Working memory	☐	☐	☐	☐
10	Realistic self-image	☐	☐	☐	☐
11	Capacity for theory of mind	☐	☐	☐	☐
12	Prosocial behavior (keeping others' interests in mind)	☐	☐	☐	☐

Next, compare your scores to your previous scores (Chapter 3, p. 63). Summarize the differences below, if you like.

Assess your wisdom- and success-related traits

Rate yourself for the traits related to wisdom and success on the list below, on a scale ranging from 'none' to 'a little,' 'sufficient,' and 'a lot.'

Trait/skill		None	A little	Sufficient	A lot
1	Grit (dedication)	☐	☐	☐	☐
2	Willpower	☐	☐	☐	☐
3	Energy/zest for life	☐	☐	☐	☐
4	Social intelligence	☐	☐	☐	☐
5	Gratitude	☐	☐	☐	☐
6	Optimism	☐	☐	☐	☐
7	Curiosity	☐	☐	☐	☐
8	Prosocial attitudes and behaviors	☐	☐	☐	☐
9	Self-reflection and self-knowledge	☐	☐	☐	☐
10	Recognizing and coping with uncertainty	☐	☐	☐	☐
11	Tolerance	☐	☐	☐	☐
12	Spirituality	☐	☐	☐	☐
13	Sense of humor	☐	☐	☐	☐

Then compare your scores with the scores you gave yourself earlier, when you filled in the list in Chapter 4 (p. 86). If you like, summarize the differences below.

Assessing your grit

SELF-KNOWLEDGE

Grit, or perseverance coupled with dedication, is key to achieving long-term goals. Presumably, the EFFECT program has had a positive influence on your grit. Take the online grit questionnaire[36] again and compare your new score to your earlier score (p. 90).

Initial grit score: ______ New grit score: ______

36 https://sasupenn.qualtrics.com/SE/?SID=SV_06f6QSOS2pZW9qR

In Chapter 7, you tested whether you were the master of your attention. If you have started implementing Flow Focus, you will have experienced some improvement in your ability to focus, sustain, release and redirect your attention. Assess once again to what extent you have (re)gained control of your attention.

PFC exercise: Focus and distraction

SELF-KNOWLEDGE

1 Try to become aware of what you pay attention to over the course of a day. Do this at night too, if you find yourself unable to sleep (from worries, for instance).

  - Is your attention drawn by stimuli from your own body – sensations, thoughts and feelings – or rather by stimuli in your surroundings, like images, sounds and smells?
  - Do these stimuli hold your attention for long?
  - Is this good or bad?

  Decide whether you are the master of your attention, focusing on whatever you choose, or more of a marionette that responds to all kinds of internal and external stimuli.

Attention drawn by	**Holds your attention yes/no**	**Positive**	**Negative**

I am the master of my attention yes ☐ no ☐
I focus my attention on what I want to develop or achieve yes ☐ no ☐

2 What do you want to focus on? Keep track of whether you succeed in doing so.

I want to focus my attention on ....

Compare your answers to see whether they have changed from the first time you answered these questions in Chapter 7 (p. 134). Summarize the differences below, if you like. ....

Improving your sleeping habits

In Chapter 8, you learned about the importance of sleep and took away a list of tips to improve your sleeping habits. If you kept a sleep diary at that point (see p. 157), you could do this again for a couple of weeks to become (even more) aware of the changes you've made and possible changes you'd still like to make.

If you did not keep a diary, you may have filled out the list below on days when you slept exceptionally long or short to understand your sleeping pattern and how it affected your mood, energy level, daytime drowsiness, stress level and patience. You could do that again and draw conclusions based on the differences. Have you improved your sleeping habits?

Do you want or need to improve your sleeping habits even more? Review the tips in Chapter 8 (p. 162) and incorporate more of them into your life.

Hours of sleep ....

Mood	☐ good	☐ okay	☐ bad
Energy level	☐ high	☐ normal	☐ low
Patience	☐ little	☐ normal	☐ a lot
Stress level	☐ high	☐ normal	☐ absent
Daytime drowsiness	☐ not at all	☐ a few times	☐ a lot
Alcohol use	☐ Type		Units ....
Caffeine use	☐ Type		Units ....
I feel like I had a good night's sleep	☐ yes ☐ no		

Compare these results with the results from Chapter 8. Summarize your conclusions below, if you like. ....

Three core executive skills

Chapter 3, 'The CEO Brain' and Chapter 10, 'Connecting Today with Tomorrow' contain several hyperlinks to sites where you can test your three core executive skills – inhibitory control, cognitive and mental flexibility and working memory. If you wish, you can retake these tests and assess how well you're doing compared to last time. This only makes sense if you last took the tests at least six months ago. This time span is necessary to ensure you don't remember your answers and therefore improve your score without actually having improved your skills. Then compare your earlier score to your new score.

Here is where you can find the tests:
- www.mathsisfun.com/games/towerofhanoi.html
- http:/zap.psy.utwente.nl/
- http:/www.cognitivefun.net/
- www.cogmed.com/working-memory-challenge
- http://cognitivefun.net/test/4
- www.gocognitive.net/demo/working-memory-capacity

First time Task	Score	Second time Task	Score

Reflecting on your goal

Presumably, you have spent time incorporating the various elements of the EFFECT program into your life to boost the executive skills you need to achieve your goal. I don't know whether you've actually been working toward that goal. If you haven't yet, now is the time to start. If you have, you should assess how far you've come, whether you've reached your goal, and if so, whether this achievement has brought you what you expected from it.

My goal was to: ______________________________

I considered my goal achieved when: ______________________________

Goal: Not achieved / Partly Achieved / Achieved

How do I benefit from this goal? (What was the reason I set it?) ______________________________

Has setting and/or achieving this goal brought me what I expected? ☐ yes ☐ no

Presumably, reading this book, doing the exercises and applying the lessons you learned has improved your skills and your chances of achieving the goal you set at the beginning. This goal is not the be-all and end-all, however, but merely the beginning. Developing your executive skills not only enables you to achieve that first goal; it also enables you to achieve future goals that require planning, grit, self-control, wise responses, self-monitoring and flexibility, or in a nutshell, goals that require you to connect the present to the future.

SELF-KNOWLEDGE

Selecting your next goal

In Chapter 1, 'A Goal to Set Your Sights on', you wrote down more goals and dreams. You defined what success and happiness look like to you and what you want to accomplish career-wise, in terms of your friends and family, your personality traits, your health and fitness, education and personal development, leisure time and wealth, and for the greater good, as well as any other goals you had.

1 Look at the list of goals below, and again rank your goals in order of importance, prioritizing the variable you value most by assigning it a 1 (e.g. your job), and the one you value most after that a 2 (e.g. your family), and so on.
2 Now it's time to rate how successful you've been at reaching these goals. If you added extra variables, include these in the list below. You can rate your success using a scale ranging from 'None' (meaning not at all successful) to 'Somewhat successful' to 'Quite successful' to 'Very successful'. This will show you in which areas you are doing well by your own standards, and which areas still need attention and effort and which of those you should prioritize.

Successfulness	None	Somewhat	Quite	Very	Ranking
Work	☐	☐	☐	☐	....
Family	☐	☐	☐	☐	....
Friends	☐	☐	☐	☐	....
Education	☐	☐	☐	☐	....
Leisure	☐	☐	☐	☐	....
Physical health	☐	☐	☐	☐	....
Wealth	☐	☐	☐	☐	....
Happiness	☐	☐	☐	☐	....
Personality traits	☐	☐	☐	☐	....
For the greater good	☐	☐	☐	☐	....
....	☐	☐	☐	☐	....
....	☐	☐	☐	☐	....
....	☐	☐	☐	☐	....
....	☐	☐	☐	☐	....

Setting a new goal

If you've identified more goals you'd like to work on, go back to Chapter 1 to set a new goal and draw up a roadmap. It may be another personal goal, but you can also use this book to help others develop their executive skills and achieve their goals. For this purpose, I've created a separate workbook with all the questionnaires and exercises and a tutorial to help others develop their prefrontal lobe and executive skills. You can use the workbook to measure the impact of the EFFECT program.

Articulating your next goal and drawing up a roadmap

SELF-KNOWLEDGE

Articulate your new goal in a realistic manner, using the 'I want to...' structure. Be as concrete as possible about what you want to achieve, so you will know when you have achieved it. Also write down what benefits you expect to reap, what you need to do to achieve it (roadmap), and what pitfalls (obstacles/temptations) you expect to encounter.

Goal: I want to ……………………………………………

I will have reached my goal when ……………………………………………

'I'm sorry, but if you feel I'm asking too much of you, you need this book all the more. Trust me, I'm speaking from experience.'

How do I benefit from this goal? (What is the reason I am setting it?)

What do I need to do to achieve my goal?

What obstacles and temptations can I expect to come across along the way?

Meet **Your Best Self**

Not only has this book given you insight in what you *are*, it has also taught you about *becoming* – in the sense of becoming aware of why you are the way you are, and, more importantly, aware of how you can keep improving and become your best self. That was my goal when I decided to write this book. It might strike you as paradoxical, this simultaneous state of being and becoming, because one is a constant and the other a dynamic factor, but it's less of contradiction than you think. The moment you commit to your life's journey, plans and dreams, and accept the fact that nothing stays the same, you'll find yourself more willing to change and develop. That willingness will become a constant in your life. The resulting mindset will foster constant evolvement, or a state of becoming, and will gradually make changing easier. You will no longer long for change as a means of escape or salvation, based on a feeling that you can't stand it where you are, but you will perceive it instead as a natural state, an openness to new experiences and opportunities for personal development. Once you've achieved this, adaptation will no longer automatically cause anxiety and stress. You will eagerly anticipate and welcome changes in your life. Developing your executive skills is an important step in that direction.

In this book, I have focused on methods that help develop your executive skills in general. I chose to focus on these techniques because they are the most basic and effective method to improve your default mindset. My next books will zoom in on developing specific executive skills, like motivation, prosocial behavior and creativity.

Executive skills enable us to be successful, happy and healthy in the complicated times we live in. Executive skills help us transcend our cravings and knee-jerk reactions. They empower us to break with stereotypical behavior, to be more proactive and innovative, resist temptation, reduce stress, take more control, see opportunities, accelerate our personal development, take greater responsibility for our lives and those of our loved ones, and so on. These are far-reaching benefits, but they are not all. Neural plasticity enables us to develop our executive skills and, in so doing, learn to steer our progress in the direction we want. This is something I'm passionate about. I believe the mechanisms I've described in this book can help us develop from homo sapiens (wise human) into homo sapiens verus (the truly wise human, or the human being that posesses all the qualities that make us human). These mechanisms can help you reach your full potential, and become your best self. They can even help the world become a better, healthier, friendlier and fairer place to live. And to think that all that potential can be developed in your very own brain! Let's not leave it untapped. I urge you to shape your brain, shape your life, and shape the world.

Shape
your brain.
Shape
your life.
Shape
the world.

Literature

Chapter 1 A Goal to Set Your Sights on

Duckworth, A. L., Kirby, T., Gollwitzer, A., & Oettingen, G. (2013). From fantasy to action: Mental contrasting with implementation intentions (MCII) improves academic performance in children. *Social Psychological and Personality Science*, 4(6), 745-753.

Hall, P. A., & Fong, G. T. (2015). Temporal self-regulation theory: A neurobiologically informed model for physical activity behavior. *Frontiers in Human Neuroscience*, 9, 117.

Heatherton, T. F., & Wagner, D. D. (2011). Cognitive neuroscience of self-regulation failure. *Trends in Cognitive Sciences*, 15(3), 132-139.

Hofmann, W., Schmeichel, B. J., & Baddeley, A. D. (2012). Executive functions and self-regulation. *Trends in Cognitive Sciences*, 16(3), 174-180.

Inzlicht, M., Bartholow, B. D., & Hirsh, J. B. (2015). Emotional foundations of cognitive control. *Trends in Cognitive Sciences*, 19(3), 126-132.

Koestner, R., Lekes, N., Powers, T. A., & Chicoine, E. (2002). Attaining personal goals: Self-concordance plus implementation intentions equals success. *Journal of Personality and Social Psychology*, 83(1), 231-244.

Mann, T., Ridder, D. de, & Fujita, K. (2013). Self-regulation of health behavior: Social psychological approaches to goal setting and goal striving. *Health Psychology*, 32(5), 487-498.

Sevincer, A. T., & Oettingen, G. (2013). Spontaneous mental contrasting and selective goal pursuit. *Personality and Social Psychology Bulletin*, 39(9), 1240-1254.

Sheldon, K. M. (2014). Becoming oneself: The central role of self-concordant goal selection. *Personality and Social Psychology Review*, 18(4), 349-365.

Chapter 2 The VUCA World

Actieagenda smart industry: Dutch industry fit for the future. (2014). Accessed via http://www.smartindustry.nl/wp-content/uploads/2014/11/Smart-Industry-actieagenda-LR.pdf.

Carr, N. G. (2010). *The shallows: What the internet is doing to our brains*. New York, NY: W.W. Norton & Company.

Carroll, L. (1871). *Through the looking-glass (and what Alice found there)*. New York: Macmillan & Co.

Chitta, K. (2014). *Change agility: Leadership, transformation and the pursuit of purpose*. North Charleston, SC: CreateSpace.

Cobb, V. (1999). *How to really fool yourself: Illusions for all your senses*. New York, NY: John Wiley & Sons.

Diamond, J. M. (2005). *Collapse: How societies choose to fail or succeed*. New York, NY: Viking Press.

Friedman, T. L. (2005). *The world is flat: A brief history of the twenty-first century*. New York, NY: Farrar, Straus and Giroux.

Goldberg, E., & Podell, K. (1999). Adaptive versus veridical decision making and the frontal lobes. *Consciousness and Cognition, 8(3), 364-377.*

Heuvel, M. van den (2014). *Vrijheid gelijkheid broederschap: Oude waarden in nieuwe tijden*. Amsterdam: Boom.

Levitin, D. J. (2014). *The organized mind: Thinking straight in the age of information overload*. New York, NY: Dutton Penguin.

May, J., & May, C. (2014). *Are you VUCA ready?* North Charleston, SC: CreateSpace.

Restak, R. (2003). *The new brain: How the modern age is rewiring your mind.* Emmaus, PA: Rodale.

Sitskoorn, M. M. (2010). *Passies van het brein: Waarom zondigen zo verleidelijk is.* [Passions of the Brain: Why Sin is so Tempting]. Amsterdam: Bert Bakker.

Sitskoorn, M. M. (2014). Het 'executive brain'. *FD Outlook*, 7(4), 126, December 19.

Spencer, H. (1864, 1867). *Principles of Biology* (2 vols., 2nd ed., 1898-99). London: Williams and Norgate.

Stichting Adverteerdersjury Nederland (2014). *SAN Jaarboek 2014*, 3-5.

Stiehm, J. H., & Townsend, N. W. (2002). *U.S. Army war college: Military education in a democracy* (p. 6). Philadelphia, PA: Temple University Press.

Toffler, A. (1970). *Future Shock*. New York, NY: Random House

Trilling, B., & Fadel, C. (2012). *21st Century skills: Learning for life in our times*. San Francisco, CA: Jossey-Bass.

Chapter 3 The CEO Brain

Anderson, J. R., & Gallup, G. G. (2011). Which primates recognize themselves in mirrors? *PLoS Biology*, 9(3), e1001024.

Ardila, A. (2008). On the evolutionary origins of executive functions. *Brain and Cognition*, 68(1), 92-99.

Asimov, I. (1981). *Asimov on science fiction*. New York, NY: Doubleday. Reprint of *My Own View, in The Encyclopedia of Science Fiction* (1978), ed. Robert Holdstock. N.p.: Wh. Smith Pub.

Barkley, R. A. (2001). The executive functions and self-regulation: An evolutionary neuropsychological perspective. *Neuropsychology Review*, 11(1), 1-29.

Bechara, A. (2004). The role of emotion in decision-making: Evidence from neurological patients with orbitofrontal damage. *Brain and Cognition*, 55(1), 30-40.

Bechara, A., Damasio, A. R., Damasio, H., & Anderson, S. W. (1994). Insensitivity to future consequences following damage to human prefrontal cortex. *Cognition*, 50(1), 7-15.

Brodmann, K. (2006). *Brodmann's Localisation in the Cerebral Cortex* (translated and edited by Laurence Garey). New York, NY: Springer.

Casey, B. J., Somerville, L. H., Gotlib, I. H., Ayduk, O., Franklin, N. T., Askren, M. K., ... Teslovich, T. (2011). Behavioral and neural correlates of delay of gratification 40 years later. *Proceedings of the National Academy of Sciences*, 108(36), 14998-15003.

Center on the Developing Child at Harvard University (2011). Building the brain's 'Air Traffic Control' system: How early experiences shape the development of executive function: Working paper No. 11. www.developingchild.harvard.edu, accessed July 24, 2015.

Chitta, K. (2014). *Change agility: Leadership, transformation and the pursuit of purpose*. North Charleston, SC: CreateSpace.

Damasio, A., R., Anderson, S. W., & Tranel, D. (2011). The frontal lobes. In K. M. Heilman & E. Valenstein (Eds.), *Clinical neuropsychology* (5th ed., pp. 417-465). New York, NY: Oxford University Press.

Dawson, P., & Guare, R. (2014). Interventions to promote executive development in children and adolescents. In S. Goldstein & J. A. Naglieri (Eds.), *Handbook of executive functioning* (table on pp. 428-429). New York, NY: Springer.

Diamond, A. (2013). Executive functions. *Annual Review of Psychology*, 64, 135-168.

Duckworth, A. L., & Seligman, M. E. (2005). Self-discipline outdoes IQ in predicting academic performance of adolescents. *Psychological Science*, 16(12), 939-944.

Duckworth, A. L., Quinn, P. D., & Tsukayama, E. (2012). What no child left behind leaves behind: The roles of IQ and self-control in predicting standardized achievement test scores and report card grades. *Journal of Educational Psychology*, 104(2), 439-451.

Duckworth, A. L., Tsukayama, E., & Kirby, T. A. (2013). Is it really self-control? Examining the predictive power of the delay of gratification task. *Personality and Social Psychology Bulletin*, 39(7), 843-855.

Duckworth, A. L., Kirby, T., Gollwitzer, A., & Oettingen, G. (2013). From fantasy to action: Mental contrasting with implementation intentions (MCII) improves academic performance in children. *Social Psychological and Personality Science*, 4(6), 745-753.

Duckworth, A. L., Weir, D., Tsukayama, E., & Kwok, D. (2012). Who does well in life? Conscientious adults excel in both objective and subjective success. *Frontiers in Psychology*, 3, 356.

Eigsti, I.-M., Zayas, V., Mischel, W., Shoda, Y., Ayduk, O., Dadlani, M. B., ... Casey, B. (2006). Predicting cognitive control from preschool to late adolescence and young adulthood. *Psychological Science*, 17(6), 478-484.

Frith, C. D., & Frith, U. (2012). Mechanisms of social cognition. *Annual Review of Psychology*, 63, 287-313.

Gallup, G. G. (1970). Chimpanzees: Self-recognition. *Science*, 167(3914), 86-87.

Goldberg, E. (2009). *The new executive brain: Frontal lobes in a complex world.* New York, NY: Oxford University Press.

Goldstein, S., & Naglieri, J. A. (2014). *Handbook of executive functioning.* New York, NY: Springer.

Hongwanishkul, D., Happaney, K. R., Lee, W. S., & Zelazo, P. D. (2005). Assessment of hot and cool executive function in young children: Age-related changes and individual differences. *Developmental Neuropsychology*, 28(2), 617-644.

Ingvar, D. H. (1984). 'Memory of the future': An essay on the temporal organization of conscious awareness. *Human Neurobiology*, 4(3), 127-136.

Kolb, B., & Whishaw, I. Q. (2009). *Fundamentals of human neuropsychology* (6th ed.). New York, NY: Worth.

Lezak, M. D., Howieson, D. B., Bigler, E. D., & Tranel, D. (2012). *Neuropsychological assessment* (5th ed.). New York, NY: Oxford University Press.

Li, W., Mai, X., & Liu, C. (2014). The default mode network and social understanding of others: What do brain connectivity studies tell us. *Frontiers in Human Neuroscience*, 8, 74.

McClelland, M. M., & Cameron, C. E. (2011). Self-regulation and academic achievement in elementary school children. *New Directions for Child and Adolescent Development*, 2011(133), 29-44.

McCloskey, G., & Perkins, L. A. (2012). *Essentials of executive functions assessment.* New York, NY: John Wiley & Sons.

Meshberger, F. L. (1990). An interpretation of Michelangelo's creation of Adam based on neuroanatomy. *JAMA*, 264(14), 1837-1841.

Mischel, W., Shoda, Y., & Rodriguez, M. I. (1989). Delay of gratification in children. *Science*, 244(4907), 933-938.

Mischel, W., Ayduk, O., Berman, M. G., Casey, B. J., Gotlib, I. H., Jonides, J., ... Shoda, Y. (2011). 'Willpower' over the life span: Decomposing self-regulation. *Social Cognitive and Affective Neuroscience*, 6(2), 252-256.

Mitchell, R. L., & Phillips, L. H. (2015). The overlapping relationship between emotion perception and theory of mind. *Neuropsychologia*, 70, 1-10.

Miyake, A., Friedman, N. P., Emerson, M. J., Witzki, A. H., Howerter, A., & Wager, T. D. (2000). The unity and diversity of executive functions and their contributions to complex 'frontal lobe' tasks: A latent variable analysis. *Cognitive Psychology*, 41(1), 49-100.

Naglieri, J. A., & Goldstein, S. (2013). *Comprehensive executive functioning inventory technical manual.* Toronto, ON: Multi-Health Systems.

Nigg, J. T. (2000). On inhibition/disinhibition in developmental psychopathology: Views from cognitive and personality psychology and a working inhibition taxonomy. *Psychological Bulletin*, 126(2), 220-246.

Rajkowska, G., & Goldman-Rakic, P. S. (1995a). Cytoarchitectonic definition of prefrontal areas in the normal human cortex: I. Remapping of areas 9 and 46 using quantitative criteria. *Cerebral Cortex*, 5(4), 307-322.

Rajkowska, G., & Goldman-Rakic, P. S. (1995b). Cytoarchitectonic definition of prefrontal areas in the normal human cortex: II. Variability in locations of areas 9 and 46 and relationship to the Talairach Coordinate System. *Cerebral Cortex*, 5(4), 323-337.

Shamosh, N. A., & Gray, J. R. (2008). Delay discounting and intelligence: A meta-analysis. *Intelligence*, 36(4), 289-305.

Shamosh, N. A., DeYoung, C. G., Green, A. E., Reis, D. L., Johnson, M. R., Conway, A. R., ... Gray, J. R. (2008). Individual differences in delay discounting: Relation to intelligence, working memory, and anterior prefrontal cortex. *Psychological Science*, 19(9), 904-911.

Sitskoorn, M. M. (2010). *Passies van het brein: Waarom zondigen zo verleidelijk is* [Passions of the Brain: Why Sin is so Tempting]. Amsterdam: Bert Bakker.

Smith, M. E. (2002). Success rates for different types of organizational change. *Performance Improvement*, 41(1), 26-33.

Uylings, H., Rajkowska, G., Sanz-Arigita, E., Amunts, K., & Zilles, K. (2005). Consequences of large interindividual variability for human brain atlases: Converging macroscopical imaging and microscopical neuroanatomy. *Anatomy and Embryology*, 210(5-6), 423-431.

Wagner, D. D., Altman, M., Boswell, R. G., Kelley, W. M., & Heatherton, T. F. (2013). Self-regulatory depletion enhances neural responses to rewards and impairs top-down control. *Psychological Science*, 24(11), 2262-2271.

Ward, J. (2015). The executive brain. In J. Ward (Ed.), *The student's guide to cognitive neuroscience* (3rd ed., pp. 345-372). New York, NY: Psychology Press.

Zelazo, P. D., Qu, L., & Müller, U. (2005). Hot and cool aspects of executive function: Relations in early development. In W. Schneider, R. Schumann-Hengsteler & B. Sodian (Eds.), *Young children's cognitive development: Interrelationships among executive functioning, working memory, verbal ability, and theory of mind* (pp. 71-93). Mahwah, NJ: Lawrence Erlbaum.

Chapter 4 A Recipe for Success

Bailey, C. E. (2007). Cognitive accuracy and intelligent executive function in the brain and in business. *Annals of the New York Academy of Sciences*, 1118(1), 122-141.

Bangen, K. J., Meeks, T. W., & Jeste, D. V. (2013). Defining and assessing wisdom: A review of the literature. *American Journal of Geriatric Psychiatry*, 21(12), 1254-1266.

Brown, T. E., & Landgraf, J. M. (2010). Improvements in executive function correlate with enhanced performance and functioning and health-related quality of life: Evidence from 2 large, double-blind, randomized, placebo-controlled trials in ADHD. *Postgraduate Medicine*, 122(5), 42-51.

Carr, N. G. (2010). *The shallows: What the internet is doing to our brains*. New York, NY: W.W. Norton & Company.

Cobb, V. (1999). *How to really fool yourself: Illusions for all your senses*. New York, NY: John Wiley & Sons.

Crescioni, A. W., Ehrlinger, J., Alquist, J. L., Conlon, K. E., Baumeister, R. F., Schatschneider, C., & Dutton, G. R. (2011). High trait self-control predicts positive health behaviors and success in weight loss. *Journal of Health Psychology*, 16(5), 750-759.

Davis, C. L., Tomporowski, P. D., McDowell, J. E., Austin, B. P., Miller, P. H., Yanasak, N. E., ... Naglieri, J. A. (2011). Exercise improves executive function and achievement and alters brain activation in overweight children: A randomized, controlled trial. *Health Psychology*, 30(1), 91-98.

Davis, J. C., Marra, C. A., Najafzadeh, M., & Liu-Ambrose, T. (2010). The independent contribution of executive functions to health related quality of life in older women. *BMC Geriatrics*, 10(1), 16.

De Sousa, A., & Cunha, E. (2012). Hominins and the emergence of the modern human brain. *Progress in Brain Research*, 195, 293-322.

Duckworth, A. L., & Seligman, M. E. (2005). Self-discipline outdoes IQ in predicting academic performance of adolescents. *Psychological Science*, 16(12), 939-944.

Duckworth, A. L., Quinn, P. D., & Tsukayama, E. (2012). What no child left behind leaves behind: The roles of IQ and self-control in predicting standardized achievement test scores and report card grades. *Journal of Educational Psychology*, 104(2), 439-451.

Duckworth, A. L., Tsukayama, E., & Kirby, T. A. (2013). Is it really self-control? Examining the predictive power of the delay of gratification task. *Personality and Social Psychology Bulletin*, 39(7), 843-855.

Duckworth, A. L., Kirby, T., Gollwitzer, A., & Oettingen, G. (2013). From fantasy to action: Mental contrasting with implementation intentions (MCII) improves academic performance in children. *Social Psychological and Personality Science*, 4(6), 745-753.

Duckworth, A. L., Peterson, C., Matthews, M. D., & Kelly, D. R. (2007). Grit: Perseverance and passion for long-term goals. *Journal of Personality and Social Psychology*, 92(6), 1087-1101.

Duckworth, A. L., Weir, D., Tsukayama, E., & Kwok, D. (2012). Who does well in life? Conscientious adults excel in both objective and subjective success. *Frontiers in Psychology*, 3, 356.

Eigsti, I.-M., Zayas, V., Mischel, W., Shoda, Y., Ayduk, O., Dadlani, M. B., ... Casey, B. (2006). Predicting cognitive control from preschool to late adolescence and young adulthood. *Psychological Science*, 17(6), 478-484.

Frankl, V. E., Kushner, H. S., & Winslade, W. J. (2006). *Man's search for meaning*. Boston, MA: Beacon Press.

Gibson, J. J. (1979). *The ecological approach to visual perception*. Boston, MA: Houghton Mifflin.

Goldberg, E. (2009). *The new executive brain: Frontal lobes in a complex world*. New York, NY: Oxford University Press.

Lhermitte, F. (1983). 'Utilization behaviour' and its relation to lesions of the frontal lobes. *Brain, 106 (Pt 2), 237-255.*

Lövdén, M., Bäckman, L., Lindenberger, U., Schaefer, S., & Schmiedek, F. (2010). A theoretical framework for the study of adult cognitive plasticity. *Psychological Bulletin*, 136(4), 659-676.

Lövdén, M., Wenger, E., Mårtensson, J., Lindenberger, U., & Bäckman, L. (2013). Structural brain plasticity in adult learning and development. *Neuroscience & Biobehavioral Reviews*, 37(9), 2296-2310.

May, A. (2011). Experience-dependent structural plasticity in the adult human brain. *Trends in Cognitive Sciences*, 15(10), 475-482.

McClelland, M. M., & Cameron, C. E. (2011). Self-regulation and academic achievement in elementary school children. *New Directions for Child and Adolescent Development*, 2011(133), 29-44.

Meeks, T. W., & Jeste, D. V. (2009). Neurobiology of wisdom: A literature overview. *Archives of General Psychiatry*, 66(4), 355-365.

Mischel, W., Shoda, Y., & Rodriguez, M. I. (1989). Delay of gratification in children. *Science*, 244(4907), 933-938.

Mischel, W., Ayduk, O., Berman, M. G., Casey, B. J., Gotlib, I. H., Jonides, J., ... Shoda, Y. (2011). 'Willpower' over the life span: Decomposing self-regulation. *Social Cognitive and Affective Neuroscience*, 6(2), 252-256.

Neubauer, S. (2014). Endocasts: Possibilities and limitations for the interpretation of human brain evolution. *Brain, Behavior and Evolution*, 84(2), 117-134.

Park, D. C., & Reuter-Lorenz, P. (2009). The adaptive brain: Aging and neurocognitive scaffolding. *Annual Review of Psychology*, 60, 173-196.

Pearce, E., Stringer, C., & Dunbar, R. I. (2013). New insights into differences in brain organization between Neanderthals and anatomically modern humans. *Proceedings of the Royal Society of London B: Biological Sciences*, 280(1758), 20130168.

Peterson, C., & Seligman, M. E. (2004). *Character strengths and virtues: A handbook and classification*. New York, NY: Oxford University Press.

Restak, R. (2003). *The new brain: How the modern age is rewiring your mind*. Emmaus, PA: Rodale.

Shamosh, N. A., & Gray, J. R. (2008). Delay discounting and intelligence: A meta-analysis. *Intelligence*, 36(4), 289-305.

Shamosh, N. A., DeYoung, C. G., Green, A. E., Reis, D. L., Johnson, M. R., Conway, A. R., ... Gray, J. R. (2008). Individual differences in delay discounting: Relation to intelligence, working memory, and anterior prefrontal cortex. *Psychological Science*, 19(9), 904-911.

Sitskoorn, M. M. (2006). *Het maakbare brein: Gebruik je hersens en word wie je wilt zijn*. [The Mutable Brain: Using Your Head to Become Who You Want to Be]. Amsterdam: Bert Bakker.

Sitskoorn, M. M. (2010). *Passies van het brein: Waarom zondigen zo verleidelijk is*. [Passions of the Brain: Why Sin is so Tempting]. Amsterdam: Bert Bakker.

Sitskoorn, M. M. (2012). *Ik wil iets van jou, jij wilt iets van mij*. [I Want Something from You, You Want Something from Me]. Amsterdam: Bert Bakker.

Tough, P. (2013). *How children succeed: Grit, curiosity and the hidden power of character*. London: Random House Books.

Valkanova, V., Eguia Rodriguez, R., & Ebmeier, K. P. (2014). Mind over matter – what do we know about neuroplasticity in adults? *International Psychogeriatrics*, 26(6), 891-909.

Wagner, D. D., Altman, M., Boswell, R. G., Kelley, W. M., & Heatherton, T. F. (2013). Self-regulatory depletion enhances neural responses to rewards and impairs top-down control. *Psychological Science*, 24(11), 2262-2271.

Chapter 5 Pitfalls

Alquist, J., & Baumeister, R. F. (2012). Self-control: Limited resources and extensive benefits. Wiley interdisciplinary reviews: *Cognitive Science*, 3(3), 419-423.

Berridge, K. C. (2009). 'Liking' and 'wanting' food rewards: Brain substrates and roles in eating disorders. *Physiology & Behavior*, 97(5), 537-550.

Berridge, K. C., Ho, C.-Y., Richard, J. M., & DiFeliceantonio, A. G. (2010). The tempted brain eats: Pleasure and desire circuits in obesity and eating disorders. *Brain Research*, 1350, 43-64.

Bishop, M., Elder, S. T., & Heath, R. G. (1963). Intracranial self-stimulation in man. *Science*, 140(3565), 394-396.

Briers, B., Pandelaere, M., Dewitte, S., & Warlop, L. (2006). Hungry for money: The desire for caloric resources increases the desire for financial resources and vice versa. *Psychological Science*, 17(11), 939-943.

Burghardt, P. R., Love, T. M., Stohler, C. S., Hodgkinson, C., Shen, P.-H., Enoch, M.-A., ... Zubieta, J.-K. (2012). Leptin regulates dopamine responses to sustained stress in humans. *The Journal of Neuroscience*, 32(44), 15369-15376.

Dutton, K. (2011). *Split-second persuasion: The ancient art and new science of changing minds*. Boston, MA: Houghton Mifflin Harcourt.

Fishbach, A., & Dhar, R. (2005). Goals as excuses or guides: The liberating effect of perceived goal progress on choice. *Journal of Consumer Research*, 32(3), 370-377.

Fishbach, A., Dhar, R., & Zhang, Y. (2006). Subgoals as substitutes or complements: The role of goal accessibility. *Journal of Personality and Social Psychology*, 91(2), 232-242.

Gardner, E. L. (2011). Addiction and brain reward and antireward pathways. *Advances in Psychosomatic Medicine*, 30, 22-60.

Heath, R. G. (1963). Electrical self-stimulation of the brain in man. *American Journal of Psychiatry*, 120(6), 571-577.

Heath, R. G. (1972). Pleasure and brain activity in man: Deep and surface electroencephalograms during orgasm. *The Journal of Nervous and Mental Disease*, 154(1), 3-18.

Heatherton, T. F., & Wagner, D. D. (2011). Cognitive neuroscience of self-regulation failure. *Trends in Cognitive Sciences*, 15(3), 132-139.

Hildebrandt, T., & Greif, R. (2013). Stress and addiction. *Psychoneuroendocrinology*, 38(9), 1923-1927.

Hofmann, W., Schmeichel, B. J., & Baddeley, A. D. (2012). Executive functions and self-regulation. *Trends in Cognitive Sciences*, 16(3), 174-180.

Khan, U., & Dhar, R. (2006). Licensing effect in consumer choice. *Journal of Marketing Research*, 43(2), 259-266.

Knutson, B., & Cooper, J. C. (2005). Functional magnetic resonance imaging of reward prediction. *Current Opinion in Neurology*, 18(4), 411-417.

Lieberman, M. D., & Eisenberger, N. I. (2009). Neuroscience: Pains and pleasures of social life. *Science*, 323(5916), 890-891.

Lüscher, C., & Malenka, R. C. (2011). Drug-evoked synaptic plasticity in addiction: From molecular changes to circuit remodeling. *Neuron*, 69(4), 650-663.

Mann, T., de Ridder, D., & Fujita, K. (2013). Self-regulation of health behavior: Social psychological approaches to goal setting and goal striving. *Health Psychology*, 32(5), 487-498.

McGonigal, K. (2012). *The willpower instinct: How self-control works, why it matters, and what you can do to get more of it*. London: Penguin.

Mick, D. G., & DeMoss, M. (1990). Self-gifts: Phenomenological insights from four contexts. *Journal of Consumer Research*, 17(3), 322-332.

Olds, J. (1956a). Pleasure centers in the brain. *Scientific American*, 195, 105-117.

Olds, J. (1956b). Runway and maze behavior controlled by basomedial forebrain stimulation in the rat. *Journal of Comparative and Physiological Psychology*, 49(5), 507-512.

Olds, J. (1958). Self-stimulation of the brain: Its use to study local effects of hunger, sex, and drugs. *Science*, 127(3294), 315-324.

Olds, J., & Milner, P. (1954). Positive reinforcement produced by electrical stimulation of septal area and other regions of rat brain. *Journal of Comparative and Physiological Psychology*, 47(6), 419-427.

Richard, J. M., Castro, D. C., DiFeliceantonio, A. G., Robinson, M. J., & Berridge, K. C. (2013). Mapping brain circuits of reward and motivation: In the footsteps of Ann Kelley. *Neuroscience & Biobehavioral Reviews*, 37(9), 1919-1931.

Rock, D. (2009). *Your brain at work*. New York, NY: Harper Business.

Sachdeva, S., Iliev, R., & Medin, D. L. (2009). Sinning saints and saintly sinners: The paradox of moral self-regulation. *Psychological Science*, 20(4), 523-528.

Sinha, R., & Jastreboff, A. M. (2013). Stress as a common risk factor for obesity and addiction. *Biological Psychiatry*, 73(9), 827-835.

Sitskoorn, M. M. (2010). *Passies van het brein: Waarom zondigen zo verleidelijk is*. [Passions of the Brain: Why Sin is so Tempting]. Amsterdam: Bert Bakker.

Vincent, A. (2009). *Believe it, be it: How being the biggest loser won me back my life*. Emmaus, PA: Rodale.

Williams, M. A., Li, C., Kash, T. L., Matthews, R. T., & Winder, D. G. (2014). Excitatory drive onto dopaminergic neurons in the rostral linear nucleus is enhanced by norepinephrine in an α_1 drenergic receptor-dependent manner. *Neuropharmacology*, 86, 116-124.

Zhang, Y., Fishbach, A., & Kruglanski, A. W. (2007). The dilution model: How additional goals undermine the perceived instrumentality of a shared path. *Journal of Personality and Social Psychology*, 92(3), 389-401.

Chapter 6 Environmental Enrichment – Challenging Your Brain

Alwis, D. S., & Rajan, R. (2014). Environmental enrichment and the sensory brain: The role of enrichment in remediating brain injury. *Frontiers in Systems Neuroscience*, 8, 156.

Barulli, D., & Stern, Y. (2013). Efficiency, capacity, compensation, maintenance, plasticity: Emerging concepts in cognitive reserve. *Trends in Cognitive Sciences*, 17(10), 502-509.

Draganski, B., Gaser, C., Busch, V., Schuierer, G., Bogdahn, U., & May, A. (2004). Neuroplasticity: Changes in grey matter induced by training. *Nature*, 427(6972), January, 311-312.

Kuboshima-Amemori, S., & Sawaguchi, T. (2007). Plasticity of the primate prefrontal cortex. *The Neuroscientist*, 13(3), 229-240.

Maguire, E.A., Spiers, H.J. Good, C.D., Hartley, T., Frackowiak, R.S., & Burgess, N. (2003). Navigation expertise and the human hippocampus: A structural brain imaging analysis. *Hippocampus*, 13(2), 208-217.

Nithianantharajah, J., & Hannan, A. J. (2009). The neurobiology of brain and cognitive reserve: Mental and physical activity as modulators of brain disorders. *Progress in Neurobiology*, 89(4), 369-382.

Petrosini, L., De Bartolo, P., Foti, F., Gelfo, F., Cutuli, D., Leggio, M. G., & Mandolesi, L. (2009). On whether the environmental enrichment may provide cognitive and brain reserves. *Brain Research Reviews*, 61(2), 221-239.

Renoir, T., Pang, T. Y., Mo, C., Chan, G., Chevarin, C., Lanfumey, L., & Hannan, A. J. (2013). Differential effects of early environmental enrichment on emotionality related behaviours in Huntington's disease transgenic mice. *Journal of Physiology*, 591(1), 41-55.

Sitskoorn, M. M. (2006). *Het maakbare brein: Gebruik je hersens en word wie je wilt zijn.* [The mutable brain: Using your head to become who you want to be]. Amsterdam: Bert Bakker.

Valkanova, V., Eguia Rodriguez, R., & Ebmeier, K. P. (2014). Mind over matter – what do we know about neuroplasticity in adults? *International Psychogeriatrics*, 26(6), 891-909.

Woollett, K., & Maguire, E.A. (2011). Acquiring 'the Knowledge' of London's layout drives structural brain changes. *Current Biology*, 21(24), December, 2109-2114.

Chapter 7 Flow Focus – Directing the Plasticity of Your Brain

Al-Hashimi, O., Zanto, T. P., & Gazzaley, A. (2015). Neural sources of performance decline during continuous multitasking. *Cortex*, 71, 49-57.

Alavash, M., Hilgetag, C. C., Thiel, C. M., & Gießing, C. (2015). Persistency and flexibility of complex brain networks underlie dual-task interference. *Human Brain Mapping*, 36(9), 3542-3562.

Arden, J. B. (2010). *Rewire your brain: Think your way to a better life.* New York, NY: John Wiley & Sons.

Chiesa, A., & Serretti, A. (2010). A systematic review of neurobiological and clinical features of mindfulness meditations. *Psychological Medicine*, 40(8), 1239-1252.

Chiesa, A., Calati, R., & Serretti, A. (2011). Does mindfulness training improve cognitive abilities? A systematic review of neuropsychological findings. *Clinical Psychology Review*, 31(3), 449-464.

Chiesa, A., Serretti, A., & Jakobsen, J. C. (2013). Mindfulness: Top-down or bottom-up emotion regulation strategy? *Clinical Psychology Review*, 33(1), 82-96.

Conrad, C. D. (2011). *The handbook of stress: Neuropsychological effects on the brain.* Hoboken, NJ: Wiley-Blackwell.

Csikszentmihalyi, M. (1990). *Flow: The psychology of optimal experience.* New York, NY: Harper & Row.

Davidson, R. J., & Lutz, A. (2008). Buddha's brain: Neuroplasticity and meditation. *IEEE Signal Processing Magazine*, 25(1), 176-174.

Diamond, A. (2013). Executive functions. *Annual Review of Psychology*, 64, 135-168.

Ding, X., Tang, Y.-Y., Tang, R., & Posner, M. I. (2014). Improving creativity performance by short-term meditation. *Behavioral and Brain Functions*, 10(9), 1-8.

Ding, X., Tang, Y.-Y., Cao, C., Deng, Y., Wang, Y., Xin, X., & Posner, M. I. (2015). Short-term meditation modulates brain activity of insight evoked with solution cue. *Social Cognitive and Affective Neuroscience*, 10(1), 43-49.

Dresler, M., & Repantis, D. (2015). Cognitive enhancement in humans. In S. Knafo & C. Venero (Eds.), *Cognitive enhancement: Pharmacologic, environmental and genetic factors* (pp. 273-306). San Diego, CA: Academic Press.

Dutton, K. (2011). *Split-second persuasion: The ancient art and new science of changing minds.* Boston, MA: Houghton Mifflin Harcourt.

Fan, Y., Tang, Y.-Y., Tang, R., & Posner, M. I. (2014). Short term integrative meditation improves resting alpha activity and Stroop performance. *Applied Psychophysiology and Biofeedback*, 39(3-4), 213-217.

Feil, J., Sheppard, D., Fitzgerald, P. B., Yücel, M., Lubman, D. I., & Bradshaw, J. L. (2010). Addiction, compulsive drug seeking, and the role of frontostriatal mechanisms in regulating inhibitory control. *Neuroscience & Biobehavioral Reviews*, 35(2), 248-275.

Feltenstein, M., & See, R. (2008). The neurocircuitry of addiction: An overview. *British Journal of Pharmacology*, 154(2), 261-274.

Froeliger, B., Garland, E., & McClernon, F. (2012). Yoga meditation practitioners exhibit greater gray matter volume and fewer reported cognitive failures: Results of a preliminary voxel-based morphometric analysis. *Evidence-based Complementary and Alternative Medicine: eCAM*, 2012, 821307-821307.

Gard, T., Taquet, M., Dixit, R., Holzel, B. K., de Montjoye, Y. A., Brach, N., ... Lazar, S. W. (2014). Fluid intelligence and brain functional organization in aging yoga and meditation practitioners. *Frontiers in Aging Neuroscience*, 6, 76.

Harp, D., & Feldman, N. (1997). *Drie minuten meditaties* [3-minute meditations]. Amsterdam: Maarten Muntinga.

Hodgins, H. S., & Adair, K. C. (2010). Attentional processes and meditation. *Consciousness and Cognition*, 19(4), 872-878.

Hofmann, W., Schmeichel, B. J., & Baddeley, A. D. (2012). Executive functions and self-regulation. *Trends in Cognitive Sciences*, 16(3), 174-180.

Hölzel, B. K., Carmody, J., Vangel, M., Congleton, C., Yerramsetti, S. M., Gard, T., & Lazar, S. W. (2011). Mindfulness practice leads to increases in regional brain gray matter density. *Psychiatry Research: Neuroimaging*, 191(1), 36-43.

Kabat-Zinn, J. (1994). *Wherever you go, there you are: Mindfulness training in everyday life*. New York, NY: Hyperion.

Levitin, D. J. (2014). *The organized mind: Thinking straight in the age of information overload*. New York, NY: Dutton Penguin.

Luders, E., Toga, A. W., Lepore, N., & Gaser, C. (2009). The underlying anatomical correlates of long-term meditation: Larger hippocampal and frontal volumes of gray matter. *NeuroImage*, 45(3), 672-678.

Lutz, A., Slagter, H. A., Dunne, J. D., & Davidson, R. J. (2008). Attention regulation and monitoring in meditation. *Trends in Cognitive Sciences*, 12(4), 163-169.

McEwen, B. S. (2004). Protection and damage from acute and chronic stress: Allostasis and allostatic overload and relevance to the pathophysiology of psychiatric disorders. *Annals of the New York Academy of Sciences*, 1032(1), 1-7.

McGonigal, K. (2012). *The willpower instinct: How self-control works, why it matters, and what you can do to get more of it*. London: Penguin.

Moore, A., & Malinowski, P. (2009). Meditation, mindfulness and cognitive flexibility. *Consciousness and Cognition*, 18(1), 176-186.

Moore, A., Gruber, T., Derose, J., & Malinowski, P. (2012). Regular, brief mindfulness meditation practice improves electrophysiological markers of attentional control. *Frontiers in Human Neuroscience*, 6, 18.

Nakamura, J., & Csikszentmihalyi, M. (2002). The concept of flow. In C. R. Snyder & S. J. Lopez (Eds.), *Handbook of positive psychology* (pp. 89-105). New York, NY: Oxford University Press.

Ophir, E., Nass, C., & Wagner, A. D. (2009). Cognitive control in media multitaskers. *Proceedings of the National Academy of Sciences*, 106(37), 15583-15587.

Opialla, S., Lutz, J., Scherpiet, S., Hittmeyer, A., Jäncke, L., Rufer, M., ... Brühl, A. B. (2014). Neural circuits of emotion regulation: A comparison of mindfulness-based and cognitive reappraisal strategies. *European Archives of Psychiatry and Clinical Neuroscience*, 265(1), 45-55.

Park, G., & Thayer, J. (2014). From the heart to the mind: Cardiac vagal tone modulates top-down and bottom-up visual perception and attention to emotional stimuli. *Frontiers in Psychology*, 5, 278.

Posner, M. I., Tang, Y.-Y., & Lynch, G. (2014). Mechanisms of white matter change induced by meditation training. *Frontiers in Psychology*, 5, 1220.

Rubinstein, J., Meyer, D., & Evans, J. (2001). Executive control of cognitive processes in task switching. *Journal of Experimental Psychology*, 27(4), 763-797.

Sapolsky, R. M. (2004). *Why zebra's don't get ulcers* (3rd ed.). New York, NY: Henry Holt and Company.

Schwartz, J. M., & Gladding, R. (2011). *You are not your brain: The 4-step solution for changing bad habits, ending unhealthy thinking, and taking control of your life.* Garden City, NY: Avery.

Slagter, H. A., Davidson, R. J., & Lutz, A. (2011). Mental training as a tool in the neuroscientific study of brain and cognitive plasticity. *Frontiers in Human Neuroscience*, 5, 17.

Song, H.-S., & Lehrer, P. M. (2003). The effects of specific respiratory rates on heart rate and heart rate variability. *Applied Psychophysiology and Biofeedback*, 28(1), 13-23.

Steckler, T., Kalin, N. H., & Reul, J. M. H. M. (2005). *Handbook of stress and the brain part 1: The neurobiology of stress.* Amsterdam: Elsevier Science.

Tang, Y.-Y., Hölzel, B. K., & Posner, M. I. (2015). The neuroscience of mindfulness meditation. *Nature Reviews Neuroscience*, 16(4), 213-225.

Tang, Y.-Y., Posner, M. I., & Rothbart, M. K. (2014). Meditation improves self-regulation over the life span. *Annals of the New York Academy of Sciences*, 1307(1), 104-111.

Tang, Y.-Y., Lu, Q., Fan, M., Yang, Y., & Posner, M. I. (2012). Mechanisms of white matter changes induced by meditation. *Proceedings of the National Academy of Sciences*, 109(26), 10570-10574.

Tang, Y.-Y., Lu, Q., Feng, H., Tang, R., & Posner, M. I. (2015). Short-term meditation increases blood flow in anterior cingulate cortex and insula. *Frontiers in Psychology*, 6, 212.

Tang, Y.-Y., Ma, Y., Fan, Y., Feng, H., Wang, J., Feng, S., ... Li, J. (2009). Central and autonomic nervous system interaction is altered by short-term meditation. *Proceedings of the National Academy of Sciences*, 106(22), 8865-8870.

Tang, Y.-Y., Ma, Y., Wang, J., Fan, Y., Feng, S., Lu, Q., ... Fan, M. (2007). Short-term meditation training improves attention and self-regulation. *Proceedings of the National Academy of Sciences*, 104(43), 17152-17156.

Teper, R., & Inzlicht, M. (2013). Meditation, mindfulness and executive control: The importance of emotional acceptance and brain-based performance monitoring. *Social Cognitive and Affective Neuroscience*, 8(1), 85-92.

Tough, P. (2013). *How children succeed: Grit, curiosity and the hidden power of character.* London: Random House.

Travis, F., & Shear, J. (2010). Focused attention, open monitoring and automatic self-transcending: Categories to organize meditations from Vedic, Buddhist and Chinese traditions. *Consciousness and Cognition*, 19(4), 1110-1118.

Winbush, N. Y., Gross, C. R., & Kreitzer, M. J. (2007). The effects of mindfulness-based stress reduction on sleep disturbance: A systematic review. *Explore: The Journal of Science and Healing*, 3(6), 585-591.

Witkiewitz, K., Lustyk, M. K. B., & Bowen, S. (2013). Retraining the addicted brain: A review of hypothesized neurobiological mechanisms of mindfulness-based relapse prevention. *Psychology of Addictive Behaviors*, 27(2), 351-365.

Xue, S.-W., Tang, Y.-Y., & Posner, M. I. (2011). Short-term meditation increases network efficiency of the anterior cingulate cortex. *NeuroReport*, 22(12), 570-574.

Xue, S.-W., Tang, Y.-Y., Tang, R., & Posner, M. I. (2014). Short-term meditation induces changes in brain resting EEG theta networks. *Brain and Cognition*, 87, 1-6.

Zanesco, A. P., King, B. G., MacLean, K. A., & Saron, C. D. (2013). Executive control and felt concentrative engagement following intensive meditation training. *Frontiers in Human Neuroscience*, 7, 566.

Zeidan, F., Gordon, N. S., Merchant, J., & Goolkasian, P. (2010). The effects of brief mindfulness meditation training on experimentally induced pain. *Journal of Pain*, 11(3), 199-209.

Zeidan, F., Johnson, S. K., Diamond, B. J., David, Z., & Goolkasian, P. (2010). Mindfulness meditation improves cognition: Evidence of brief mental training. *Consciousness and Cognition*, 19(2), 597-605.

Zeidan, F., Martucci, K. T., Kraft, R. A., McHaffie, J. G., & Coghill, R. C. (2014). Neural correlates of mindfulness meditation-related anxiety relief. *Social Cognitive and Affective Neuroscience*, 9(6), 751-759.

Chapter 8 Fixed Sleeping Pattern – Unleashing the Power of Sleep

Arden, J. B. (2010). *Rewire your brain: Think your way to a better life*. New York, NY: John Wiley & Sons.

Buysse, D. J., Reynolds, C. F., Monk, T. H., Berman, S. R., & Kupfer, D. J. (1989). The Pittsburgh Sleep Quality Index: A new instrument for psychiatric practice and research. *Psychiatry Research*, 28(2), 193-213.

Dhand, R., & Sohal, H. (2006). Good sleep, bad sleep! The role of daytime naps in healthy adults. *Current Opinion in Pulmonary Medicine*, 12(6), 379-382.

Diekelmann, S. (2014). Sleep for cognitive enhancement. *Frontiers in Systems Neuroscience*, 8, 46.

Diekelmann, S., Wilhelm, I., & Born, J. (2009). The whats and whens of sleep-dependent memory consolidation. *Sleep Medicine Reviews*, 13(5), 309-321.

Dresler, M., & Repantis, D. (2015). Cognitive enhancement in humans. In S. Knafo & C. Venero (Eds.), *Cognitive enhancement: Pharmacologic, environmental and genetic factors* (pp. 273-306). San Diego, CA: Academic Press.

Durmer, J. S., & Dinges, D. F. (2005). Neurocognitive consequences of sleep deprivation. *Seminars in Neurology*, 25(1), 117-129.

Durning, S. J., Capaldi II, V. F., Artino Jr, A. R., Graner, J., Van der Vleuten, C., Beckman, T. J., ... Schuwirth, L. (2014). A pilot study exploring the relationship between internists' self-reported sleepiness, performance on multiple-choice exam items and prefrontal cortex activity. *Medical Teacher*, 36(5), 434-440.

Elmenhorst, D., Elmenhorst, E.-M., Luks, N., Maass, H., Mueller, E.-W., Vejvoda, M., ... Samel, A. (2009). Performance impairment during four days partial sleep deprivation compared with the acute effects of alcohol and hypoxia. *Sleep Medicine*, 10(2), 189-197.

Ficca, G., Axelsson, J., Mollicone, D. J., Muto, V., & Vitiello, M. V. (2010). Naps, cognition and performance. *Sleep Medicine Reviews*, 14(4), 249-258.

Filevich, E., Dresler, M., Brick, T. R., & Kühn, S. (2015). Metacognitive mechanisms underlying lucid dreaming. *The Journal of Neuroscience*, 35(3), 1082-1088.

Genzel, L., Quack, A., Jäger, E., Konrad, B., Steiger, A., & Dresler, M. (2012). Complex motor sequence skills profit from sleep. *Neuropsychobiology*, 66(4), 237-243.

Genzel, L., Kiefer, T., Renner, L., Wehrle, R., Kluge, M., Grözinger, M., ... Dresler, M. (2012). Sex and modulatory menstrual cycle effects on sleep related memory consolidation. *Psychoneuroendocrinology*, 37(7), 987-998.

Gorgoni, M., D'Atri, A., Lauri, G., Rossini, P. M., Ferlazzo, F., & De Gennaro, L. (2013). Is sleep essential for neural plasticity in humans, and how does it affect motor and cognitive recovery? *Neural Plasticity*, 2013.

Jackson, M. L., Gunzelmann, G., Whitney, P., Hinson, J. M., Belenky, G., Rabat, A., & Van Dongen, H. P. (2013). Deconstructing and reconstructing cognitive performance in sleep deprivation. *Sleep Medicine Reviews*, 17(3), 215-225.

Killgore, W. D. (2010). Effects of sleep deprivation on cognition. *Progress in Brain Research*, 185, 105-129.

Killgore, W. D., Balkin, T. J., & Wesensten, N. J. (2006). Impaired decision making following 49 h of sleep deprivation. *Journal of Sleep Research*, 15(1), 7-13.

Killgore, W. D., Lipizzi, E. L., Kamimori, G. H., & Balkin, T. J. (2007). Caffeine effects on risky decision making after 75 hours of sleep deprivation. *Aviation, Space, and Environmental Medicine*, 78(10), 957-962.

Kubitz, K. A., Landers, D. M., Petruzzello, S. J., & Han, M. (1996). The effects of acute and chronic exercise on sleep. *Sports Medicine*, 21(4), 277-291.

Lahl, O., Wispel, C., Willigens, B., & Pietrowsky, R. (2008). An ultra short episode of sleep is sufficient to promote declarative memory performance. *Journal of Sleep Research*, 17(1), 3-10.

Nettersheim, A., Hallschmid, M., Born, J., & Diekelmann, S. (2015). The role of sleep in motor sequence consolidation: Stabilization rather than enhancement. *The Journal of Neuroscience*, 35(17), 6696-6702.

O'Connor, P., & Youngstedt, S. (1995). Influence of exercise on human sleep. *Exercise and Sport Sciences Reviews*, 23, 105-134.

Perrier, J., Clochon, P., Bertran, F., Couque, C., Bulla, J., Denise, P., & Bocca, M.-L. (2015). Specific EEG sleep pattern in the prefrontal cortex in primary insomnia. *PLoS one*, 10(1).

Rechtschaffen, A. (1971). The control of sleep. In W. A. Hunt (Ed.), *Human behavior and its control* (pp. 75-92). Cambridge, MA: Schenkman.

Ritter, S. M., Strick, M., Bos, M. W., Van Baaren, R. B., & Dijksterhuis, A. (2012). Good morning creativity: Task reactivation during sleep enhances beneficial effect of sleep on creative performance. *Journal of Sleep Research*, 21(6), 643-647.

Siengsukon, C. F., & Boyd, L. A. (2009). Does sleep promote motor learning? Implications for physical rehabilitation. *Physical Therapy*, 89(4), 370-383.

Sitskoorn, M. M. (2008). Masterclass besluitvorming. [Masterclass in decision making]. *Management Scope*, June 23.

Stickgold, R., & Walker, M. (2004). To sleep, perchance to gain creative insight? *Trends in Cognitive Sciences*, 8(5), 191-192.

Venkatraman, V., Chuah, Y., Huettel, S., & Chee, M. (2007). Sleep deprivation elevates expectation of gains and attenuates response to losses following risky decisions. *Sleep*, 30(5), 603-609.

Vercoulen, J. H., Swanink, C. M., Fennis, J. F., Galama, J. M., van der Meer, J. W., & Bleijenberg, G. (1994). Dimensional assessment of chronic fatigue syndrome. *Journal of Psychosomatic Research*, 38(5), 383-392.

Verleger, R., Rose, M., Wagner, U., Yordanova, J., & Kolev, V. (2013). Insights into sleep's role for insight: Studies with the number reduction task. *Advances in Cognitive Psychology*, 9(4), 160-172.

Werf, Y. D. van der, Altena, E., Schoonheim, M. M., Sanz-Arigita, E. J., Vis, J. C., Rijke, W. de, & Someren, E. J. van (2009). Sleep benefits subsequent hippocampal functioning. *Nature Neuroscience*, 12(2), 122-123.

Chapter 9 Exercise – Shaping and Training Your Brain

Angevaren, M., Aufdemkampe, G., Verhaar, H., Aleman, A., & Vanhees, L. (2008). Physical activity and enhanced fitness to improve cognitive function in older people without known cognitive impairment. *The Cochrane Database of Systematic Reviews* (2), CD005381.

Best, J. R., Nagamatsu, L. S., & Liu-Ambrose, T. (2014). Improvements to executive function during exercise training predict maintenance of physical activity over the following year. *Frontiers in Human Neuroscience*, 8, 353.

Burdette, J. H., Laurienti, P. J., Espeland, M. A., Morgan, A., Telesford, Q., Vechlekar, C. D., ... Kraft, R. A. (2010). Using network science to evaluate exercise-associated brain changes in older adults. *Frontiers in Aging Neuroscience*, 2, 23.

Calfas, K. J., Sallis, J. F., Oldenburg, B., & Ffrench, M. (1997). Mediators of change in physical activity following an intervention in primary care: PACE. *Preventive Medicine*, 26(3), 297-304.

Cassilhas, R. C., Viana, V. A., Grassmann, V., Santos, R. T., Santos, R. F., Tufik, S., & Mello, M. T. (2007). The impact of resistance exercise on the cognitive function of the elderly. *Medicine and Science in Sports and Exercise*, 39(8), 1401.

Chang, Y.-K., Labban, J., Gapin, J., & Etnier, J. (2012). The effects of acute exercise on cognitive performance: A meta-analysis. *Brain Research*, 1453, 87-101.

Chang, Y.-K., Labban, J., Gapin, J., & Etnier, J. (2012). Corrigendum to 'The effects of acute exercise on cognitive performance: A meta-analytic review' [Brain Res. 1453 (2012) 87-101]. *Brain Research*, 1470, 159.

Chang, Y.-K., Pan, C., Chen, F., Tsai, C., & Huang, C. (2012). Effect of resistance-exercise training on cognitive function in healthy older adults: A review. *Journal of Aging and Physical Activity*, 20(4), 497-517.

Cotman, C. W., Berchtold, N. C., & Christie, L.-A. (2007). Exercise builds brain health: Key roles of growth factor cascades and inflammation. *Trends in Neurosciences*, 30(9), 464-472.

Courneya, K. S., Friedenreich, C. M., Quinney, H. A., Fields, A. L., Jones, L. W., & Fairey, A. S. (2004). Predictors of adherence and contamination in a randomized trial of exercise in colorectal cancer survivors. *Psycho-Oncology*, 13(12), 857-866.

Cress, M., Buchner, D., Prohaska, T., Rimmer, J., Brown, M., Macera, C., ... Chodzko-Zajko, W. (2005). Best practices for physical activity programs and behavior counseling in older adult populations. *Journal of Aging and Physical Activity*, 13(1), 61-74.

Curlik, D., & Shors, T. (2013). Training your brain: Do mental and physical (MAP) training enhance cognition through the process of neurogenesis in the hippocampus? *Neuropharmacology*, 64, 506-514.

Diamond, A. (2015). Effects of physical exercise on executive functions: Going beyond simply moving to moving with thought. *Annals of Sports Medicine and Research*, 2(1), 1011.

Dresler, M., & Repantis, D. (2015). Cognitive enhancement in humans. In S. Knafo & C. Venero (Eds.), *Cognitive enhancement: Pharmacologic, environmental and genetic factors* (pp. 273-306). San Diego, CA: Academic Press.

Dupuy, O., Gauthier, C. J., Fraser, S. A., Desjardins-Crèpeau, L., Desjardins, M., Mekary, S., ... Bherer, L. (2015). Higher levels of cardiovascular fitness are associated with better executive function and prefrontal oxygenation in younger and older women. *Frontiers in Human Neuroscience*, 9, 66.

Endo, K., Matsukawa, K., Liang, N., Nakatsuka, C., Tsuchimochi, H., Okamura, H., & Hamaoka, T. (2013). Dynamic exercise improves cognitive function in association with increased prefrontal oxygenation. *The Journal of Physiological Sciences*, 63(4), 287-298.

Erickson, K. I., Leckie, R. L., & Weinstein, A. M. (2014). Physical activity, fitness, and gray matter volume. *Neurobiology of Aging*, 35, S20-S28.

Guiney, H., & Machado, L. (2013). Benefits of regular aerobic exercise for executive functioning in healthy populations. *Psychonomic Bulletin & Review*, 20(1), 73-86.

Haller, J., Raczkevy-Deak, G., Gyimesine, K. P., Szakmary, A., Farkas, I., & Vegh, J. (2014). Cardiac autonomic functions and the emergence of violence in a highly realistic model of social conflict in humans. *Frontiers in Behavioral Neuroscience*, 8, 364.

Holzschneider, K., Wolbers, T., Röder, B., & Hötting, K. (2012). Cardiovascular fitness modulates brain activation associated with spatial learning. *NeuroImage*, 59(3), 3003-3014.

Hötting, K., & Röder, B. (2013). Beneficial effects of physical exercise on neuroplasticity and cognition. *Neuroscience & Biobehavioral Reviews*, 37(9), 2243-2257.

Imayama, I., Alfano, C. M., Mason, C. E., Wang, C., Xiao, L., Duggan, C., ... McTiernan, A. (2013). Exercise adherence, cardiopulmonary fitness, and anthropometric changes improve exercise self-efficacy and health-related quality of life. *Journal of Physical Activity and Health*, 10, 676-689.

Labelle, V., Bosquet, L., Mekary, S., Vu, T., Smilovitch, M., & Bherer, L. (2014). Fitness level moderates executive control disruption during exercise regardless of age. *Journal of Sport & Exercise Psychology*, 36(3), 258-270.

Lakes, K. D., Bryars, T., Sirisinahal, S., Salim, N., Arastoo, S., Emmerson, N., ... Kang, C. J. (2013). The Healthy for Life Taekwondo pilot study: A preliminary evaluation of effects on executive function and BMI, feasibility, and acceptability. *Mental Health and Physical Activity*, 6(3), 181-188.

Liu-Ambrose, T., Nagamatsu, L. S., Graf, P., Beattie, B. L., Ashe, M. C., & Handy, T. C. (2010). Resistance training and executive functions: A 12-month randomized controlled trial. *Archives of Internal Medicine*, 170(2), 170-178.

Manjunath, N., & Telles, S. (2001). Improved performance in the Tower of London test following yoga. *Indian Journal of Physiology and Pharmacology*, 45(3), 351-354.

Martins, A. Q., Kavussanu, M., Willoughby, A., & Ring, C. (2013). Moderate intensity exercise facilitates working memory. *Psychology of Sport and Exercise*, 14(3), 323-328.

Matta Mello Portugal, E., Cevada, T., Sobral Monteiro-Junior, R., Teixeira Guimarães, T., da Cruz Rubini, E., Lattari, E., ... Camaz Deslandes, A. (2013). Neuroscience of exercise: From neurobiology mechanisms to mental health. *Neuropsychobiology*, 68(1), 1-14.

Nanda, B., Balde, J., & Manjunatha, S. (2013). The acute effects of a single bout of moderate-intensity aerobic exercise on cognitive functions in healthy adult males. *Journal of Clinical and Diagnostic Research*, 7(9), 1883-1885.

Nouchi, R., Taki, Y., Takeuchi, H., Sekiguchi, A., Hashizume, H., Nozawa, T., ... Kawashima, R. (2014). Four weeks of combination exercise training improved executive functions, episodic memory, and processing speed in healthy elderly people: Evidence from a randomized controlled trial. *Age*, 36(2), 787-799.

Park, G., & Thayer, J. F. (2014). From the heart to the mind: Cardiac vagal tone modulates top-down and bottom-up visual perception and attention to emotional stimuli. *Frontiers in Psychology*, 5, 278.

Prakash, R. S., Voss, M. W., Erickson, K. I., & Kramer, A. F. (2015). Physical activity and cognitive vitality. *Annual Review of Psychology*, 66, 769-797.

Rattray, B., & Smee, D. (2013). Exercise improves reaction time without compromising accuracy in a novel easy-to-administer tablet-based cognitive task. *Journal of Science and Medicine in Sport*, 16(6), 567-570.

Reynard, A., Gevirtz, R., Berlow, R., Brown, M., & Boutelle, K. (2011). Heart rate variability as a marker of self-regulation. *Applied Psychophysiology and Biofeedback*, 36(3), 209-215.

Roig, M., Nordbrandt, S., Geertsen, S. S., & Nielsen, J. B. (2013). The effects of cardiovascular exercise on human memory: A review with meta-analysis. *Neuroscience & Biobehavioral Reviews*, 37(8), 1645-1666.

Rooks, C. R., Thom, N. J., McCully, K. K., & Dishman, R. K. (2010). Effects of incremental exercise on cerebral oxygenation measured by near-infrared spectroscopy: A systematic review. *Progress in Neurobiology*, 92(2), 134-150.

Sitskoorn, M. M. (2006). *Het maakbare brein: Gebruik je hersens en word wie je wilt zijn.* [The mutable brain: Using your head to become who you want to be] Amsterdam: Bert Bakker.

Sitskoorn, M. M. (2012). *Ik wil iets van jou, jij wilt iets van mij.* [I want something from you, you want something from me] Amsterdam: Bert Bakker.

Smith, P. J., Blumenthal, J. A., Hoffman, B. M., Cooper, H., Strauman, T. A., Welsh-Bohmer, K., ... Sherwood, A. (2010). Aerobic exercise and neurocognitive performance: A meta-analytic review of randomized controlled trials. *Psychosomatic Medicine*, 72(3), 239-252.

Suls, J. (2013). Anger and the heart: Perspectives on cardiac risk, mechanisms and interventions. *Progress in Cardiovascular Diseases*, 55(6), 538-547.

Thayer, J. F., Hansen, A. L., Saus-Rose, E., & Johnsen, B. H. (2009). Heart rate variability, prefrontal neural function, and cognitive performance: The neurovisceral integration perspective on self-regulation, adaptation, and health. *Annals of Behavioral Medicine*, 37(2), 141-153.

Thomas, L. E., & Lleras, A. (2009). Swinging into thought: Directed movement guides insight in problem solving. *Psychonomic Bulletin & Review*, 16(4), 719-723.

Verburgh, L., Königs, M., Scherder, E., & Oosterlaan, J. (2014). Physical exercise and executive functions in preadolescent children, adolescents and young adults: A meta-analysis. *British Journal of Sports Medicine*, 48(12), 973-979.

Voelcker-Rehage, C., & Niemann, C. (2013). Structural and functional brain changes related to different types of physical activity across the life span. *Neuroscience & Biobehavioral Reviews*, 37(9), 2268-2295.

Weinstein, A. M., Voss, M. W., Prakash, R. S., Chaddock, L., Szabo, A., White, S. M., ... Kramer, A. F. (2012). The association between aerobic fitness and executive function is mediated by prefrontal cortex volume. *Brain, Behavior, and Immunity*, 26(5), 811-819.

Williams, P., & Lord, S. R. (1997). Effects of group exercise on cognitive functioning and mood in older women. *Australian and New Zealand Journal of Public Health*, 21(1), 45-52.

Yanagisawa, H., Dan, I., Tsuzuki, D., Kato, M., Okamoto, M., Kyutoku, Y., & Soya, H. (2010). Acute moderate exercise elicits increased dorsolateral prefrontal activation and improves cognitive performance with Stroop test. *NeuroImage*, 50(4), 1702-1710.

Chapter 10 Connecting Today with Tomorrow – Start Changing the Future

Anda, R. F., Felitti, V. J., Bremner, J. D., Walker, J. D., Whitfield, C., Perry, B. D., ... Giles, W. H. (2006). The enduring effects of abuse and related adverse experiences in childhood. *European Archives of Psychiatry and Clinical Neuroscience*, 256(3), 174-186.

Baniqued, P. L., Lee, H., Voss, M. W., Basak, C., Cosman, J. D., DeSouza, S., ... Kramer, A. F. (2013). Selling points: What cognitive abilities are tapped by casual video games? *Acta Psychologica*, 142(1), 74-86.

Barkley, R. A. (2001). The executive functions and self-regulation: An evolutionary neuropsychological perspective. *Neuropsychology Review*, 11(1), 1-29.

Bierman, K. L., Domitrovich, C. E., Nix, R. L., Gest, S. D., Welsh, J. A., Greenberg, M. T., ... Gill, S. (2008). Promoting academic and social-emotional school readiness: The Head Start REDI program. *Child Development*, 79(6), 1802-1817.

Blair, C., & Diamond, A. (2008). Biological processes in prevention and intervention: The promotion of self-regulation as a means of preventing school failure. *Development and Psychopathology*, 20(3), 899-911.

Blair, C., & Raver, C. C. (2012). Child development in the context of adversity: Experiential canalization of brain and behavior. *American Psychologist*, 67(4), 309-318.

Blair, C., Zelazo, P. D., & Greenberg, M. T. (2005). The measurement of executive function in early childhood. *Developmental Neuropsychology*, 28(2), 561-571.

Blair, C., Granger, D. A., Kivlighan, K. T., Mills-Koonce, R., Willoughby, M., Greenberg, M. T., ... Fortunato, C. K. (2008). Maternal and child contributions to cortisol response to emotional arousal in young children from low-income, rural communities. *Developmental Psychology*, 44(4), 1095-1109.

Bodrova, E., & Leong, D. J. (2005). Promoting student self-regulation in learning. *Education Digest*, 71(2), 54-57.

Bodrova, E., & Leong, D. J. (2007). Play and early literacy: A vygotskian approach. In K. A. Roskos & J. F. Christie (Eds.), *Play and early literacy in early childhood: Research from multiple perspectives* (2nd ed., pp. 185-200). Mahwah, NJ: Lawrence Erlbaum Associates.

Bogg, T., & Lasecki, L. (2015). Reliable gains? Evidence for substantially underpowered designs in studies of working memory training transfer to fluid intelligence. *Frontiers in Psychology*, 5, 1589.

Bowlby, J. (1988). *A secure base: Parent-child attachment and healthy human development.* New York, NY: Basic Books.

Bush, G., Luu, P., & Posner, M. I. (2000). Cognitive and emotional influences in anterior cingulate cortex. *Trends in Cognitive Sciences*, 4(6), 215-222.

Center on the Developing Child at Harvard University (2011). Building the brain's 'Air Traffic Control' system: How early experiences shape the development of executive function: Working paper No. 11. www.developingchild.harvard.edu, accessed July 24, 2015.

Chen, X.-J., Wang, Y., Liu, L.-L., Cui, J.-F., Gan, M.-Y., Shum, D. H., & Chan, R. C. (2015). The effect of implementation intention on prospective memory: A systematic and meta-analytic review. *Psychiatry Research*, 226(1), 14-22.

Drevets, W. C., & Raichle, M. E. (1998). Reciprocal suppression of regional cerebral blood flow during emotional versus higher cognitive processes: Implications for interactions between emotion and cognition. *Cognition and Emotion*, 12(3), 353-385.

Goldsmith, D. F., & Rogoff, B. (1997). Mothers' and toddlers' coordinated joint focus of attention: Variations with maternal dysphoric symptoms. *Developmental Psychology*, 33(1), 113-119.

Gollwitzer, P. M., & Sheeran, P. (2006). Implementation intentions and goal achievement: A meta-analysis of effects and processes. *Advances in Experimental Social Psychology*, 38, 69-119.

Grusec, J. E., Goodnow, J. J., & Kuczynski, L. (2000). New directions in analyses of parenting contributions to children's acquisition of values. *Child Development*, 71(1), 205-211.

Harlow, H.F. (1958). The Nature of Love. *American Psychologist*, 13, 573-685.

Hofmann, W., Schmeichel, B. J., & Baddeley, A. D. (2012). Executive functions and self-regulation. *Trends in Cognitive Sciences*, 16(3), 174-180.

Kane, M. J., Brown, L. H., McVay, J. C., Silvia, P. J., Myin-Germeys, I., & Kwapil, T. R. (2007). For whom the mind wanders, and when: An experience-sampling study of working memory and executive control in daily life. *Psychological Science*, 18(7), 614-621.

Klingberg, T. (2010). Training and plasticity of working memory. *Trends in Cognitive Sciences*, 14(7), 317-324.

Kochanska, G., & Aksan, N. (2006). Children's conscience and self-regulation. *Journal of Personality*, 74(6), 1587-1618.

Kochanska, G., & Knaack, A. (2003). Effortful control as a personality characteristic of young children: Antecedents, correlates, and consequences. *Journal of Personality*, 71(6), 1087-1112.

Kochanska, G., Murray, K., & Coy, K. C. (1997). Inhibitory control as a contributor to conscience in childhood: From toddler to early school age. *Child Development*, 68(2), 263-277.

Kochanska, G., Murray, K., Jacques, T. Y., Koenig, A. L., & Vandegeest, K. A. (1996). Inhibitory control in young children and its role in emerging internalization. *Child Development*, 67(2), 490-507.

Kuhl, J., & Kazén, M. (1999). Volitional facilitation of difficult intentions: Joint activation of intention memory and positive affect removes Stroop interference. *Journal of Experimental Psychology: General*, 128(3), 382-399.

Landsinger, K. L., & Corts, D. (2002). Effects of stress on prospective memory. *Journal of Undergraduate Study and Independent Research*, 3, 24-29.

Lengua, L. J., Honorado, E., & Bush, N. R. (2007). Contextual risk and parenting as predictors of effortful control and social competence in preschool children. *Journal of Applied Developmental Psychology*, 28(1), 40-55.

Liu, D., Diorio, J., Tannenbaum, B., Caldji, C., Francis, D., Freedman, A., ... Meaney, M. J. (1997). Maternal care, hippocampal glucocorticoid receptors, and hypothalamic-pituitary-adrenal responses to stress. *Science*, 277(5332), 1659-1662.

Macan, T., Gibson, J. M., & Cunningham, J. (2010). Will you remember to read this article later when you have time? The relationship between prospective memory and time management. *Personality and Individual Differences*, 48(6), 725-730.

McDaniel, M. A., Einstein, G. O., Graham, T., & Rall, E. (2004). Delaying execution of intentions: Overcoming the costs of interruptions. *Applied Cognitive Psychology*, 18(5), 533-547.

McGowan, P. O., Sasaki, A., D'Alessio, A. C., Dymov, S., Labonté, B., Szyf, M., ... Meaney, M. J. (2009). Epigenetic regulation of the glucocorticoid receptor in human brain associates with childhood abuse. *Nature Neuroscience*, 12(3), 342-348.

Nouchi, R., Taki, Y., Takeuchi, H., Hashizume, H., Nozawa, T., Kambara, T., ... Nouchi, H. (2013). Brain training game boosts executive functions, working memory and processing speed in the young adults: A randomized controlled trial. *PLoS One*, 8(2), e55518.

O'Donnell, K., Gaudreau, H., Colalillo, S., Steiner, M., Atkinson, L., Moss, E., ... Lydon, J. (2014). The maternal adversity, vulnerability and neurodevelopment project: Theory and methodology. *Canadian Journal of Psychiatry*, 59(9), 497-508.

Plotsky, P. M., & Meaney, M. J. (1993). Early, postnatal experience alters hypothalamic corticotropin-releasing factor (CRF) mRNA, median eminence CRF content and stress-induced release in adult rats. *Molecular Brain Research*, 18(3), 195-200.

Redick, T. S., Shipstead, Z., Harrison, T. L., Hicks, K. L., Fried, D. E., Hambrick, D. Z., ... Engle, R. W. (2013). No evidence of intelligence improvement after working memory training: A randomized, placebo-controlled study. *Journal of Experimental Psychology: General*, 142(2), 359-379.

Rodriguez, M. L., Ayduk, O., Aber, J. L., Mischel, W., Sethi, A., & Shoda, Y. (2005). A contextual approach to the development of self-regulatory competencies: The role of maternal unresponsivity and toddlers' negative affect in stressful situations. *Social Development*, 14(1), 136-157.

Rudebeck, S., Bor, D., Ormond, A., O'Reilly, J., & Lee, A. (2011). A potential spatial working memory training task to improve both episodic memory and fluid intelligence. *PLoS One*, 7(11), e50431.

Sethi, A., Mischel, W., Aber, J., Shoda, Y., & Rodriguez, M. (2000). The role of strategic attention deployment in development of self-regulation: Predicting preschoolers' delay of gratification from mother-toddler interactions. *Developmental Psychology*, 36(6), 767-777.

Shinaver, C. S., Entwistle, P. C., & Soderqvist, S. (2014). Cogmed WM training: Reviewing the reviews. *Applied Neuropsychology: Child*, 3(3), 163-172.

Shipstead, Z., Redick, T., & Engle, R. (2012). Is working memory training effective? *Psychological Bulletin*, 138(4), 628-654.

Shiv, B., & Nowlis, S. M. (2004). The effect of distractions while tasting a food sample: The interplay of informational and affective components in subsequent choice. *Journal of Consumer Research*, 31(3), 599-608.

Takeuchi, H., Taki, Y., Nouchi, R., Hashizume, H., Sekiguchi, A., Kotozaki, Y., ... Kawashima, R. (2013). Effects of working memory training on functional connectivity and cerebral blood flow during rest. *Cortex*, 49(8), 2106-2125.

Thompson, T. W., Waskom, M. L., Garel, K.-L. A., Cardenas-Iniguez, C., Reynolds, G. O., Winter, R., ... Alvarez, G. A. (2013). Failure of working memory training to enhance cognition or intelligence. *PloS One*, 8(5), e63614.

Tough, P. (2013). *How children succeed: Grit, curiosity and the hidden power of character.* London: Random House.

Turecki, G., & Meaney, M. J. (2014). Effects of the social environment and stress on glucocorticoid receptor gene methylation: A systematic review, online December 13. *Biological Psychiatry*. 79(2), 87-96.

Ursache, A., Noble, K. G., & Blair, C. (2015). Socioeconomic status, subjective social status, and perceived stress: Associations with stress physiology and executive functioning. *Behavioral Medicine*, 41(3), 145-154.

Chapter 11 Time – Giving Your Brain Time to Change

Cohen, J.M. & Cohen, M. J.(1980) *The Penguin Dictionary of Modern Quotations*. London: Penguin

Diamond, A. (2013). Executive functions. *Annual Review of Psychology*, 64, 135-168.

Dweck, C. S. (2008). *Mindset: The new psychology of success*. New York, NY: Ballantine Books.

Friedman, R., & Elliot, A. J. (2008). The effect of arm crossing on persistence and performance. *European Journal of Social Psychology*, 38(3), 449-461.

Inzlicht, M., Bartholow, B. D., & Hirsh, J. B. (2015). Emotional foundations of cognitive control. *Trends in Cognitive Sciences*, 19(3), 126-132.

Schroder, H. S., Moran, T. P., Donnellan, M. B., & Moser, J. S. (2014). Mindset induction effects on cognitive control: A neurobehavioral investigation. *Biological Psychology*, 103, 27-37.

Chapter 12 The Effect: Assessing the Impact of the EFFECT Program

Duckworth, A. L., Peterson, C., Matthews, M. D., & Kelly, D. R. (2007). Grit: Perseverance and passion for long-term goals. *Journal of Personality and Social Psychology*, 92(6), 1087-1101.

Sitskoorn, M. M. (2006). *Het maakbare brein: Gebruik je hersens en word wie je wilt zijn.* [The mutable brain: Using your head to become who you want to be] Amsterdam: Bert Bakker.

Sitskoorn, M. M. (2010). P*assies van het brein: Waarom zondigen zo verleidelijk is*. [Passions of the brain, Why sin is so tempting.] Amsterdam: Bert Bakker.

Online Sources

Chapter 1 A Goal to Set Your Sights on

http://www.archimedes-lab.org/weekly_optical.html
https://www.goodreads.com/author/quotes/9399.Jeanette_Winterson
http://www.goodreads.com/quotes/141245-if-you-want-to-live-a-happy-life-tie-it

Chapter 2 The VUCA World

https://en.wikipedia.org/wiki/Future_Shock
http://en.wikipedia.org/wiki/Red_Queen_hypothesis
http://en.wikipedia.org/wiki/Volatility,_uncertainty,_complexity_and_ambiguity
http://gereports.eu/post/99052496229/whats-next-the-six-technologies-that-will-shape
http://www.inc.com/erik-sherman/12-disruptive-technologies-you-need-to-know-about.html
http://www.kennisnet.nl/themas/21st-century-skills/vaardigheden/benodigde-vaardigheden-voor-de-21ste-eeuw/
http://www.kvk.nl/advies-en-informatie/innoveren/internet-of-things/?gclid=CJ_th6KJtMMCFaHJtAodUQUAIQ
http://www.marketingfacts.nl/berichten/pim-trendrapport-2014-welkom-in-het-tijdperk-van-de-homo-socius
http://newscenter.berkeley.edu/2013/06/20/the-red-queen-was-right-life-must-continually-evolve-to-avoid-extinction/
http://opite.pbworks.com/w/fi le/fetch/61995295/White%20Paper%2021stCS_Final_ENG_def2.pdf
http://www.p21.org/our-work/p21-framework
http://vara.nl/Vrijheid-gelijkheid-broeders.10996.0.html

Chapter 3 The CEO Brain

http:/www.cognitivefun.net/
http://en.wikiquote.org/wiki/Isaac_Asimov
http://www.goodreads.com/quotes/110684-it-is-change-continuing-change-inevitable-change-that-is-the
http://en.wikipedia.org/wiki/Mirror_test
http://www.mathsisfun.com/games/towerofhanoi.html
http:/zap.psy.utwente.nl/

Chapter 4 A Recipe for Success

http://www.brainyquote.com/quotes/quotes/v/viktorefr160380.html
http://character.org/
https://sasupenn.qualtrics.com/SE/?SID=SV_06f6QSOS2pZW9qR
https://sites.sas.upenn.edu/duckworth/pages/research

Chapter 5 Pitfalls

https://www.coach.me/ http://www.davidrock.net/fi les/NLJ_SCARFUS.pdf
http://web.archive.org/web/20100705024057/http://www.your-brain-at-work.com:80/files/NLJ_SCARFUS.pdf
http://www.nasonline.org/publications/biographical-memoirs/memoir-pdfs/olds-james.pdf
https://play.google.com/store/apps/details?id=uk.amimetic.habitspro
http://www.quotationspage.com/quote/42360.html
https://sasupenn.qualtrics.com/SE/?SID=SV_06f6QSOS2pZW9qR
https://www.youtube.com/watch?v=KhoXFVQsIxw

Chapter 6 Environmental Enrichment – Challenging Your Brain

http://www.boston.com/bostonglobe/ideas/graphics/011109_hacking_your_brain/
https://www.goodreads.com/author/quotes/1203736.Oliver_Wendell_Holmes_Sr_

Chapter 7 Flow Focus – Directing the Plasticity of Your Brain

http://www.apa.org/news/press/releases/2008/10/stress-in-america.pdf
http://news.stanford.edu/2009/08/24/multitask-research-study-082409/
http://www.brainyquote.com/quotes/quotes/a/alberteins104873.html
http://buddhify.com/
https://en.wikipedia.org/wiki/Flow_(psychology)
https://en.wikipedia.org/wiki/Heart_rate_variability
https://www.headspace.com/headspace-meditation-app
http://www.healthline.com/health/mental-health/top-meditation-iphone-android-apps#5
http://www.mentalworkout.com/store/programs/mindfulness-meditation/
https://www.mindful.org/free-mindfulness-apps-worthy-of-your-attention/
https://www.theguardian.com/technology/2016/may/26/five-of-the-best-meditation-apps
http://www.theregister.co.uk/2009/08/26/multitasking_study/
https://www.youtube.com/watch?v=92i5m3tV5XY

Chapter 8 Fixed Sleeping Pattern – Unleashing the Power of Sleep

http://www.artofmanliness.com/2012/08/08/12-concentration-exercises-from-1918/
www.azumio.com
http://www.zoominfo.com/p/Allan-Rechtschaffen/456564911
http://www.dokterdokter.nl/gezond-leven/psyche/10-redenen-om-meer-te-slapen/
http://educatie.ntr.nl/beterslapen/index.jsp?nr=574728
http://www.kempenhaeghe.nl/upload/_1117_pageitems_613_slaapwaakkalender%20volwassenen%20-%20voor%20web.pdf
https://www.nhg.org
https://www.nhg.org/sites/default/files/content/nhg_org/uploads/standaard/download/slaapdagboek.pdf

https://play.google.com/store/apps/details?id=nl.uu.science.sleepcare&hl=nl
https://www.radboudumc.nl/Zorg/Afdelingen/nkcv/Pages/default.aspx
http://sleep.org/
www.sleepcycle.com
http://sleepfoundation.org/how-sleep-works/how-much-sleep-do-we-really-need
http://sleepfoundation.org/sites/default/files/STREPchanges_1.png
http://sleephealthjournal.org/
http://www.thuisarts.nl
http://www.thuisarts.nl/sites/default/files/slaapdagboek.pdf
http://www.vermoeidheid.nl/vermoeidheid/tips-voor-een-goede-nachtrust.asp

Chapter 9 Exercise – Shaping and Training Your Brain

http://www.azumio.com/s/argus/index.html
http://www.azumio.com/s/fitnessbuddy/index.html
http://www.fysiotherapiewetenschap.com/bestanden/38.pdf
http://internal.psychology.illinois.edu/~alleras/videos.htm
https://itunes.apple.com/app/trainingpeaks/id408047715?mt=8
http://www.joggycoach.com/home.html
http://www.myfitnesspal.com/mobile/iphone
http://www.nhs.uk/LiveWell/Fitness/Pages/Fitnesshome.aspx
http://onlinelibrary.wiley.com/doi/10.1038/oby.2002.193/full
http://www2.open.ac.uk/openlearn/olympisize_html/?state=0,
https://runkeeper.com/running-app
http://www.topendsports.com/fitness/karvonen-formula.htm
http://www.topendsports.com/fitness/sportspecific.htm
https://www.youtube.com/playlist?list=PL9NYvjxBy6SOxm8UjvbqXmpBDsvJLDClw

Chapter 10 Connecting Today with Tomorrow – Start Changing the Future

www.acestudy.org
http://www.brainyquote.com/quotes/keywords/today.html
http://www.cogmed.com/working-memory-challenge
http://cognitivefun.net/test/4
http://www.gocognitive.net/demo/working-memory-capacity
https://itunes.apple.com/nl/app/iowa-gambling-task/id807409936?mt=8
http://www.lumosity.com/
https://play.google.com/store/apps/details?id=com.zsimolabs.iowa&hl=en
https://support.apple.com/nl-nl/HT202335
https://www.youtube.com/watch?v=39A3z3S6aY0
http://zap.psy.utwente.nl/zaps/zaps/zaps/sternbergsearch.res/frames.html

Chapter 11 Time – Giving Your Brain Time to Change

http://www.bbc.com/future/story/20120827-how-to-make-time-stand-still
https://www.beeminder.com/overview
http://www.citatenverzameling.com/trefwoorden-werk.html
http://www.dosomethingdifferent.com/
http://www.goalsontrack.com/
https://www.omnigroup.com/omnifocus?pk_campaign=tmga
http://www.sociidot.com/
http://www.stridesapp.com/
https://www.superbetter.com/
http://www.unstuck.com/

Chapter 12 The Effect: Assessing the Impact of the EFFECT Program

http://www.cogmed.com/working-memory-challenge
http:/www.cognitivefun.net/
http://cognitivefun.net/test/4
http://www.gocognitive.net/demo/working-memory-capacity
http://www.goodreads.com/quotes/44719-it-is-good-to-have-an-end-to-journey-toward
http://www.mathsisfun.com/games/towerofhanoi.html
https://sasupenn.qualtrics.com/SE/?SID=SV_06f6QSOS2pZW9qR
https://sites.sas.upenn.edu/duckworth/pages/research
http:/zap.psy.utwente.nl/

Acknowledgements

First of all I would like to thank all the patients, test subjects and researchers whose cooperation, knowledge and insight into the brain and human behavior made this book possible. I would also like to thank the team at Vakmedianet publishing house for their advice during the entire writing process and for creating room for many new ideas to spring up as I was working. Their efforts inspired me to keep going and to try new directions. Gerri Reimert and Freek Talsma deserve special thanks for believing in this project when it was still in the outline stage.

My gratitude is also due to Joost Sitskoorn and Maarten van den Heuvel for their comments on the first draft of the book (again). I have always been able to count on them and sound them out about all kinds of ideas. My thanks also go to Karin Gehring, Martijn Stuiver and Ivan Niklicek for contributing their expertise. Sophie van der Linden and Jimme Bruijn deserve recognition for their assistance regarding articles and references. Desiree Kruijt provided crucial moral support during the entire project.

This book is dedicated to my mother. To put it in scholarly terms, she laid the foundations for the development of my prefrontal cortex. In daily life, that came down to an endless supply of love and structure in a social environment in which enrichment and consideration for others were the norm. I am very grateful to her for this.

About the author

MARGRIET SITSKOORN Ph.D. is a Full Professor of Clinical Neuropsychology at Tilburg University (Netherlands).

Her research focuses on the relationship between the brain and human behavior. She explores how behavior and environment affect the brain and how we can use this knowledge to influence and develop human emotions, skills and behavior. Her additional interest lies in popularizing brain research and integrating scientific knowledge into education, politics and the business world.

Sitskoorn is the director of Neuro-Cognitief Centrum Nederland. She is a sought-after public speaker and consultant.

In addition to her scientific research, she writes columns for several magazines and is a frequent guest on television. Earlier, she wrote three non-fiction bestsellers *Het maakbare brein* (2006), *Passies van het brein* (2010) and *Ik wil iets van jou, jij wil iets van mij* (2012).

Margriet Sitskoorn also offers training sessions on the EFFECT program.

Irene Sitskoorn | fotografie